AF850435

Racial and Ethnic Economic Inequality

aus
american
university
studies

Series XVI
Economics

Vol. 10

PETER LANG
New York • Washington, D.C./Baltimore • Bern
Frankfurt am Main • Berlin • Brussels • Vienna • Oxford

Racial and Ethnic Economic Inequality

An International Perspective

Samuel L. Myers, Jr. and Bruce P. Corrie,
Editors

PETER LANG
New York • Washington, D.C./Baltimore • Bern
Frankfurt am Main • Berlin • Brussels • Vienna • Oxford

Library of Congress Cataloging-in-Publication Data

World Conference on Remedies to Racial and Ethnic Inequality (1st: 1996:
Roy Wilkins Center for Human Relations and Social Justice)
Racial and ethnic economic equality: an international perspective /
edited by Samuel L. Myers, Jr., Bruce P. Corrie.
p. cm. — (American university studies. Series XVI, Economics; vol. 10)
Papers, some rev., presented at the First World Conference on Remedies
to Racial and Ethnic Inequality, held May 16–19, 1996, Roy Wilkins
Center for Human Relations and Social Justice.
Includes bibliographical references and index.
1. Racism—Congresses. 2. Ethnocentrism—Congresses.
3. Discrimination—Congresses. 4. Social justice—Congresses.
I. Myers, Samuel L. II. Corrie, Bruce P. III. Title. IV. American university
studies. Series XVI, Economics; v. 10.
HT1505.W646 305.8—dc21 2003011712
ISBN 0-8204-5656-X
ISSN 0740-2150

Bibliographic information published by **Die Deutsche Bibliothek**.
Die Deutsche Bibliothek lists this publication in the "Deutsche
Nationalbibliografie"; detailed bibliographic data is available
on the Internet at http://dnb.ddb.de/.

Photo of Samuel L. Myers, Jr. by Bill Alkofer

© 2006 Peter Lang Publishing, Inc., New York
29 Broadway, New York, NY 10006
www.peterlang.com

All rights reserved.
Reprint or reproduction, even partially, in all forms such as microfilm,
xerography, microfiche, microcard, and offset strictly prohibited.

Contents

• CHAPTER ONE •

Introduction

BRUCE P. CORRIE
Associate Dean
Undergraduate Studies, College of Business and Organizational Leadership
Professor of Economics
Concordia University—St. Paul
Editor, www.policybriefs.org

SAMUEL L. MYERS, JR.
Roy Wilkins Professor of Human Relations and Social Justice
Hubert H. Humphrey Institute of Public Affairs
University of Minnesota

The papers in this volume provide a range of global perspectives and policy prescriptions for a critical and enduring problem in human history: the deliberate exclusion and exploitation of one group of people by another in the form of racial and ethnic inequality. Are legal solutions the answer? Is political mobilization the answer? Is deliberate goal setting a solution? Is policy and program mainstreaming the answer?

Over the years, the Wilkins Forum at the Hubert H. Humphrey Institute of Public Affairs at the University of Minnesota has wrestled with these issues and brought scholars and activists together to gain insight and new perspectives on remedies to racial and ethnic inequality. This journey of policy discovery began with the First World Conference on Remedies to Racial and Ethnic Inequality. From May 16–19, 1996 more than 200 scholars, community leaders, university officials, and thinkers convened at the Hubert H. Humphrey's Roy Wilkins Center for Human Relations and Social Justice at the University of Minnesota for the First World Conference on Remedies to Racial and Ethnic Inequality. This policy journey took the Forum members to Australia and New Zealand for the Second World Conference on Remedies to Racial and Ethnic Inequalities to study the experience of the indigenous people of these two countries in 1998. The Third World Conference was held in in 2001 in conjunction with the United Nation's World Conference against Racism in Durban, South Africa. Here Forum members experienced the practical dilemmas of policy making on a global scale.

Many of the papers presented at the First World Conference are included in this volume. Some new papers have been added. These papers set the stage for the policy dialogue that continued in the Second and Third World Conferences.

The issues raised in this volume remain pertinent today. For example, the recent elections in India underscore the point made in the papers on Dalits in India in this volume: economic development has to be broad based and inclusive. Many of the arguments in this volume, around affirmative action in the United States, were deliberated in the 2003 Supreme Court rulings on affirmative action. As state governments across the United States attempt to change agreements with American Indian tribes over the extent and control of gambling, the article in this volume on gaming as an economic development strategy provides a perspective for policy makers to consider. September 11th and its ensuing "war on terrorism" can be viewed in a historical perspective when one reads the articles in this volume on the exclusion of "Arabs" or "Turks" across countries.

The papers in this volume address a broad range of issues relating to racial and ethnic inequality. The first set of papers by Pinar Batur, Hernán Vera, and Yanick St. Jean present global facets of racism. For instance, racism is culturalized as in the case of the "Haitian" in the Dominican Republic or the white Caucasian Muslim who is called "Black" in Russia. In Latin America as Vera points out, racism is practiced openly but denied passionately. These authors point to the need to understand both global patterns of racism and its link with global capitalism as well as local structures and processes that reproduce these unjust relations.

The authors in this volume also point to the lack of both solid academic research on the patterns and processes of racial and ethnic discrimination, as well as appropriate academic approaches to study the issue. For instance in the discipline of economics, the paper by Jomo calls for a movement from pure economistic approaches to study ethnic discrimination in employment and remuneration to more eclectic approaches that could include factors such as culture, ideology and alternative methodological approaches.

Nacoste makes the case that the analyses of the political stigma of affirmative action policies should be formally social-psychological for two reasons: first such analyses could pinpoint the sources and conditions that lead to stigma and second, it can be used to clarify the informal social-psychological analyses followed by the U.S. Supreme Court to develop constitutional standards.

Deale and Stafford review recent court rulings challenging affirmative action and observe that these rulings fail to recognize the historical justification for affirmative action. They encourage the use of international legislation, such as the Convention on the Elimination of All Forms of Racial Discrimination, which the U.S. ratified in 1994, as a new tool to protect effective remedies against racial and ethnic discrimination.

Colin and Eleanor Bourke, reflecting the Australian experience, make the case for an indigenous Australian university to help address the problem of low educational achievement among indigenous people in Australia.

Three papers by Dhesi, Thorat, and Corrie consider the experience of India's Dalit or Untouchable castes. Dhesi finds patterns of discrimination in the education and labor markets in India against Dalits. Thorat examines the various development programs initiated by the Indian government and finds that they have not helped Dalits rise above poverty and destitution in a significant way. Corrie points to the need for comprehensive strategies for Dalit empowerment in India.

Similarly, Lashley examines the experience of the Maoris of New Zealand and the major strategies adopted to improve their lives, including negotiated Treaty rights, biculturalism, and affirmative action and development programs. Lashley finds a poor record of success and is concerned that with free market reforms the situation of Maoris has worsened in New Zealand.

Anders examines the recent strategy of gaming as an approach to indigenous development and empowerment and suggests ways to make the strategy more effective.

Collins presents a framework to address the issue of racial and ethnic discrimination that includes the following core elements: full employment, affirmative action, income support, protection of workers' rights, corporate responsibility and accountability, capital controls, reduction in military spending, universal health insurance, universal and life-long education, rebuilding of cities and environmental conservation and protection.

Finally, Myers' paper concludes the volume with a challenge to policy makers to devise meaningful strategies for eliminating racial and ethnic discrimination both in the United States as well as globally.

• CHAPTER TWO •

Just a Link in the Chain: Global Racism and the Concept of "Blackness" in Russia

PINAR BATUR
Associate Professor of Sociology, Director of Urban Studies
Vassar College

Introduction

Two main questions confront anti-racist intellectuals today: how has racism integrated into capitalism to become a global reality, and how to oppose and resist global racism? Rather than examining the historical development of global racism, this work concentrates on racism as a globally interconnected contemporary reality by using Russia as a case study. Global racism is a product of capitalism, anchored in institutions, as well as knowledge and imagination, and the patterns of global racism are tied to the articulation of racism in everyday life. Only through understanding this complex connection is it possible to explore ways to oppose and resist racism globally.

Racism has become a process of defining and building communities and societies based on a racialized hierarchy of power. The root of this process lies in the expansion of capitalism through colonialism. This expansion casts new formulas of division and opposition, fostering inequality even while integrating all previous forms of inequality so long as they met the needs of capitalist arrangements (Batur-VanderLippe 1996). In this historical development, colonialism built upon the hierarchy of the "superiority" of the colonizer and the "inferiority" of the colonized to legitimize the domination and violence of colonial administration, exploitative trade and labor, and the imposition of Christianity. In this process, the various antagonisms and images merged, for example, representing religious conflict in racialized symbolism.

As racism came to embrace a multitude of intersecting inequalities and oppositions, they were summarized in violent dichotomies of "color," creating what Frantz Fanon calls the "Manichean world" of colonial oppression (Fanon 1963). In this sense, "color" became a way to reduce divisions to racialized symbols, representing the brutal hierarchy of superiority and inferiority in "color lines." This reductionism has led complex relations to be summarized in seemingly simple juxtapositions of "color," and this process has produced a "global color line," (Mazrui 1991) imposing and inventing "color" even where color differences do not exist. As a result, all political, economic and social relations and culture are racialized, reinforcing patterns of global racism and dominating reconstruction of the past, understanding of the present and imagination of the future. Etienne Balibar argues that the global culture of racism has become "not only [a way to tie] words with objects, but more profoundly a way to connect words with images to create concepts" (Balibar 1994, 200). For example, in 1994 when Muslims began to build a mosque in Moscow, the foundation stone was defaced, and "Blacks Out!" was written on nearby walls.

While "Caucasian" has come to mean "White" in Western societies, many Russians construct Caucasian Muslims and some Central Asian Muslims, who have "white" skin, as "blacks." This merging is meant to justify exclusion of Muslims by a "color line" in a manner similar to American segregation. Russian residents living near the mosque organized to block its construction, while searching for ways to prevent Muslims from moving into the neighborhood: "We know these Caucasians—one shows up, then a hundred more follow." Another said, "when some [Caucasians] rented the apartment next to mine, I tried to get them evicted...They've brought their ways into my building." Yet another said, "...if 'blacks' lived here? You might go in and never come out again..." They tried to justify exclusion as the only way to meet the "Muslim menace" against Russians, Russian society and Russian culture: "all those...mountain people—the Mafiosi. You mean you don't see what's happening? Russia is under a real attack..." Father Gregory, a local priest, echoed these sentiments: "Moscow is and will continue to be a holy city for the Orthodox...Moscow is the third Rome, not the second Mecca" (Lebedeva 1994, 1–4).

"Blackness" and the Links in the Chain of Racism

According to the All-Russian Center for the Study of Public Opinion, in 1993 over 60 percent of Russians in Moscow were "anti-black," meaning anti-Muslim. Even though Muslims have settled around Moscow since the fifteenth century, and make up approximately 10 percent of the population of

Moscow and surrounding provinces, they are considered to be outsiders (Lebedeva 1994, 1–4). Violence and policies of exclusion against Muslims reveal that racist stereotypes and racism are part of everyday life in Russia. Yet, the imagery that constructs Muslims as "blacks" makes this everyday racism a global property. Henri Lefebvre argues that the global and everyday are symbiotically interconnected, meaning that "at any given historical moment the everyday has already been created within a determined global space, and global relations are the product of everyday existence" (Holt 1995, 10; Lefebvre 1991). In this context, "space" represents layers of praxis, a site that displays the collective impact of economic, political and social relations and production of culture. Global space frames human activity in its abstract and cumulative meaning, while everyday life redefines and reformulates the abstract and cumulative, allowing for integration into individual consciousness, revealed in the social space of everyday life.

The abstractness of the global allows the multiplicity of connections in everyday experience to be summarized on the global level. In this context, the graffiti that screams "Blacks Out!" is not a single incident confined to the everyday racism in some street in Moscow, but is part of the global racism that connects Moscow to Washington, D.C., to Johannesburg to Rio de Janeiro to Paris to London and to Moscow. Thus, every racist action reinforces the connection between the abstract global space of racism and the social space of everyday racism. This connection is renewed and revitalized by accumulative racist action, knowledge and ideology, and is reproduced in economic, political and social forms. In this context, the use of the term "black" together with the violence of exclusion in a Moscow neighborhood connects the social space of everyday racism in one context to discrimination, segregation and apartheid in a multitude of other contexts, making each a link in the global chain of racism.

The Confluence of Everyday Racism and Global Racist Discourse

Russian authorities in Moscow have been trying to "cleanse" the capital of Muslims by expelling them, a policy that has received wide support among Russians. As one reader wrote to a Soviet periodical, "Everybody knows that a fish rots from the head, so the first thing we need to do is cleanse Moscow of all this filth." In the letter, the author complained of seeing "fewer and fewer kind Russian faces [in Moscow]," but seeing more Muslims and Jews: "The streets are filthy with former 'quota-fillers' who settled down in the capital" (Shakrina 1990, 211).

"Quota-filler" is a contemptuous term for non-Russian residents of Moscow, some of whom migrated to the capital as part of Soviet diversity programs. In racist speech, both Muslims and Jews are described as "quota-fillers," making them subject to similar prejudice and discriminatory actions. Even the racist stereotypes overlap. At an anti-Muslim rally organized by the Congress of Russian Communities, horror stories circulated among the crowd, such as "your children will be dismembered [by the Muslims] and roasted on skewers for shish kebab" (Musin 1994, 4). The stories about cannibalism are reminiscent of anti-Semitic narrative from the turn of the century, and anti-Semitism is also on the rise in Russia. Since the mid-1980s, the Pamyat (Memory) Society, an ultra-nationalist, para-military organization, has gained support with racist slogans, such as "give us de-Zionization." According to a witness, activities at one Pamyat Society meeting ranged from applauding racist speeches to circulating a petition demanding that all Jews be expelled from Moscow, while some members wearing Nazi-style clothing chanted anti-Semitic slogans (Kalner 1990, 212–3). But anti-Semitism is not restricted to Pamyat. According to a Moscow professor, during a meeting of the Union of Writers, when Andrey Chernov, a Russian poet, accused an anti-Semitic speaker of supporting fascism, he was dragged from the auditorium by people who beat him and threw him down the stairs while police watched (Sinyavsky 1990, 491–2).

Intellectuals are instrumental in forging the symbiotic connections between the abstract space of global racism and the social space of everyday racism through knowledge and ideology. For example, Viktor Bezverkhy, a former professor at the Russian Academy of Sciences' Institute of Ethnology and Anthropology in Moscow, has written that "...Jews, Gypsies and people of mixed race...have no place in a 'socially organized society'" (Rich 1995, 27). Igor Shafarevich, a Professor of Mathematics at Moscow's Steklov Institute, has argued that "Jews were responsible for the Bolshevik Revolution and Jewish intellectuals were intent on destroying Russian culture." (Leary 1992, B8) The notion of a "Jewish conspiracy" is an aspect of global racism, and its articulation in Russia exhibits the permeation of global racism in everyday discourse (Kohan 1990, 40). This confluence of global and everyday racism is apparent in the results of surveys that have shown that approximately two out of ten respondents believe Russia may be the victim of a "Zionist plot" (Brym 1994, 844; Brym and Degtyarev 1993; Gibson 1994, 796–806).

Making Connections in the Sphere of Global Racism

When the Soviet Union collapsed in 1991, some were quick to claim that the "black problem," the "Muslim mafia" or a "Jewish conspiracy," were hampering Russia's advancement and integration into the capitalist economy. Some intellectuals like Solzhenitsyn, politicians like Zhirinovsky and Lebed provided a simple solution: recapturing the past glory of Russia by uniting Slavs against Muslims and Jews, recreating Russia in the image of its former empire (Elliott 1994. 41; Bohlen 1994, A1). The promise of violence emerging from this rhetoric is dismissed by some Russian as well as Western intellectuals as fringe politics, but it is being used to justify the war in Chechnya and the deaths and devastation of more than half of the Chechens. When the "official" war as a Russian response to Chechnya's Independence Movement began in December 1994, an army officer insisted that "Chechnya must not merely [be] defeated but destroyed," stressing that "extermination rather than pacification is the way to secure long-term control of [this] region" of the Caucasus. Another Russian official argued that "we need a new Stalin [to] show us how to deal with these blacks" (Socor 1994).

The racism surrounding the war in Chechnya is one link between international politics and the everyday racism of defacing a foundation stone on a mosque in Moscow. The war in the former Yugoslavia is another. The war between Serbs, Croats and Bosnians has exhibited the kinds of violence reminiscent of World War II, such as "ethnic cleansing," death by starvation in concentration camps, the rape of more than twenty thousand Muslim Bosnian women by Serbian soldiers, and mass burials of massacred civilians. Since the beginning of the war, Serbian forces have engaged in a well-documented "slow-motion genocide," (Ali and Lifeshultz 1993, xvii) particularly targeting Muslims. American policy towards the former Yugoslavia has been ambivalent, dramatically revealed by a series of protest resignations by American government officials charged with the Yugoslavian case (Holmes 1993, A12; Pomfret 1996, A1). But Russia has strongly supported Slavic Serbia, and it is not alone. A senior French diplomat has been quoted as saying, "our interests are closer to the Serbs than you think...We worry more about Muslims than about Serbs" (Ali and Lifeshultz 1993, xvii). And a French parliament member said, "What many in my party fear is the emergence of a kind of Gaza Strip in the midst of the Balkans" (Cohen 1994, D3). According to United Nations sources, two French soldiers stationed with U.N. forces in Sarajevo, left to join Serbian military forces to prepare to "fight the Muslims who have flooded France" (Reuters 1994).

As a result of immigration from France's colonies and former colonies in North Africa and West Africa, it is estimated that one in every four French citizens has a "non-White" parent or grandparent (Silverman 1992, 10). According to polls, 75 percent of French people think there are "too many Arabs [Muslims]" in France (Bilski and Geddes 1992, 36). Immigrants and their communities live under four levels of racist violence: cultural criticism, social isolation, political marginalization and economic exploitation. In France, the "old racist discourse" emphasized color and physical features, while the "new racist discourse" stresses the conflict between the "superior" French culture and the "inferior" culture of immigrants. In this "new racist discourse" "I am not racist" means "I do not care what color they are, I do not want to live with them, talk to them, or want them in France" (Todorov 1990, 47–8). This "popular racism" became a base for the French National Front Party of Jean-Marie LePen and its racist rhetoric, which gained 5 percent of votes in national elections in the 1980s, later 10 percent, and close to 25 percent in some regions during recent elections.

How have intellectuals responded to the rise of racist discourse in France? There are three important postures. The first one, employed by the left, proposes "repression" of racist discourse, such as making it a crime to advocate that the "holocaust never happened," and civic pressure, such as not renting town halls for racist meetings. The second position minimizes the importance of racist discourse, as a "cruel and undesirable" result of liberty and freedom, and the "price of democracy." The third approach rejects both racist and anti-racist discourse as "two demagogic movements of opposite meaning," in favor of advocating a united "French national identity" (47–8).

The attitudes of Russian intellectuals are similar to those in France. Those who oppose racism and racist discourse claim that "after all, there is the article in the Criminal Code against fanning nationalist hatred; there is public opinion, and finally, the moderate opinions of the Russian intelligentsia" (Kalner 1990, 212–3). They raise outrage that racist violence actually happens: "all in the presence of policemen, deputies, monitors, a huge cast of people entrusted with maintaining public order" (Sinyavsky 1990, 491–2). Some Russian intellectuals see both the Pamyat Society and Zhirinovsky as "problems" resulting from rapid transition to democracy, and believe they will gradually disappear as mature ideas reduce their appeal. In addition, there are intellectuals who find racists "irrational" and anti-racists "reactionary," and argue that there are more important questions facing Russia. All these approaches to racist discourse in France and Russia overlook the fact that racism is integrated into everyday experience, and has become a defining discourse for communities. Furthermore, they disregard the global connections of racism linking, reinforcing and justifying racist beliefs and actions from one place to another such as from Russia to Chechnya to Bosnia to France.

Confronting Global Racism

The symbiotic connections between the global and the everyday allow racism to integrate into institutions, knowledge, imagination and experience, through which the violence of racism replicates itself. In this context, racism is a property of both social and global space. These connected spaces exhibit the impact of racism in terms of violence, oppression and devastation in economic, political and social relations, and the production of culture. Not only does everyday racism invade the social space of homes, factories and churches, global racism ties all activities of prejudice, discrimination, racist knowledge and imagination to a globally racialized past, present and future. As one example, images in the mainstream media connect the global abstract space of racism and the everyday social space of racism. The racist paradigm uses the multiplicity of this connectedness to justify thought and actions. As one Russian said, "You do not want to live with blacks in America; we do not want to live with blacks here."

The two main questions confronting anti-racist intellectuals involve exploring the process of globalization of racism and searching for ways to oppose global racism. These two questions carry theoretical and practical burdens. On a theoretical level the questions demand a reconceptualization of racism, with attention to global connections, in order to understand the process of how racism became a globally interconnected contemporary reality, permeating institutions, knowledge and imagination. On a practical level, these questions necessitate action that unites local anti-racist movements globally. Thus, anti-racist intellectuals and anti-racist movements carry the practical task of combining efforts with theoretical arguments to question racism both locally and globally. This combination will facilitate praxis, creating connections between everyday confrontation of racism and the global confrontation of racism.

While the ultimate goal of anti-racist movements is to eradicate racism, their immediate goal should be to understand the global realities of racism and racist history. This will facilitate building bridges between local anti-racist movements and their historical memory to generate a global anti-racist movement. Furthermore, anti-racist movements should be rooted in organizing societies based on cooperation rather than competition. Competition is a product of the commodification of social relations under capitalism and colonialism, and not only severs individuals from their communities, but also makes them the property of the market rather than part of humanity. In addition, anti-racist movements should foster the survival and legitimacy of autonomous cultural identities, and promote common respect for the heterogeneous character of multi-cultural communities.

But could recognition of the global extent of racism discourage and fragment anti-racist movements leading them to confront only local manifestations of racism? Racism divides people across the global color line and these divisions can permeate anti-racist movements. As much as racism has the propensity to keep anti-racist movements marginalized, isolated and separated by the color line, anti-racist movements should reconceptualize themselves to insist on unity and the importance of confronting racism both locally and globally. Anti-racist European organizations coordinated by UNITED (European Network Against Racism) organized an "Action Week Against Racism" around March 21st, in remembrance of the Sharpeville massacre in South Africa. While the U.N. reserved this week as a "Week of Solidarity with the Peoples Struggling Against Racism and Racial Discrimination," ninety anti-racist organizations from forty European countries met in Prague, and groups in thirty countries held mass demonstrations, conferences, exhibitions and concerts, from Spain to Sweden to Lithuania to Belarus to Greece.

By confronting racism globally, are these anti-racist organizations pursuing an unattainable dream? Martin Luther King raised the challenge to have the courage to dream. Dreaming and acting upon the dream puts theory into practice and is the key to eradicating the crushing power of racism. It is time to take the challenge and make this global struggle an everyday reality.

References

Ali, Rabia and Lawrence Lifschultz. 1993. In plain view. In *Why Bosnia? Writings on the Balkan War*, edited by Rabia Ali and Lawrence Lifschultz. Stony Creek, CT: The Pamphleteer's Press.

Balibar, Etienne. 1994. *Masses, classes, ideas: Studies on politics and philosophy before and after Marx*. Translated by James Swanson. New York: Routledge.

Batur-VanderLippe, Pinar. 1996. Colonialism and Post-Colonialism: Global expansion of racism. In *Racial and Ethnic Relations*, 5th edition, edited by Joe Feagin and Clarice Feagin. New York: Prentice-Hall.

Bilski, Andrew and Diana Geddes. 1992. Panic in Calais: Frightened residents drive out an Arab. *McLean's* 105(47): 36.

Bohlen, Celestine. 1994. Zhrininovsky cult grows: All power to the leader. *The New York Times*, 5 April, p. A1.

Brym, Robert J. 1994. Anti-Semitism in Moscow: A re-examination. *Slavic Review* 53: 844.

Cohen, Roger. 1994. West's fears in Bosnia 1) Chaos, 2) Islam. *The New York Times*, 13 March, p. D3.

Elliott, Dorinda. 1994. Solzhenitsyn goes home. *Newsweek*, 6 June, p. 41.

Erlanger, Steven. 1994. Russia's nationalists love a man in uniform. *The New York Times*, 9 October, p. D5.

Fanon, Frantz. 1963. *The wretched of the earth*. New York: Grove Press.

Gibson, James L. 1994. Understandings of Anti-Semitism in Russia: An analysis of the politics of anti-Jewish attitudes. *Slavic Review* 53: 796–806.

Holmes, Steven. 1993. State Dept. Balkan aides explain why they quit. *The New York Times*, 26 August, p. A12.

Holt, Thomas C. 1995. Marking: Race, race-making, and the writing of history. *American Historical Review* 100: 10.

Kalner, Sasha. 1990. How Fascism starts. Letter in *Small fires: Letters from the Soviet people to* OGONYOK *Magazine 1987–1990*, edited by Christopher Cerf and Marina Albee. New York: Simon & Schuster.

Kohan, John. 1990. Still in love with mother Russia. *Time*, 12 March, p. 40.

Leary, Warren. 1992. Alleging bias, science group urges Russian to quit. *The New York Times*, 29 July, p. B8.

Lebedeva, Yelena. 1994. Planned Muslim center disturbs Muscovites. *The Current Digest of the Post-Soviet Press*, 7 September, pp. 1–4.

Lefebvre, Henri. 1991. *The production of space*. Translated by Donald Nicholson-Smith. Oxford: Blackwell.

Musin, Valery. 1994. Orthodox believers don't want Muslim culture. *The Current Digest of the Post-Soviet Press*, 4 September, p. 4.

Pomfret, John. 1996. Bosnia's vote may hasten partition. *Washington Post*, 13 June, p. A1.

Reuters. 1994. Two French soldiers go over to Serbs. 26 July.

Rich, Vera. 1995. Anthropology Institute accused of racism. *Science*, 7 July, p. 27.

Shakrina, L. 1990. Market relations. Letter in *Small fires: Letters from the Soviet people to* OGONYOK *Magazine 1987–1990*, edited by Christopher Cerf and Marina Albee. New York: Simon & Schuster.

Silverman, Maxim. 1992. *Deconstructing the nation: Immigration, racism and citizenship in Modern*

France. London: Routledge.

Sinyavsky, Andrey. 1990. Russian nationalism. *The Massachusetts Review* 31: 491–492.

Socor, Vladimir. 1994. Fighting spirit in Russia's task force for Chechnya. *RFE/RL*, 9 December.

Todorov, Tzvetan. 1990. Racism (in France). Translated by Mary Maxwell. *Salmagundi* 88–89: 47–8.

• CHAPTER THREE •

Local Global Racism in Latin America

HERNÁN VERA
Professor of Sociology
University of Florida

Racism is practiced openly, and passionately denied in Chile. As a result, broad segments of the population are excluded from participation in the economy, polity, and society or else their participation is made painful and humiliating. Consider the case of the owner of an exercise club, himself the son of relatively recent German immigrants, who refused admittance to Korean and other Asian people, claiming that his act was not racial or ethnic discrimination but motivated by "the foul smell in the saunas resulting from the Korean citizens' food habits" (Sevicio Nacional del Consumidor contra Centro de Salud y Recreacion Gunter Mund y Cia. Limitada 1993). Convinced of the righteousness of his actions, in court he produced two witnesses who declared they had complained to him about "the foul smell produced by the Koreans and Asians in general." In spite of the fact that Chilean tribunals, including the Supreme Court, affirmed the illegality of the exclusion, implicit in the tribunals' decisions was the opinion that restrictions based on race or ethnicity would be allowable if previously announced to the public (Bertelsen 1993). In one of my interviews, a manager, after explaining to me the "achievement-only" hiring policy of his mid-size corporation, added that people who "looked Indian" were not hired because "The fact that most Indians in Chile are confined to poverty reveals their 'inferior culture' and 'inferior racial quality.'"

These practices of overt exclusion justified or denied openly in racist terms, I would like to call "candid racism." These practices are not exclusive to Chile, but ubiquitous in most Latin American countries. A measure of how overt is racial exclusion in Chile can be obtained from considering a type of newspaper want ad soliciting "*señorita buena presencia*," which can be literally translated "single women of good bearing." In these ads "*buena presencia*" is a code word for "White skin," as I confirmed by calling—introducing myself as a relative of a potential applicant—fifteen telephone numbers listed in ads of this kind appearing one week in March 1999 in two Santiago newspapers. In eight cases "light" or "white" skin (*tez clara*) was volunteered as part of what "*buena presencia*" meant. In six additional cases, in response to my direct question, it was admitted that skin tone might make a difference. Only in one case was I told that the color of the skin made no difference. I had also asked a dozen university students for the meaning of "*buena presencia*" in these ads. They all volunteered that the key component was skin tone and ethnicity.

Racial inequality, racism, and the language categories on which they rest, are unique and distinct to each of the thirty-five South American and Caribbean nations. But at the same time, these practices and categories are, and have historically been, a part of the global processes of political, economic and ideological dependence. Racism in Chile and Latin America must be examined as an ongoing process of reproduction that builds layer upon layer, on patterned social relations left behind by historical events in which local and global factors intertwine. To illustrate this process of reproduction, I will examine a single event, so that from its analysis I can propose a direction for research on the roots of current racism, on the racial and ethnic inequality that leads to the exclusion of "minorities" and broad "majorities" from the mainstream of Chilean social life. I want to show how what I call "the vanished majority" can be understood as a local/global process that requires the examination of layers of social relations.

Racism is the socially organized set of attitudes, ideas, and practices that denies people of color and ethnic minorities the dignity, opportunity, freedom, and rewards that a nation has to offer the dominant segments of the population (Feagin and Vera 1995, 7). As such, it impinges directly on the process of national integration and the way in which citizenship is conceived of and exercised. I prefer to use the term "racism," to avoid the many euphemisms that plague the field of "race relations." In doing this, I will lose some analytical precision. Racism does not stand alone as a monolithic, easily recognizable phenomenon. It is deeply rooted in class, ethnic, and gender distinctions as well as in the ideologies of national and regional pride taken for granted in society. It is deeply embedded in the somatic and moral sense of personal identity and the everyday rhythm of life. Very often, as I will show, class, gender, and ethnic identities are articulated in racial terms.

The Case of the Vanished Majority

An advantage of focusing on racism, rather than "race relations," is that it can be examined as a project; that is, as practices seeking to achieve specific goals.

From this perspective, the aesthetic goals of racist projects stand out as having been a badly neglected research topic. Racism seeks to impose the body features of the oppressor as the standard by which bodily beauty and normalcy are to be appraised. It seeks to impose the aesthetic judgments and sensitivity of the oppressor as universal ideals. Racial privilege rests not only on taken-for-granted superior intelligence, morality and spirituality, but also on notions of authentic beauty. In contradistinction, the oppressed are not only defined as inferior in intelligence, morality and spirituality, but are defined also as ugly.

One need only to walk the streets of Latin America's capital cities to realize that the layout of streets, the display of religious and political symbols—cathedrals, government buildings, courthouses, statues of heroes and historical events—the power and tastes of the conqueror and its descendants are represented. The media, especially its advertisements, also express this power and those tastes. And so it is that the fashion models and the actors in magazine ads and TV commercials in Chile *all* have an Anglo-Saxon or Northern European look. In a visit to Chile in 1996, I bought a collection of the most popular local magazines at a downtown kiosk to examine the pictures in advertisements. I also systematically watched different channels of prime time TV for one week. I did not find a single Mestizo or Indian-looking actor or actress, although Mestizos and people of aboriginal descent represent more than seventy percent of the population. I replicated the magazine study in Quito, Ecuador, in December 1996. I found an overwhelming number of Northern-European and Anglo looking models; however, I could detect Mestizo features in roughly a tenth of the models. In these countries, imported Colors of Benetton ads are often the only models of dark skin.[1]

In September 1997, *Paula* (1997), the best selling woman's magazine in Chile, celebrated its 30th year with a special 200-page full-color issue and a black-and-white brochure, *Madres Niñas* (1997), devoted to the problem of teenage mothers. The main issue had a pull out front cover portraying thirty starved-to-perfection young women, all dressed in white jeans and T-shirts. All were of Nordic European or Anglo-Saxon looks. Not one of the women, looked Mediterranean, none could be said to be Mestiza, the type to which most of the population of Chile belongs. In case one missed the message of the whiteness of the models' bodies, they were all dressed in white jeans and white T-shirts. To reinforce this message the background is also white. These white women dressed in white against a white background contrasted starkly with the all Indian or mestizo girls featured in the dark grey brochure. All the 25 or so girls pictured in this brochure had recognizable Indian or Mestizo features and were often poorly dressed. In summary, the good, desirable life was portrayed by the bodies of white females dressed in white against a white backcloth. The social problem of teen pregnancy was represented—in black and grey tones—by the bodies of all dark skinned Indian and Mestizo child-mothers and their children.

I asked a producer of television commercials who works for an important advertising firm in Chile to explain the absence of the racial type of the overwhelming majority of the population from the commercials she produced. Her answer was that agencies contracted with their clients for a certain type of actor. "North American and Chilean clients clearly specify that the TV commercial must be shot with white models of fair complexion, light hair, and upper class looks," she told me. Then she added that "there is nothing racial about that choice: all marketing surveys show that Mestizo, Oriental, or Arab looking people have a low aspirational[2] value. Surveys show that no one wants to imitate them."

She thus justified racial/ethnic exclusion in the dominant prejudices of the population as captured by marketing research. Her words also reveal the vitality of the categories of white European and Mestizo, which were already a part of the caste society of colonial and early independence times (Wade 1993, 8–10), and observe how immigrant groups (Asians and Arabs) that have a strong presence in Chile and other Latin American countries have joined Mestizos (Indians and black people) as targets for exclusion in the image of what is good and desirable in consumer life. Finally, it is notable that the exclusion of immigrant groups is justified by the same prejudices that support the exclusion of people of color.

The vanishing of images of the preponderant racial/ethnic type from commercial advertising is a prime illustration of two main ways in which Latin American racism is part of a global phenomenon. First, according to the producer of the local commercials, international clients demanded a specific race, ethnicity, and social class body image in their advertisements. At least some of the surveys she mentions as justification for this policy are most probably done in the United States and Europe. Second, Chile exports the advertisements and TV spots it produces to 15 other Latin American countries and several countries in Eastern Europe, another reason to make sure the images conform to global prejudicial stereotypes.

The Conquest Today

The conquest of the Americas by Spain was made in the name of a superior God, a superior religion, and a superior monarch to whom the aboriginal peoples owed servitude. The doctrines justifying the servitude of aboriginal populations and African slaves were global in the sense that they applied to Spain and all its colonies.

The dominance of the European, established in the sixteenth century through raw violence and economic subjugation, has continued to be reproduced locally to the present day, despite the changing socioeconomic conditions of the colonial order, and the establishment and development of independent Latin American nations. A social scientist I recently interviewed in Chile believed that the "model" of interaction between the dominant Spaniard and the subjected Indian and Mestizo strata is still the operative model in many Latin American nations. In his view this "model," with only minor adaptations, dominates the mind-set and expectations of industrial entrepreneurs in these countries, and is a crucial obstacle to Latin American development.

The active importance of the conquest to today's Latin America can be readily observed in the fact that in practically all Latin American countries, one finds communities, peoples and persons who still live by and practice the cultures that were here upon the arrival of the European 500 years ago. Aboriginal groups and runaway slave communities in Jamaica, Haiti, Cuba, Suriname, the Dominican Republic, Brazil, Venezuela, Colombia, Ecuador, Bolivia, Paraguay, and Chile, reject the European culture and way of life. In the parlance of the social sciences, they refuse to "assimilate;" to become a part of the Europeanized national mainstream that reserves for them a place at the very bottom of the social structure. The Mapuche, for example, the aboriginal group in Chile who still consider themselves to be undefeated by the Spanish invaders, currently engage in rituals decrying the brutal and treacherous nature of the conquest. In their contemporary songs and poems, they depict Europeans and their descendants as "cold, evil foreigners" (Bengoa 1992). But the Mapuche are not alone. In the Peruvian highlands, hundreds of little towns stage a show called Inca-Capitán, which depicts the events of Cajamarca in 1532 and 1533, in which the Inca Atahualpa was finally captured and killed. A similar ritual is staged in Bolivia in numerous feasts. In Mexico and Guatemala the foundational acts of the Conquest are also re-enacted in ritual song and dance by the descendants of many aboriginal communities (Bengoa 1992).

Thus, to understand the current exclusion of Mestizos, Indians, and Africans from the advertised images of the good life, one needs to understand the establishment of the relations of white Europeans and these groups in the colonial era. These relations evolved into different racial orders in each Latin American nation as re-elaborations of a religious, political and economic order of the Spanish world domain.

The Nineteenth Century Imperialist Wave

The incorporation of Southern European, Asian, and Middle Eastern immigrants as targets for racial exclusion in the case we are analyzing is the sediment of another global racist impetus. Colonial relations did not become fully conceptualized in racial terms until the second half of the nineteenth century, following the European doctrines that supported the wave of colonialism in that century. These conceptualizations, which were rejected, accepted, and adapted in different ways in particular Latin American Countries, are also global in reach. Within the Latin American continent the works by authors such as those I am about to mention had a continental, not just a local, influence.

Latin American nations gained political independence from Europe in the early nineteenth century, when they were racially and ethnically highly heterogeneous societies. In spite of political independence, their elites were for the most part creole; that is, locally born Whites of Spanish origin, or in Brazil of Portuguese origin. These elites had a closer contact with and knowledge of Europe than they did with their own countries, thus adopting social aims and views that were truly foreign in their nations (Helg 1990).

In the last quarter of the nineteenth century, Latin American intellectuals re-elaborated the European and North American ideologies with original results. This re-elaboration, obsessed with "colored races," had little or nothing to do with their countries' realities. For example, by 1880 Africans and Indians were insignificant minorities in Argentina. Yet prominent writers such as Jose Ingenieros, Domingo Faustino Sarmiento, and Carlos Octavio Bunge, were concerned with the superiority of the White race over colored races. These writers were extremely influential in the rest of Latin America. "Men of colored races," wrote Ingenieros, who is considered a progressive writer, "should not be politically and juridically our equal; they are unfit for the exercise of civil rights and they should not be juridically considered as 'individuals'" (Helg 1990, 37).

Notwithstanding, Latin Americans did not share in the European and North American horror of miscegenation, which was the means that would supposedly bring about the future "improvement of the race" through "whitening" (Wright 1993). The evolutionary inferiority of some races proposed in Europe and North America, Sarmiento thought, would be overcome through education.

These re-elaborated racist ideas would end up targeting not only people of color but also Europeans. In 1883, for example Domingo Faustino Sarmiento, prominent educator and President of Argentina (1868–1874), wrote that the brains of Spaniards, who were a strong immigrant current into Argentina at the time, had been atrophied by five centuries of Inquisition and intermarriage with races possessing lesser brains. The faculties needed for self-government and democracy belonged to the superior Anglo-Saxon. He deplored the fact that Argentina had attracted so few of them as their immigrants and such a high proportion of Latins (Spaniards and Italians)(Helg 1990, 40).

In the era of German hegemony, Nicolás Palacios (1996), in a book that is still in print, wrote in 1903 that the superiority of the Chilean Mestizo race derived from its being a mixture of two very similar racial stocks. The Spanish conqueror, he claimed, descended from "those warrior and conquering blond barbarians...the Gothic, prototype of the Teutonic, German or Nordic race" (44). The Araucanian Indian was seen as similar to the conqueror in his warrior ways, as being "of similar brain and heart." To this felicitous mixture, Palacios attributes a "lively race sentiment" among Chileans and the fact "that we all think identically in all cardinal questions" (43). However, the most important similarity was in the gender relations within these "races."

> The Gothic and the Araucanians, so different in the physical aspect, both possessed, with the same clarity and fixity, all the characteristic traits of what the experts call virile or patriarchal psychology, in which the opinion of the male weighs absolutely over that of women in all spheres of mental ability.

Palacios' writing illustrates the intimate connection between sexism and racism. Patriarchy, in his thought, is a sign of racial supremacy.

Palacios argues strongly against the immigration of "Latin races" to Chile because their mixture with the local stock would produce, according "to one of the most solidly established conclusions of modern science," a "mediocre offspring" (47). He explains, "The cross of two races of diverse psychology, and I am not speaking of different degrees of culture, brings about an imbalance of the peripheral nervous relations with the receptive and moderating brain centers." As a consequence, "These Mestizos lack what is called brain control, and they constitute the social burden of the passionate, the impulsive, the atavistic and moral degenerates of all sorts..." (48).

Needless to say, Palacios' history was as bad as his biological and social science. According to reputable historians, the touted "homogeneous race" of Chile was formed by the Spaniard's absorption "of the scarce pacific Indians" to which "the bellicose Araucanian of the south of the Biobio was not integrated" (Eyzaguirre 1967).

Racism, Ethnic Prejudice and Xenophobia

Thus, racism in Latin America cannot be understood in terms of the binary relations between Whites of European origin and people of color, excluding the experience of European immigrants, as it is usually conceived of and theorized in the United States. Latin American racism must be understood also in terms of the relations between different groups of European extraction. I propose that the distinction between racism, ethnic prejudices, and xenophobia is largely academic in Latin America. These phenomena, as the thought of Nicolás Palacios clearly illustrates, draw from the same ideological pool which propounds biological explanations, glorifies inheritance, and attributes inferior physical, intellectual, and moral traits to the excluded populations. For example, Polish immigrants in Brazil, as reported by Octavio Iani (1960) were allegedly given to alcoholism, were excessively religious, and were intellectually inferior. In the dominant ideology, Polish immigrants and their descendants were not seen as Brazilians, but as "polacos," a separate and inferior category comparable to Negroes (336). Antonia Rebolledo has called "turcofobia" (Turk phobia) the discrimination faced by Arab immigrants in Chile, "Turk" being the pejorative term with which Arabs have been designated in many Latin American countries. She notes that the "hostility directed at Arab immigrants is part of a more general situation of rejection of the foreigner as such" (Rebolledo 1994). In Chile, in 1996, two young professionals explained to me the superiority of the "Chilean and Latin American race" which was "not afflicted by the flaws of laziness, arrogance and stupidity that traditionally plague the Spanish and Italian races." Thus, important elements of turn-of-the-century theorizing about race and culture appear to be still as much in vogue in Latin America as they are in the United States and Europe.

I must leave aside a "racism of class" to be found among dominant groups in many Latin American countries. This racism of class explains the need for working class subordination in the same terms used against denigrated racial/ethnic groups.

Most Latin American nations define themselves officially as racial democracies, and adhere, in different ways, to that official myth. In Chile, scholars and politicians agree that racism is not a national problem. A minister of education said in a press interview that Chile is a homogeneous race, not like the United States that has a black problem (Bezama 1991). Other countries, such as Venezuela, declare their racial democracy by officially defining themselves as Mestizo, "Café Con Leche" societies. Racism is considered non-existent there. In fact throughout the 20th century, racism in Latin American countries has been defined as existing solely as the virulent anti-black type of discrimination and segregation in the United States. By looking at the closed system in the United States as the true racism, Latin Americans overlook the signs of discrimination in their own countries. In all Latin American countries, generations of elites have maintained a somatic image of themselves that has emphasized whiteness. These racial democracies and "racially homogeneous" nations do not exist.

Conclusion

I hope to have shown that the aesthetic choices at the case of the vanishing of images that represent the majority of the population in Chile and other Latin

American countries is difficult to understand without reference to colonial categorizations and the racial ideologies elaborated to justify the European colonial expansions of the nineteenth century still in use. However, the analysis of the historical layers on which contemporary Latin American racism rests is only a part, perhaps the least important part, of the story. Understanding of contemporary racism requires an examination of the local social structures and the social process that propel its reproduction today. While I do not have the space here to outline these structures and processes, we must remember that racism is about privilege: the economic, social, and cultural privilege that dominant groups want to perpetuate, at considerable cost to themselves and their societies.[3] For these groups the past—local and global—is filled with ideological elements with which to construct and reconstruct the dominant ideologies of each society. In an age of United States hegemony, these groups also feed on the propaganda of the United States Information Agency (USIA) and aggressively marketed U.S. media products, including books such as *The Bell Curve* (Herrnstein and Murray 1994).

In searching for the remedies for economic racial/ethnic inequalities, we must keep in mind that in Latin America these remedies are no easier to implement than are solutions for these countries' economic dependency. Both are global processes with deep local consequences and need to be approached as such. Both processes determine the integration and exclusion from national life of broad segments of Latin American populations. Economic dependency and racial/ethnic inequality mutually support each other, to the extent that they could be considered one and the same process of racism/imperialism.

References

Bengoa, Jose. 1992. *Conquista y barbarie: Ensayo crítico acerca de la conquista de Chile.* Santiago, Chile: Ediciones Sur.

Bertelsen R., Raul. 1993. *Denuncia por infraccion a la ley de proteccion al consumidor: Sevicio Nacional del Consumidor contra Centro de Salud y Recreación Gunther Mund y Cia.Limitada.* Santiago, Chile: Informe Constitucional, September.

Bezama, Boris. 1991. Racismo en Chile: Prejuicios, mentiras y dominación. *Página Abierta* 9(22)(December): 18.

Eyzaguirre, Jaime. 1967. *Historia de las instituciones políticas y sociales de Chile.* Santiago, Chile: Editorial Universitaria.

Feagin, Joe R. and Hernán Vera. 1995. *White racism: The basics.* New York and London: Routledge.

Helg, Aline. 1990. Race in Argentina and Cuba, 1880–1930: Theory, policies, and popular reaction. In *The idea of race in Latin American, 1870-1940.* Edited by Graham, Richard. Austin: University of Texas Press.

Herrnstein, Richard J. and Charles Murray. 1994. *The Bell Curve: Intelligence and class structure in American life.* New York: The Free Press.

Iani, Octavio. 1960. Do Polonês ao Polaco. *Revista do Museu Paulista,* Nova Series, XII, São Paulo, pp. 315–338.

Madres Niñas, Postdata? 1997. *Number 1.* Santiago, Chile: Fundación América, Cochrane Impresores.

Palacios, Nicolás. 1996. *La raza Chilena.* Santiago, Chile: Editorial Andujar.

Paula: 30 años. *764.* September 1997. Santiago, Chile: Paula Comunicaciones S.A.

Rebolledo Hernández, Antonia. 1994. "La 'Turcofobia': Discriminación antiarabe en Chile, 1900-1950." *Historia 28*: 249–272.

Sevicio Nacional del Consumidor contra Centro de Salud y Recreación Gunther Mund y Cia. Limitada. Juzgado de Policía Local de Vitacura, 6 de Enero de 1993. Decision by Judge Sergio Villalobos Ríos.

Wade, Peter. 1993. *Blackness and race mixture: The dynamics of racial identity in Colombia.* Baltimore: John Hopkins University Press.

Wright, Winthrop R. 1993. *Café con leche: Race class and national image in Venezuela.* Austin: University of Texas Press.

• CHAPTER FOUR •

A Case of Culturalization: Haitians in the Dominican Republic

YANICK ST. JEAN
Visiting Assistant Professor, Department of Sociology
University of Wisconsin-Eau Claire

Modern racism is culturalized (Essed 1991). One need not be Jewish to be a cultural Jew, but only perceived as thinking, acting and feeling like a Jew on the basis of prevailing characterizations of Jew. Jew is a position of difference vis-a-vis a referent (Guillaumin 1992) thus, the difference is denigrated and culturalized. Jewishness is a minority position, a vilified symbol that can apply to any individual or group, in light of this referent, perceived to deviate from cultural standards.

Likewise the notion "black" carries with it a set of meanings based on the cultural referent's assessment of black difference. Thus, blackness is not necessarily associated with physical traits, but an abstraction that reflects difference from a referent as viewed by a referent. Culturalized blackness means more than somatic characteristics; it reflects a disapproval of black difference and disciplines, individuals or groups, black or non-black, that dares to diverge from this accepted referent. With culturalization, blackness becomes more symbolic, more complex, more fluid, and more easily incorporated into a global code.

Consider the term "Haitian" in Dominican thinking. The term is not always an objective identification of inhabitants of the other half of Hispaniola. Haitian is often pejorative and applied to anyone, of Haitian origin or not, daring to violate or appearing to be a potential violator of Dominican standards. A student who once received a poor grade from a Dominican teacher called the teacher "a Haitian s.o.b." (Menendez-Alarcon 1994). So Haitian in the Dominican Republic is a culturalized, denigrated category with a specific, subjective set of meanings—not necessarily racial. Anyone who acts like a s.o.b. is a culturalized Haitian.

Note how Haitian is also synonymous with black. In the view of Dominican sociologist, Adelfina Pontier, "When [Dominicans] say black, or when they say Haitian, it's the same thing" (cited in Wucker 1996, 83). Mistaken for Haitians on the basis of color, Dominican citizens may be arrested, and sent to Haiti. One farmer, stripped of identity papers and other belongings, as he and his family were being put on a bus to Haiti, exclaimed, "We are black, but not Haitians!" (Caroit 1999) The culturalization of Haitian is also a culturalization of blackness and, as such, derives meaning from Dominican representations of blackness.

Once culturalized, racial notions are dissociated from specific groups. So while old practices continue, victimization is less obvious. For that reason, the direct and indirect impact of racial notions on these groups is obscured, even while the groups' minority positions vis-a-vis cultural referent are strengthened. Additionally, with dissociation and culturalization, racial change becomes more difficult, since change necessitates understanding how notions and their sources interact. For example, to refute the conceptualization "Haitian" in the Dominican Republic, an understanding of reasons behind the Dominican thinking is key. How did "Haitian" become associated with a negative image? What are contributing historic circumstances? What is the role of the Dominican cultural referent in this denigration? Particles need reconnecting.

Unfortunately, coherence and clarity are not defining characteristics of modern racism. Moreover, as Haitian anthropologist and historian Michel-Rolph Trouillot (1995) suggested, societies tend to silence the past. Silencing is beneficial because when combined with diffusion through culturalization it can effectively repress the sources of racial notions, and, eventually, stifle change. In a silencing society, individuals and groups interact without the knowledge, or with only a vague understanding, of how structures from the past influence actions and interactions in the present. It is therefore silence—national and global—that must first be broken, to understand how notions relate to sources, and to refute conceptualizations. Knowledge of Dominican-Haitian history, and roots of Dominican culture in colonization, can provide reasons behind the culturalization of "Haitian," and continued oppression of Haitians in the Dominican Republic.

Breaking Silence on Haitian Mistreatment

It is 1937. Blaming Haitians for economic problems of the Dominican-Haitian frontier, President Raphael Trujillo orders their extermination. Everyone suspected of being Haitian is asked to pronounce two words: Perejil and Cotorrito. The order is executed by the military. In this ordeal named *El Corto*, approximately 17,000 Haitian men, women, and children who fail the linguistic identification perish (d'Ans 1992).[1] Only the lives of Haitian sugar cane cutters are spared. Cane cutters' lives are probably precious, and sacred enough to be protected (d'Ans 1992).

Critical to the Dominican economy is the sugar industry (Calder 1985). Haitian scholar Jean Price-Mars (1953) who has written extensively on Haitian-Dominican relations noted, "Nous avons toujours été et nous sommes encore les fournisseurs les plus fidèles de la main-d'oeuvre agricole de la communauté dominicaine" [We (Haitians) have always been and still are the most committed suppliers of agricultural workers to the Dominican community] (309).[2] If cane cutters were exterminated, who, then, would do this harsh, tedious, back-breaking "Haitian work?"(Griffin 1995). Deploring this massacre, an angered international community compared Trujillo to Hitler and Mussolini (Rooarda 1996).

It is 1946. One Dominican writer recaptures the incident, calling it "a message to the Dominican youth, to men and women in whose hands the future of the [Dominican] nation reposes" (d'Ans 1992). Thus, the extermination was being presented to future generations by this writer, probably a collaborator of Trujillo (d'Ans 1992), as an expression of nationhood, an example of how cherished Dominican ideals, borders and territory ought to be protected, and a symbol to be inscribed in Dominican memory.

It is 1996. The Dominican-Haitian situation in the Dominican Republic has not changed. If not a massacre similar to what took place in 1937, "arbitrary roundups of what Dominican officials call 'Haitian-looking individuals'" continue to be carried out by the Dominican police (Gavigan 1996). The past is present.

Beyond 1996 is little if any change (Wucker 1999). The detention and repatriation of Haitians continue. The children of Haitian workers born in the Dominican Republic are excluded from citizenship (Caroit 1999). A dynamic past flows into present and future.[3]

But what exactly makes a Haitian in the Dominican Republic "Haitian-looking?" Haitians and Dominicans share similar "looks." Any Haitian could be Dominican. Do linguistic abilities have a role in Haitian identification as in 1937? Are there subtle factors that form this Haitian look? Perhaps it is the ability to read and write? "Haitian-looking" is a symbol for a set of subjective characteristics that Dominicans (the cultural referents), on the basis of a dominant referent, associate with the position "Haitian." A Haitian look is not strictly about visible traits, but a culturalized, diffused notion applicable to non-Haitian persons or groups, for whatever reason, deviate from Dominican norms. An image with deep racial roots appears non-racial. Detention, repatriation, and exclusion from citizenship are anchored in tradition.

More Explanations

The mistreatment of Haitians in the Dominican Republic is likely due to additional historical factors as well. Haiti occupied that country twice, once before 1809, and again from 1822 to 1844. Moreover, in 1849 and from 1855–1856 there were attempts by Haiti to regain power in the Dominican Republic and unify Hispaniola (Prince 1994). Interestingly, "the Dominican Republic now celebrates its independence not from any European colonial power but from the 22 years of Haitian rule that ended in 1844" (Wucker 1996, 81).

A continued sense of threat thus loomed large in the minds of Dominican political elites—a threat legitimate, perhaps, since during their occupation Haitians promoted the immigration of African American Protestants in an attempt to "blacken" the Dominican population. This action was a direct attack on Dominican culture, its preference for White, whitening, and Catholicism. Thus from a Dominican view, arrogant Haitians should be feared and, whenever possible, punished. Moreover, in the 19th century, the anti-Haitianess of Dominican political regimes received support from the Dominican Catholic Church whose lands were nationalized, priests salaries discontinued and their status diminished during the twenty-two-year Haitian occupation (Martinez-Fernandez 1995). Violations of geographic and cultural borders made Haitians despicable to Dominicans. What appears as anti-Haitian racism on the part of Dominicans thus could well express a noble sense of Dominican nationhood, and a desire to retain national autonomy, protect norms, religion, and culture, from recurrence of an authoritarian, oppressive history, in the views of Dominicans, that might best be forgotten. Dominican attitudes and actions towards Haitians may be based on factors other than racial hatred.

But while nationhood may play some role in the treatment of Haitians, Dominican legends and beliefs, the racial attitudes of students, and the words and writings of some Dominican officials and intellectuals, speak differently (Menendez-Alarcon 1994). They indicate that anti-Haitian prejudice in the Dominican Republic is likely anti-black prejudice.[4] Indeed, social scientists in the Caribbean and elsewhere have reported their concern with anti-Haitian racism in the Dominican Republic (Rios 1980).

Dominican Intellectuals

Former President Joaquín Balaguer once remarked, "the black abandoned to his instinct...imposes in all the countries the reproduction of barbarian customs" (d'Ans 1992). This Balaguerian thinking that associates black with animality and lack of civilization is consistent with his reported aversion towards Haitians, and people of Haitian descent (Norton 1994). Balaguer's thinking is also consistent with his concern regarding increases in permanent

Haitian immigration in the Dominican Republic, his closing of the border in 1967 (Prince 1994), his ridicule and denigration of political opponent José Francisco Peña Gómez, "very palpably black," and, ironically like Balaguer himself,[5] is said to be of "Haitian origin" (Norton 1994). If, as Balaguer put it, "the black abandoned to his instinct...imposes in all the countries the reproduction of barbarian customs" (d'Ans 1992), in order for the Dominican nation to be protected from barbarity, black, Haitian and Haitian-looking people must be excluded.

Legends and Attitudes

Myths, stories and legends can have a powerful impact on the imagination and actions of a community (St. Jean and Feagin 1998). Dominican legends nurture the dominant referent. They imbue Dominican culture and feed racial attitudes. Consider the following myth about the origins of blackness (Menendez-Alarcon 1994, 305).

> People became black because Cain killed his own brother Abel, leaving his imprint of the crime ingrained on earth (apparition of stain on the skin of human beings). But, later on, to save humanity from such a sentence, a river of silvered and crystalline water—the purpose of which was to purify humans from this terrible spell—spurted on earth. This river was a divine sign of the sin's purgation. All humanity went to the big river bed to dip into the water and recover their white skin. Since so many people were bathing, the water became tainted color, gradually losing its celestial faculties. Some could only lighten a little of their skin and those who came later could only wash the palms of their hands and the soles of their feet. The river was exhausted and the mark of Cain remained in those who went later to the purification ceremony.

In light of this Dominican legend of the origins of blackness, dark-skinned Haitians are either Cain himself, or among those who dipped in the river late, very late, too late to be whitened. Thus, in Dominican thinking, Haitians still carry a strong epidermal expression of Cain's sin. In order to protect themselves, Dominicans would want to exclude Haitians and the Haitian-looking, regardless of empathy, and interact only with those purified from sin—the lightest, Spaniards and other Europeans in the referent. As Dominicans dip into this cleaner river of interactions, they, too, can become lighter, more Spanish and moral, therefore saved from the sin of Cain. Told again and again, such stories and the messages they carry cement the Dominican community while nurturing their collective memory of racism.

De-Haitianization

Efforts to purge Dominican culture of Haitians on the one hand, and to Hispanicize on the other, arise for reasons other than the protection of national autonomy (Menendez-Alarcon 1994). Though nationalism may play some role, anti-Haitian actions in the Dominican Republic seem more anti-black and pro-white than pro-nation. In light of the cultural referent, should trespassers be of European origin, Dominicans might welcome, or even invite, territorial and cultural invasion. But such encouragement is not likely when trespassers are black. Dominicans never classify themselves as black. They see themselves as Indians, and identify as *indio claro, indio oscuro, indio* (Menendez-Alarcon 1994). This classification is interesting since Dominicans are a mulatto population. Racial characteristics of Dominicans are a mixture of Caucasian and African (Menendez-Alarcon 1994).

The fictitious self-classification as Indian is symbolic of a Dominican repudiation of African origins (Menendez-Alarcon 1994). Self-classification is consistent also with the Dominican preference for things European and, ultimately, negative attitudes towards blacks, Haitians, and the "Haitian-looking." The traditional exclusion of Haitians from participation in the Dominican nation, beginning with its most extreme form in 1937, seems designed to protect a dream, and what Dominicans wish the Dominican to become, physically and culturally (Menendez-Alarcon 1994). One would expect anti-Haitian racism to be even more prevalent among educated segments in the Dominican Republic, who likely share Balaguer's devotion to Spanish culture (Menendez-Alarcon 1994). To the extent that intermarriage is an accurate measure of acceptance of the "other," it makes sense that a majority of Dominican college students said they would not marry someone black (see Menendez-Alarcon 1994).

According to Price-Mars, "the Dominican people have rejected their own [racial] conditions" (Menendez-Alarcon 1994). They "have for the most part, denied their blackness" (Torres-Saillant 1998). Illustrations in this paper, including the Indian classification, support these claims. It is therefore not surprising that Dominicans would want to improve physically by lightening skin (even Balaguer reportedly did so),[6] and to improve culturally by rejecting norms, values and other elements associated with blackness (Menendez-Alarcon 1994). Dominican rejection of the "Haitian-looking" is consistent with these goals.

The culturalization of Haitian in the Dominican Republic is likely due to a complex of factors, but is primarily due to Dominican identification with the culture of Spaniards (as evident in legends, and the thinking of intellectuals). This identification was challenged by Haitians during their occupation. Negative culturalization is thus consistent with a Dominican dream to be physically and culturally as close as possible to their European referent. The Dominican-Haitian relationship, and culturalized meaning of the term "Haitian," exemplify how racism rooted in a historical past lingers, affecting present and future, while remaining hidden and unrecognized (though blatant) due to historical silencing, dissociation from a particular group, diffusion, and culturalization. Under certain circumstances Dominican citizens are Haitian.

Long after the independence of the Dominican Republic from Haiti, Juan Pepen, a priest, noted, "The history of Dominican heterodoxy remains unwritten; but experience demonstrates that our [Dominican] nationality ends where the [Protestant] 'Churches' and 'voodoo' begin" (Martin-Fernandez 1995, 88). While his statement has multiple meanings (some will point that the statement is taken out of context), Pepen may be recalling the unwelcome immigration of African American Protestants to the Dominican Republic during the Haitian occupation and (perhaps unconsciously) stereotyping Haitians. Given the Dominican preference for white, and the interchangeability of black with Haitian in everyday Dominican language, one might add, "...where the color black begins." Martinez-Fernandez, who cited Pepen, concludes, "This kind of sentiment reveals the persistence of such ideas far into the twentieth century" (Martinez-Fernandez 1995, 88). Past is present, and shaping a future.

While "this kind of sentiment" towards Haitians permeates Dominican culture, it is difficult to grasp and link to sources because these sources are dissolved and dissipated. "Haitian" is an abstraction. It is beyond literal meaning. It applies to the Haitian-looking, as defined by Dominicans. Violators of Dominican standards are symbolic Haitians. The Dominican-Haitian relationship of the past has lost its representative force in the collective imagination of the Dominican (and perhaps also Haitian) people.

To refute the conceptualization of "Haitian" in the Dominican Republic, knowledge of reasons behind popular Dominican thinking is needed. It is necessary to be familiar with the role of history in shaping the present, and the power of diffusion and culturalization in silencing history. Such renewed vision would move Haitians and Dominicans closer to resolving long-term problems permeating their interactions. A careful look at that past must precede reconciliation.

Holocaust, African slavery, or *El Corto*—what society wants known its atrocities? One observer noted that Dominican history emerged as an intellectual pursuit only after the death of Trujillo in 1961. During Trujillo's dictatorship the writing of history could be "a life-threatening" exercise (Calder 1985). Trujillo is not alone among political leaders in attempting to bury a dishonorable historical knowledge. Are not shameful markers best forgotten? And, is not "one group's need to remember...often grist for another's desire to forget"? (Lustiger-Thaler 1998, 190). Moreover, are not racial characterizations more aggressive in their impact, and also more lasting, when dissociated from their historical source? The Haitian Creole proverb, "bay kou bliyé, poté mak, sonjé"[7] [Give a blow, forget; carry its mark, remember] seems appropriate here. Reshaping the collective Dominican imagination will likely meet resistance from those, like Trujillo, who prefer to bury a shameful past.

Conclusion

In the Dominican Republic, one need not be Haitian to be a cultural Haitian, but need only be perceived as thinking, acting, feeling, and "looking" like a Haitian on the basis of prevailing characterizations of Haitian. "Haitian" is a position of difference vis-a-vis a cultural referent (Dominican and ultimately Spanish). Difference is denigrated and culturalized. Culturalized Haitianess, a symbol of vilification, applies to any individual or group perceived to deviate, in a "Haitian" way, from Dominican standards.

Change is implemented by breaking silence. Silence—national and global—must be shunned to refute conceptualizations. Past shapes present and future. Imaginative visions of change begin with historic underpinnings of the present, and their reflections, or suppression, in the collective memory of the people.

References

Calder, Bruce. 1985. The Dominican Republic: Surveying a century of development and change. *Latin American Research Review* 20: 253–261.

Caroit, Jean-Michel. 1999. Saint Domingue procède à de nouvelles expulsions massives d'Haïtiens. *Le Monde Interactif*, vendredi 26 novembre.

Corten, André and Isis Duarte. 1995. Five hundred thousand Haitians in the Dominican Republic. *Latin American Perspectives* 86: 94–110.

D'Ans, André Marcel. 1992. Le racisme: Théorie avant l'acte ou théorisation en trompe-l'oeil et après coup? In *Racisme et modernité*, edited by M. Wieviorka. Paris: Editions de la découverte.

Essed, Philomena. 1991. *Understanding everyday racism*. Newbury Park, CA: Sage.

Gavigan, Patrick. 1996. Haitians in the Dominican Republic. *Haiti Insight*, February/March.

Griffin, Regina. 1995. Hidden from sight: Cane cutters in the Dominican Republic. *America* (July): 22–24.

Guillaumin, Colette. 1992. La différence culturelle. In *Racisme et modernité*, edited by M. Wieviorka. Paris: Editions de la découverte.

Lustiger-Thaler, Henri. 1998. Remembering forgetfully. In *Re-situating identities*, edited by Vered Amit-Talai and Caroline Knowles. Canada: Broadview Press.

Martinez-Fernandez, Luis. 1995. The sword and the crucifix: Church-state relations and nationality in the Nineteenth-century Dominican Republic. *Latin American Research Review* 30: 69–91.

Menendez-Alarcon, Antonio V. 1994. Racial prejudice: A Latin American case. *Research in race and ethnic relations* 7: 299–319.

Norton, Graham. 1994. Flashpoint Hispaniola. *The World Today* 50: 122–3.

Price-Mars, Dr. Jean. 1953. *La République d'Haiti et la République Dominicaine*. Port-au-Prince, Haiti: Collection du Tricinquantenaire de l'Indépendance d'Haiti.

Prince, Rod. 1994. Haiti in the eyes of the world. In *Haiti files: Decoding the crisis*, edited by James Ridgeway. Washington D.C.: Essential.

Ridgeway, James. 1994. *The Haiti files: Decoding the crisis*. Washington, D.C.: Essential.

Rios, Palmira N. 1980. The growing concern about racism among Spanish-Speaking scholars of the Caribbean. *Black Sociologist* 7: 13–8.

Rooarda, Eric Paul. 1996. Genocide next door: The good neighbor policy, The Trujillo Regime, and The Haitian Massacre of 1937. *Diplomatic History* 20: 301–319.

St. Jean, Yanick, and Joe R. Feagin. 1998. *Double burden: Black women and everyday racism*. New York, NY: M.E. Sharpe.

Torres-Saillant, Silvio. 1998. The tribulations of blackness. *Latin American Perspectives* 25: 126–147.

Trouillot, Michel-Rolph. 1995. *Silencing the past: Power and the production of history*. Boston: Beacon.

Wucker, Michele. 1996. Democracy comes to Hispaniola. *World Policy Journal* 13: 80–88.

———. 1999. *Why the cocks fight: Dominicans, Haitians, and the struggle for Hispaniola*. New York: Hill and Wang.

• CHAPTER FIVE •

Ethnic Discrimination: A Critical Survey of Economic Explanations

JOMO K.S.
Assistant Secretary General for Economic Development
United Nations, New York
Formerly Professor, Faculty of Economics and Administration
University of Malaya, Kuala Lumpur

Ethnic discrimination has not been the subject of much theoretical consideration in economics. Typically, ethnic relations are relegated to the realm of sociology, and less commonly to politics, social psychology or social anthropology. Nevertheless, perhaps owing to its political significance in the United States, various economists have attempted to offer economic explanations for the phenomenon of ethnic discrimination, drawing largely on the U.S. experience, particularly Black-White relations, for empirical reference. The existence of ethnic discrimination elsewhere has not inspired similar theoretical contributions, although there is an abundance of empirical studies of economic differentiation along ethnic lines in many societies, much of which is attributed to discrimination.

Not surprisingly, most of the economic literature on ethnic discrimination in the U.S. is informed by neoclassical economic analysis, the dominant approach in that society and, probably, in the world today. It is worth noting, however, that the professional establishment received rather unenthusiastically the pioneering effort by Gary Becker to extend neoclassical economic analysis to the study of ethnic discrimination. As Becker notes in his introduction to the 1971 second edition of his *The Economics of Discrimination*, based on his Ph.D. thesis and originally published in 1957 by the University of Chicago Press, his colleagues at Chicago were skeptical, the university press was reluctant to publish the book, and only a few professional economic journals reviewed it.

Nevertheless, the growth of the civil rights movement in the U.S. from the late fifties, and especially the sixties, resulted in various contributions offering different explanations, largely from within the neoclassical economic paradigm but often carrying rather different policy implications. With the mixed record of affirmative action policies since the sixties and a strong backlash by established interests adversely affected by such policies, and bolstered by the resurgence of conservative market ideologies broadly opposed to stated intervention of most kinds, interest has shifted again, this time away from the analysis of ethnic discrimination itself to the consideration of ethnic preferential policies, with a lively debate ensuing.

This paper attempts a critical review of the major contributions to the economic analysis of ethnic discrimination in the U.S., highlighting what they may offer for the economic analysis of ethnic discrimination more generally.

Neoclassical or marginalist economics is defined primarily by its approach to microeconomics; i.e., by considering the interactions of individual economic agents in markets and the consequences of market clearing activities under different conditions. Hence, while neoclassical economics shares a broad consensus on the methodology of market analysis, there are varied positions on the desirability of market outcomes. Hence, for example, the Chicago School monetarists epitomized by Milton Friedman, favour competitive markets and generally oppose state intervention, while those supporting Paul Samuelson's neoclassical synthesis with Keynesian macroeconomics, tend to favour government intervention to correct market failure and other undesirable market outcomes.

Most neoclassical economists view racism as irrational, and expect it to be wiped out by market forces. Competition among employers in the labor market is expected to eliminate racial wage differences and ethnically discriminating employers. In short, the market is seen as the best cure for ethnic discrimination. (Such a view is paralleled by sociological modernization theory's expectation that the transition from traditional social hierarchies to modern meritocracies will eliminate ethnic and other discrimination based on ascriptive criteria.)

Discrimination Models

Reich (1981, 107–8) argues that none of the neoclassical discrimination models are both logically coherent and empirically plausible. Nevertheless, as we shall see, a number of models have drawn attention to various microeconomic issues which need to be incorporated into the theory of ethnic discrimination, e.g. market imperfections (Becker 1957; 1971), economic motives (Krueger 1963; Thurow 1969) and ethnic cartels and employment relations within the firm (Welch 1967; Arrow 1962). At the macroeconomic level, Thurow has also highlighted the role of the State and of unemployment. Nevertheless, individually or together, they fail to offer a coherent and empirically plausible explanation for the persistence of discrimination. The challenge for economists then is to explain why ethnic discrimination persists in the market economy, despite the expectation of neoclassical economics market forces should serve to eliminate ethnic discrimination regardless of whether individual capitalists, individual workers or ethnic coalitions are the main discriminating agents.

Employer Discrimination

Becker's main model begins by assuming an international trade-like situation, with black economy *(B)* labor abundant and the White economy *(W)* relatively abundant in capital, with identical production functions in both, and labor perfectly substitutable. If not for discrimination, labor would be exported by *B* and the quantity of capital exported by *W*. For Becker, the monetary compensation equivalent to the psychic disutility of working with black labor is lost to White net income; i.e., it falls as a result of discrimination.

Two main criticisms of Becker have been made. First, if, as Becker argues, competition works to eliminate ethnic earnings differentials his analysis does not enable us to understand the persistence of those inequalities. As Arrow (1972, 172) notes, "The employer discrimination model predicts the absence of the phenomenon it was designed to explain." As Becker (1957, 36–37) acknowledges, the assumption of identical tastes is crucial to the model. Otherwise, employers with lower than average discrimination performances will gain by employing black labor. Their higher than normal profits will then either bid up the market wage rate for black labor or eliminate discriminatory employers by lowering output prices. Becker then explains the persistence of discrimination by pointing to the prevalence of monopoly and oligopoly, but his evidence does not conclusively show that wage discrimination is greater in monopolistic firms than in competitive ones as it is subject to different interpretations and explanations, i.e., he fails to demonstrate that empirically observed discrimination persists because of monopoly or oligopoly.

Second, Becker's assumption that Whites prefer not to hire blacks begs the question: What needs to be explained is instead treated as exogenous. As Samuelson (quoted by Reich 1981, 83) puts it, "Becker's conceptual framework...was empty; tastes for discrimination are not an explanation of behavior but merely a ghost that gets blamed for observed events."

As Thurow (1969, 117) has argued, Becker's international trade analogy seems inappropriate: "Much of the impact of discrimination comes from the monopoly powers of the discriminators rather than from his inability to distort perfect competition with trade barriers...The dominant group controls much more than its willingness to trade with the minority group...Negroes live in a white supremacist society, not just a segregated society." Thurow (1969, Ch. 7) also argues that Whites generally seem more concerned with keeping social, rather than physical, distance from Blacks, reducing the significance of Becker's emphasis on physical proximity, and hence on the Black presence in and proportion of the workforce.

Becker's pioneering effort, using distastes (preferences) and market imperfections to explain continuing ethnic inequality under competitive capitalism is not very convincing. He does not explain the origins of ethnic inequalities and also ignores unemployment. While market imperfections may well influence discrimination, his evidence does not show that they are responsible for ongoing discrimination.

Ethnic Cartel

In contrast, Krueger (1963) and Thurow (1969) have argued that economic gain—rather than psychic preference—is the main motive for discrimination, with the benefit achieved through collective action by the economically dominant ethnic group; e.g., Whites in the U.S.

Krueger

Using the analogy of international trade, Krueger argues that Whites can increase their total income by discriminating against blacks, in effect imposing an "optimum tariff" on that export of capitol. In Kruger's model, it is likely that participating in an ethnically discriminatory cartel with White workers who stand to gain reduces White capitalists' income. The obvious questions then arise: Why should White capitalists participate in such a discriminatory cartel which causes them to lose potential income, and why do individual employers not cheat? Kruger recognizes these objections and tries to overcome them by positing a relatively equal distribution of (both physical and human) capital among the White population. This, of course, is empirically implausible in view of the known inequalities among Whites. Thus, Krueger does not explain why Whites continue to discriminate when they lose income by doing so.

Thurow

Retaining Krueger's assumption that the motive for discrimination is economic gain (rather than taste), Thurow distinguishes seven types of discrimination which Whites seek to maximize when they act as a cartel against blacks in the U.S.:

1. employment discrimination (higher black unemployment)
2. wage discrimination (lower black remuneration for equivalent work)
3. occupational discrimination (occupational entry barriers against blacks)
4. human capital discrimination (poorer investment in black schooling)
5. capital discrimination (limited black access to the capital market)
6. monopoly power discrimination (black relegation to the secondary labor market)
7. price discrimination (black buyers pay higher prices and black sellers get lower prices)

Thurow's cartel analysis framework can specify the conditions under which Whites as a whole stand to gain or lose from discrimination. Unlike Kruger's cartel, then, Thurow can show how and when a White cartel offers economic advantage to Whites. He proceeds to estimate the gains against inefficiency losses due to restrictions on free market operations to show how much Whites benefit from discrimination and why they will not voluntarily put an end to it.

Reich (1981, 93) has argued that besides ignoring fundamental problems in cartel theory, Thurow's apparently impressive evidence does not systematically validate his theory. Also, Thurow is unable to prove, but merely assumes, that all Whites gain from a cartel. His analysis does not have much to say about the distribution of alleged gains among Whites, and does not explain how—in the absence of state sanctioned discrimination—the cartel is "policed" to prevent individual Whites from "cheating" on the cartel.

Crowding

According to Bergmann (1971) and Arrow (1972), discrimination forces blacks to "crowd" into low paying jobs, limiting black labor supply to other occupations, and depressing marginal productivity and wages. Meanwhile, Whites gain from working in higher paying jobs closed to blacks. Reducing labor supply to such jobs, due to black exclusion, pushes up wages for Whites in general, including those who might otherwise lose their jobs but for discrimination. In Bergmann's model, Whites gain from black losses. Chiswick (1973) offers a variant to this "crowding model," asserting that non-Whites substitute better for unskilled Whites than for skilled Whites. Consequently, a higher portion of non-Whites results in a greater rate of return to schooling for, and hence greater inequality among, Whites.

Bergmann overestimates the magnitude of White gains from discrimination by underestimating the elasticity of substitution among different kinds of labor and by ignoring the possibility of product substitution, which would further increase the overall elasticity of labor substitution and further weaken the crowding mechanism effect (Reich 1981, 96). Also, Bergmann does not systematically prove the validity of her model. She does not even attempt to explain why blacks have access to some jobs but not to others, or how restriction occurs.

The cartel approach assumes the possibility of collective action in ethnic discrimination. Unlike Becker, the ethnic cartel theorists suggest that economic gain—rather than prejudice—may be responsible for discrimination realized through collective action. This suggests that the study of coalition formation—at the workplace, through unions, in residential communities, through ethnic or religious congregation, or otherwise—both economically and politically, may be fruitful for the analysis of discrimination. However, the cartel theorists have thus far not persuasively proved their key assumption of the existence of variable ethnic cartels involving millions of people. Nor have they demonstrated how ethnic cartels have shaped government policy except where it can be presumed to be self-evident, as with apartheid in South Africa or other state-sanctioned ethnic discrimination elsewhere, e.g., in Malaysia.

Employee Discrimination

Becker's pioneering book also provides a secondary model of ethnic discrimination. Instead of employers discriminating (his central model) he suggests alternatively that it may be White workers who discriminate. According to Becker's second theory, White employees enjoy higher wages to compensate for their distaste for working with blacks; as the proportion of White employees declines, White wages increase correspondingly to compensate, raising the wage bill in ethnically mixed workforces compared to ethnically homogenous ones.

If employers are ethnically indifferent about whom they hire, wage rates will be equal between ethnic groups, and employers will profit more from having ethnically homogeneous workforces. Thus, employee discrimination may explain ethnic segregation among firms where there are no ethnic wage differentials. In response, Welch (1967) tried to explain persistent employee discrimination in ethnically mixed workforces with blacks receiving lower wages. For Welch, assuming that workers with different human capital endowments complement rather than supplant each other, and that Whites have more human capital than blacks, employers employ both blacks and Whites. Employee discrimination then occurs with external inefficiencies. For Welch, discrimination occurs when black employees' marginal productivity, and hence wages are lower than their White counterparts with similar skills, etc., because White resentment causes inefficiencies borne entirely by black workers—not by either White workers or employers. However, this outcome is heavily dependent of Welch's assumptions, and Reich (1981, 100) has argued that a "slight change in (Welch's) assumptions leads to different results."

Arrow (1972) elaborates on Welch's model with two types of labor. Since White workers dislike working under black workers, the latter are confined to poorly paid jobs; however, the higher marginal productivity of the more productive black workers raises the productivity of the workers generally, enabling White workers in the same category to benefit at the expense of their more productive black counterparts. The Welch and Arrow models are logically coherent, unlike most other models of discrimination, though they do not provide empirical evidence in support of their assumption that Black-White interactions at work involve friction and efficiency losses. Instead, Reich (1981, 101) argues that available evidence suggests that other effects dominate and black employees tend to be more productive as they have fewer job alternatives.

Employment Relations

Another view sees discrimination arising from rational efforts by employers to minimize personnel costs—including information and transaction costs (Arrow 1972). Since personnel changes are not without cost, they constrain what competitive forces might otherwise dictate. This introduces an element of inertia into the workforce dynamics. However, while persuasive for the short term, one wonders why the forces of competition and profit maximization do not eventually eliminate labor market discrimination. The model is advanced by Arrow to consider the phenomenon of "statistical discrimination" where employers form an ethnic stereotype about worker characteristics to minimize the information costs which might otherwise be required to make well informed hiring decisions. Ethnic discrimination is thus attributed to rational cost minimizing decision-making.

Such arguments exaggerate the difficulty and costs of getting information on applicants' abilities and of acting on it (Reich 1981, 105–6). Also, the models assume that all employers are equally prejudiced. Otherwise, competitive forces in the labor market should eventually eliminate ethnic inequality. In other words, the misperceptions of prejudiced employers do not explain the persistence of ethnic discrimination in hiring practices.

Furthermore, the "signaling model" (Spence 1974) maintains that with such employer prejudices prevailing, feedback mechanisms may serve to generate self-fulfilling prophecies, which reinforce the stereotypes. For example, if blacks think that investment in schooling yields lower returns for them than for Whites, they may invest in less schooling.

Employee discrimination and employment relations models demonstrate that it is quite rational for individual economic agents to discriminate, and thus obviate the need for the mass conspiracy assumption required by the cartel models.

Social Hierarchy

Darity (1989) maintains that preferred positions in a system of occupational stratification can be monopolized by the workers of a particular ethnic group, thus generating ethnic conflict. In his social (occupational) hierarchy, different clusters of occupations are associated with different class positions (see also Wright 1979). Ethnic culture then becomes the means for ethnic mobilization in the competitive processes among ethnic groups of workers, rather than among capitalists or between capital and labor. Different social also critical of affirmative action efforts to achieve inter-ethnic parity within the existing social hierarchy, favoring instead a generalized struggle for equality, eliminating existing social hierarchies, thus rendering irrelevant the question of inner-ethnic parity within these hierarchies. Darity rejects the standard neoclassical economic (comparative static) approach to competition, and instead favors the Austrian school as well as Marxist views of competition as a process. In this sense then, Darity's position is a modified combination of both ethnic cartel and employee discrimination, with (ethnic) collective action working itself out of different levels, including the firm or workplace. While quite plausible and avoiding some of the objections to both models, he does not offer supporting evidence for his key proposition, which remains to be tested.

Class Conflict

Reich (1981) views income distribution as an outcome of both market process and class conflict. Broadly speaking, capitalists attempt to organize workers and work to obtain the most work for the least pay, and workers resist, both individually and collectively. Profitability depends on limiting workers' collective resistance. Jobs are therefore organized to take advantage of ethnic and other differences among workers. Government activity is influenced by economic and political power, mediated by political parties, lobbies and pressure groups as well as corruption in democratic polities.

Reich's formal analysis explains the persistence of ethnic inequality regardless of employers' motives in both competitive as well as oligaopilistic labor markets and explains why market forces by themselves do not eliminate ethnic inequality. He also demonstrates that in the U.S., most White workers do not benefit from ethnic inequality while capitalists do, which differs from the conclusions drawn by most neoclassical theories of ethnic discrimination.

Reich's econometric tests support his analysis and contradict the neoclassical propositions, but do not reveal where the processes underlying ethnic inequality are located. Reich's econometric evidence suggests that wealthy Whites' share of White income benefits disproportionately from ethnic inequality. Ethnic inequality is positively correlated with profits, but inversely linked to unionism and wages. He also invokes historical evidence to show that the capacity of U.S. farmers and workers to forge inter-ethnic coalitions has been affected by macroeconomic conditions relating to unemployment, the role of the state and variations in Black-White economic positions.

While recognizing White working class racism, Reich's emphasis on employer effort to divide the working class (and other oppressed groups) along ethnic lines has led others (e.g., Darity 1989) to dismiss his analysis as dependent on employers' conspiring to "divide and rule" their workers. Insofar as his analysis does not explain White working class racist collective action, it is vulnerable to such criticism. After all, it is the perception of relative (ethnic) advantage—rather than actual absolute deprivation—which sustains ethnic discrimination and racism.

Conclusion

It is remarkable that so little effort has gone into developing a theoretical framework for the economic analysis of ethnic discrimination. Such rare "timidity" among economists may well reflect widespread recognition of the difficulties inherent in advancing theoretical analysis transcending historical specifics; i.e., time, space, cultures. And despite the eminence of many of the economists involved in these efforts, there is probably a certain professional condescension toward such mundane concerns, reinforced by the marginalization of those with "special" interests, e.g., black economists or female economists. The historical and cultural specifics of ethnic relations probably further reinforce contrary position, especially insofar as certain commonalties seem to emerge from the rather various circumstances of contemporary ethnic discrimination.

Despite the limitations of Becker's book, his work—like Arrow's and Thurow's—reminds us of the multi-dimensionality and aggregate character of what we refer to as "discrimination," e.g., that it might involve distinct though related phenomena of employer as well as employee discrimination. And insofar as ideology and cultural preferences have lives of their own, whatever their original motives—including economic ones—may be, it would be wise not to dismiss Becker's assumption of non-economic intent (e.g., ethnic distaste) altogether.

This, however, is not to deny the economic motives that ethnic cartel theorists (e.g., Kruger, Thurow) have emphasized. While all or most workers may well be worse off as a result of discrimination, as Reich points out, relative (ethnic) advantage is sufficient to explain ethnically disadvantaged employee's condoning—if not actively participating in or even promoting—ethnic discrimination in employment, which considering bounded rationality seems very reasonable in such circumstances. Hence, while employees may be worse off due to discrimination, privileged workers would be relatively better off than those discriminated against and may not realize that they are worse off than if there was no discrimination.

Besides the gains to be made by employers from ethnic discrimination by lowering the total wage bill, it is quite possible that statistical discrimination and other employment relations considerations (e.g., ethnic patronage involving ethnically partial firm-level corporatism resulting in greater company loyalty among ethnically privileged employees) may well reinforce employer prejudices.

All this suggests that an eclectic analysis of ethnic discrimination in employment and remuneration may well be more fruitful than attempts to develop a single explanatory model. Such eclecticism enables us to recognize:

- economic motives without being economistic, e.g., by denying the role of racist ideology.
- the distinct role of culture and ideology
- the significance of relative rather than absolute advantage as a motive for discrimination, especially considering employees' bounded rationality.
- the assumption of an ethnic cartel—requiring coordinated collective action by large numbers of people—is not necessary for explaining ethnic discrimination if we consider employee discrimination, statistical discrimination and other employment relations models explaining individual discriminatory behavior.
- that gains enjoyed by employers due to the existence of discrimination does not require assuming either an employer conspiracy or collective action to divide employees and limit workers' collective resistance as such behavior can be presumed to emerge "spontaneously" from the industrial relations of firms.

References

Arrow, Kenneth. 1972. Some mathematical modes of race discrimination in the labor market. In *Racial discrimination in economic life*, edited by Anthony H. Pascal. Lexington, Mass: Lexington Books.

———. 1973. The theory of discrimination. In *discrimination in labor markets*, edited by Orley Ashenfelter and Albert Rees. Princeton, NJ: Princeton University Press.

Becker, Gary S. 1957, 1971. *The economics of discrimination*. Chicago: University of Chicago Press.

Bergmann, Barbara R. 1971. The effect of White incomes of discrimination in employment. *Journal of Political Economy* 79(2) (March-April): 294–313.

Chiswick, Barry R. 1973. Racial discrimination in the labor market: A test of alternative hypotheses. *Journal of Political Economy* 81(6) (November-December): 1330–1352.

Darity Jr., William A. 1989. What's left of the economic theory of discrimination? In *The question of discrimination: Racial inequality in the U.S. labor market*, edited by Steven Shulman and William A. Darity, Jr. Middletown, Conn.: Wesleyan University Press.

Krueger, Anne O. 1963. The economics of discrimination. *Journal of Political Economy* 71(5) (October): 481–486.

Marshall, Ray. 1974. The economics of racial discrimination: A survey. *Journal of Economic Literature* 12(3) (September): 849–871.

Reich, Michael. 1981. *Racial inequality: A political-economic analysis*. Princeton: University Press.

Spence, A. Michael. 1974. *Market signaling: Informational transfer in hiring and related screening processes*. Cambridge: Harvard University Press.

Thurow, Lester C. 1969. *Poverty and discrimination*. Washington D.C.: Brookings Institute.

Welch, Finis. 1967. Labor-market discrimination: An interpretation of income differences in the rural south. *Journal of Political Economy* 75(3) (June): 225–240.

Wright, Erik O. 1979. *Classes*. London: New Left Books.

• CHAPTER SIX •

Affirmative Action by the Numbers: Why and How the Psychology of Affirmative Action Matters

RUPERT W. NACOSTE
Alumni Distinguished Undergraduate Professor
Department of Psychology
North Carolina State University

Successful implementation of a policy of affirmative action can only occur when certain psychological conditions are met. That may not seem like a new idea because the psychology of affirmative action has been widely debated. Unfortunately most of the commentaries on the psychology of affirmative action are theoretically simplistic. That is why the debate on the stigma of affirmative action is filled with what appear to be strong arguments confirming and refuting stigmatizing effects. These problems arise because the point of departure for both supporters and detractors of affirmative action is political rather than social-psychological.

Supporters of affirmative action make the psychologically naive assumption that the stigma of race or gender based purely on group membership is not different than the stigma attributed to affirmative action. Supporters see no difference between the generalized group stigma and a personal stigma. A generalized group stigma, however, is not the same as a stigma that says that what a particular individual has attained is not legitimate because government pressure required that standards be lowered to make the achievement attainable for that person. Not only that, a stigma that focuses on how an achievement is reached is more concrete than a global group stigma.

Detractors of affirmative action make the similarly naive assumption that the simple fact of group membership automatically causes stigmatization and group antagonisms. It turns out, however, that very few social-psychological outcomes are automatic. Outcomes such as stigma are determined by dynamic relations between variables, not the presence or absence of one variable.

Aside from avoiding the naïveté of the commentaries on the psychological effects of affirmative action, there are two reasons that the analyses of the potential stigma of affirmative action policies should be formally recognized as social-psychological. First, formal social-psychological analyses pinpoint the sources and conditions that lead to stigma. Second, formal social-psychological analyses can be used to clarify the informal social-psychological analyses followed by the U.S. Supreme Court to develop constitutional standards.

The Science of the Social Psychology of Affirmative Action

One of the problems with all informal analyses of the social psychology of affirmative action is a tendency to focus on group outcomes as opposed to system outcomes. Following the usual pattern of "naive psychology" (Heider 1954), the informal analyses are focused on the individual; the psychology of a target group member or nontarget group member. The more comprehensive formal analysis has focused on the system or ecology that might be influenced by psychological dynamics associated with a policy of affirmative action (Nacoste 1992). The ecological analysis shows that the system in question includes three, not two, potential groups that are subject to psychological influence: decision makers, target group members and non target group members. Furthermore the ecological analysis assumes that these groups are connected through various social-psychological links.

That is, even without affirmative action those groups are linked either through their respective positions in society (blacks and Whites, women and men), and/or through organizational necessity. Theoretically, affirmative action requirements influence the links between these groups by (in the long run) making equitable each group's relative opportunities through the enactment of a set of procedures. Social-psychologically these procedures are reacted to by members of each group in ways that bear on the relationship between the groups.

The issue of stigma has received the most focus in the scientific literature on the psychology of affirmative action. Based on the scientific literature we can now make a number of definitive statements about the relationship between affirmative action and stigma (for reviews see, Kravitz, Harrison, Turner, Levine, Chaves, Brannick, Denning, Russell and Conrad 1997; Skedsvold and Mann 1996). First, affirmative action can cause systemic stigma. Affirmative action can cause target group members to feel less competent, to feel emotionally down, and to experience evaluation apprehension (Nacoste 1990). Likewise, affirmative action can cause non-target group members (including decision-makers) to negatively evaluate the competence of target group members (Nacoste 1994a; Nacoste and Hummels 1994). These are systemic effects because they influence all of the relations in the ecology.

Second, the extent to which affirmative action causes systemic stigma depends on the nature of the procedures used to implement the policy, and the nature of the effects of those procedures. Procedures can be put into the categories of Universalistic or Particularistic based on how the (ethnic, gender or racial) group membership of individuals is considered in deciding who gets what is available (e.g., admission to college, a job or promotion). Universalistic procedures give weight to group membership but still most of the weight to technical (or traditional) credentials. Particularistic procedures give more weight to group membership than to technical credentials. Stigma occurs when the procedure used is Particularistic because such a procedure is perceived to be unfair (Nacoste 1990). Another part of the effect of procedures has to do with the intended function of affirmative action. Without doubt, the point of affirmative action procedures is to effect change. Generally speaking affirmative action procedures should neutralize the forces of discrimination acting on the opportunities for minority group members (U.S. Civil Rights Commission 1977). Systemic stigma will only occur when the procedures used go beyond neutralizing discrimination to creating an advantage for members of the target group (Nacoste 1994a; Nacoste 1997; Nacoste and Hummels 1994).

Third, when concrete information about procedures is unavailable, people guess about the nature of the procedure, and the nature of the effects of the procedures. Systemic stigma also occurs with guesses about procedures, when the guess is that the procedures are Particularistic (Nacoste 1989; Nacoste 1994b).

One benefit, then, of the formal analysis of the psychology of affirmative action is that it points out that the source of stigma is not the policy but the policy procedures. Another benefit of focusing on procedure is that procedures can serve as a common point of departure for discussions among policy analysts interested in the economic, social and legal ramifications of affirmative action policy. For example, Nacoste (1996) has made a connection between the established social-psychological dynamics of affirmative action procedures, and the standards developed by the U.S. Supreme Court for evaluating the constitutionality of affirmative action policies. That is not to say, however, that the social-psychological analysis simply mimics the Supreme Court's position. Indeed, as already demonstrated the formal social-psychological analysis indicates that it is not the mere consideration of group membership that sets off stigma.

Constitutional Analyses

For an affirmative action policy to have long-term effectiveness, that policy must pass a test of legality. That means the policy must be able to pass the "strict scrutiny" test used by the U.S. Supreme Court. For the last 40 years (Davis and Graham 1995), the Supreme Court has interpreted the Fourteenth Amendment of the Constitution to mean that any differentiation among citizens that is based on group membership (e.g., race) is suspect. The Supreme Court has established the standard of strict scrutiny for the evaluation of the constitutionality of government action that involves differential treatment of citizens by their group membership. Strict scrutiny necessitates that any government action involving differential treatment of citizens by group status must be justified by a compelling state interest, and must be narrowly tailored to prevent that action from having invidious effects; that is be designed to avoid reinforcing common and negative group stereotypes.

From this strict-scrutiny foundation, the Court has developed two standards—the procedural-weighting standard and the procedural-effect standard—for the evaluation of affirmative action policies and programs. Specified most clearly by Justice Lewis Powell in the *Bakke* ruling, the procedural-weighting standard is that race or any group membership may be used as a weighting factor in admissions but only as one of a number of selection factors and group membership cannot be given the most weight.

Most clearly stated by Justice Sandra Day O'Connor in the cases of *City of Richmond vs. Croson* (1989) and *Adarand Co. vs. Pena* (1995), the procedural-effect standard is that the procedures used to enact a policy of affirmative action must be narrowly tailored to match the level of discrimination present in the relevant environment. Neutralizing policies, or policies that do not give an advantage to the target group and go beyond neutralizing the level of discrimination against the target group, will not be invidious.

These particular standards have emerged because the Supreme Court is so concerned with the social psychology of affirmative action that they have developed standards that the Court thinks will screen out policies that would have negative social psychological effects. Yet these are not standards that block the implementation of effective affirmative action programs. All these standards do is block the implementation of affirmative action programs that have invidious effects.

We now know that there is scientific evidence on the matter of whether the implementation of affirmative action through the use of group membership has invidious effects. The scientific evidence addresses the more sophisticated question: under what conditions is affirmative action likely to have invidious effects? The scientific evidence from my work and that of others (Turner and Pratkanis 1994) indicates that invidious effects do not occur with certain conditions being present. First, invidious effects do not occur just because group membership is given weight, but do occur when group membership is given dominant weight in a set of decision criteria. Second, invidious effects do not occur just because affirmative action increases the number of target group members admitted, but do occur when the policy-procedures effect the distribution of admissions so that target group members are more likely to be admitted than nontarget group members, or vice versa. Unfortunately those standards are not always applied by the Supreme Court and lower courts in ways that are consistent with the scientific analyses of the social psychology of affirmative action.

Hopwood v. State of Texas

In the case of *Hopwood v. State of Texas* (1995), the University of Texas Law School said that it was doing the kind of affirmative action that the U.S. Supreme Court had approved in the *Bakke* case: using race as one factor among other selection factors when making admissions decisions. Despite that argument the Court of Appeals for the 5th Circuit ruled that Texas law's use of race to increase diversity was improper. That ruling was taken by some to mean that all affirmative action in higher education was in jeopardy of being declared unconstitutional.

That is why legal scholars, in particular, need to understand that the reasoning used by lower courts and the Supreme Court is based on an implicit theory of the social psychology of affirmative action. The context for the Supreme Court's application of social psychology is the Fourteenth Amendment of the Constitution, which specifies that citizens shall be afforded the equal protection of the law. Consequently, any law or government action that causes differential treatment of a particular class of citizens (e.g., race) is suspect, because distinctions based on group membership are assumed to be odious and invidious. What is invidious, we know, is that which tends "to cause discontent, animosity or envy." The Supreme Court has taken great care in its attempts to avoid and prevent government actions that are invidious because such action will be "reinforcing of common and negative group stereotypes." That caution has come in the form of the court's working assumption that any use of race to differentiate the treatment of citizens must be subject to strict scrutiny. Strict scrutiny,[1] however, has been applied to affirmative action policies so that any use of race is not simply subject to harsh scrutiny, but is almost automatically ruled as causing stigma.

We have already seen that the research on the social psychology of the procedures of affirmative action does not support that assumption. In the case of *Hopwood v. Texas*, as it relates to the procedural-weighting standard, there was an inconsistency between the procedures used by the University of Texas Law School and the procedural-weighting standard. The University of Texas Law School's color coding the applications by race was itself too much, but to then put those applications through different evaluation committees made it plain that the dominant weight was being given to race and ethnicity in admissions decisions. That, however, is a matter of procedures, and procedures can be revised. On this basis there is no foundation for the claim that all affirmative action is in jeopardy. Legal scholars should use the scientific evidence related to the issue of whether the use of group membership is invidious. The scientific evidence indicates which procedural conditions cause invidious effects, and indicates that not all uses of group membership will have invidious effects. That evidence waits to be used in arguments before any court.

Legal scholars can also make use of the implications of the procedural-effect standard specified by the Supreme Court, to clarify the kind of "facts" on which the courts are likely to rely. Again, the procedural-effect standard specifies that the use of group membership can only neutralize the effects of group discrimination and not guarantee results. In an attempt to gauge the procedural-effect of the affirmative action policy used by Texas law, the 5th Circuit Court cited group differences in LSAT scores and college GPAs. For Whites (W) and Blacks (B) the average scores were:

LSAT(W)	164	LSAT(B)	157
GPA(W)	3.53	GPA(B)	3.25

Those numbers were taken as evidence that African-American applicants who were admitted were marginally qualified, and thus that the affirmative action procedures used had gone beyond neutralizing discrimination by giving that group an advantage to guarantee a certain percentage of admissions would go to African American applicants. How meaningful are these group differences as an indicator of the procedural-effect of affirmative action?

With that question in mind, I looked at the criteria used in undergraduate admissions at North Carolina State University. I found this:

	SATM	SATV	HSGPA
Group 1	586.7	506.4	3.63
Group 2	571.8	496.5	3.56

On each indicator, Group 2 has lower credentials, and by the 5th Circuit Court's reasoning is marginally qualified, and has been given an advantage.

Clearly this was "reverse discrimination." Or was it? No, because the group scores are based only on White applicants admitted to North Carolina State University in the fall of 1995. Not only that but the numbers are based on a "group" variable that receives no formal consideration and certainly no preference in the selection process (Dixon 1996). These summary scores are based on a nominal group characteristic like race, which in this case is the size of the high school the applicant attended: Group 1 = large (>400), Group 2 = small (<150). How then could the apparent differences in average scores occur on the basis of these arbitrarily chosen, though still nominal, groups? I investigated further and found that it is a more general "size discrimination." Here is the evidence:

Counties with	SATM	SATV	HSGPA	HSRANK
>150,000 pop.	593.2	510.2	3.64	78.3
<150,000	575.7	498.1	3.64	85.0

What is going on here? In agreement with the Supreme Court most Americans say they prefer that selection procedures afford to applicants individualized evaluation. Yet we have not realized that individualized treatment means that each applicant must be evaluated not on any one criterion, but on the basis of a profile of criteria. Why? Because where one individual has high standardized test scores, another individual may have "marginal" test scores, but a strong GPA, and be at the top of their class. Individualized treatment means that applicants must be determined to be qualified or unqualified by a profile of relevant factors. As a consequence, applicants may be qualified differentially. Not by group, but by the individual profile on the criteria used to make selections. So individualized treatment introduces variation in qualification on any one criterion, and especially variation in qualifications on criteria aggregated by (racial or nonracial) nominal group.

Administrators have allowed others to make fallacious, spurious arguments based on aggregation of standardized test scores, GPAs and the like. Administrators have not argued against the implicit claim that consideration of group membership is preference by group membership. Yet, using almost any arbitrary, nominal group comparison (e.g., county size), any college or university will find variation in the extent to which "groups" are equal on the criteria used for making admissions decisions. The racial group comparisons are as meaningless as the county size group comparisons. In view of this problem, the use of group comparisons is itself invidious.

Suggesting that this reasoning has the potential to influence the courts, the District Court to which the *Hopwood* case was remanded, reasoned in a way that was consistent with this view. Because by then the University of Texas had changed its procedure, the U.S. Supreme Court refused to hear the appeal of the *Hopwood* decision (Denial of Writ, July 1, 1996). What that left the District Court to consider was the question of whether damages should be paid to the plaintiffs who won at the level of the 5th Circuit Court of Appeals. To do so the District Court had to decide, (1) what was the evidence that the Law School engaged in reverse discrimination, (2) what was the severity of any found reverse discrimination, (3) what level of compensation would match any established reverse discrimination?

Looking at the evidence cited by the 5th Circuit Court, the lower District Court (U.S. District Court, Austin Division, June 19, 1998) was quick to point out that any differences between admissions criteria scores did not, by itself, indicate unequal treatment. According to the District Court, differences in scores on the LSAT, college GPA's between the groups were differences that occurred in the largest group of applicants to the Law School. Those were applicants who had credentials that put them in the middle category of applicants, not extremely high and not extremely low scores. Moreover, the District Court argued, those in the middle category were "relatively close" in scores and as a consequence received individual review because within this middle category "...a difference of a few points does not necessarily correlate with more successful work in law school." In that context, the District Court scrutinized the scores by groups and concluded that the disparity between high minority and low majority numbers was "only a couple of points." With that established the District Court ruled that the differences between groups on admissions scores was not evidence of reverse discrimination, since applicant files had been evaluated using both objective and subjective admission factors.

Still, according to the District Court the Law School did engage in reverse discrimination. The District Court saw this in the set up of two different admissions committees. Two admission committees obviously meant that applicants did not receive equal treatment. But this was a ruling on the procedure of the affirmative action policy, not on the policy itself. That is especially clear since when considering damages to be paid to the plaintiffs, the District Court ruled that in view of the full picture which showed that the Law School had acted in good faith in its affirmative action efforts, the plaintiffs would not be awarded punitive damages. As for compensation for the found unequal treatment by procedure, the District Court ruled that the plaintiffs should be allowed to reapply (to be considered through the new admissions procedure), and be awarded monetary damages in the amount of One Dollar ($1) per plaintiff.

Conclusion

According to the principle of strict scrutiny, any government action based on racial distinctions between citizens is suspect, and should be assumed to be odious and invidious. Although the goal of the comparison of criterion scores by racial groups is on the surface benign, because of strict scrutiny the action must be assumed to be invidious and we must ask whether this is the best or even the only way to reach the goal. In this case, the 5th Circuit Court's reliance on racial comparisons to establish "reverse discrimination" was in fact "odious and invidious" because it was based on the false assumption that the comparison directly reflected objective racial differences. The evidence presented, however, makes clear the falsehood of that assumption since nominal group comparisons show similar "group" disparities that are not accounted for by any institutional policy. Not only that, but the Court used the racial comparison to conclude (or support the conclusion) that members of an already stereotyped group are marginally qualified. That use of the racial comparison is likewise reinforcing of common and negative stereotypes of the minority group.

What the 5th Circuit Court and others have been trying to do through these group comparisons is to measure the procedural-effect of affirmative action. Although it is important to gauge the effect of the policy-procedures, it is not clear whether that measurement should occur at the point of organizational entry or exit. Attempts to measure procedural-effects at the point of implementation are problematic where each applicant is evaluated on objective and subjective information in order to give each applicant individualized treatment. At that point, applicants by group will appear to be different on aggregated selection criteria because individualized treatment allows for variation in the extent to which a person matches the standard on any one criterion.

As an alternative strategy, we may learn something about the effects of procedures by looking at some measure of performance after entry. Having matriculated for a year, university students for example, may or may not drop out of a degree program. Or after four to five years, graduation rates can be checked. Then the question becomes is the university graduating students consistent with the affirmative actions taken at the entry point? If not, why not? Is it the selection procedure? Is it something on the campus that needs to be fixed? What is it? Moving the evaluation of the effects of procedure to the exit point opens the door to questions that go beyond should we have affirmative action or not, to what are the forces acting in the environment (affirmative action included) that need to be improved.

We have not thought to work this way, I think, because administrators have also bought the fallacious claim that consideration of group membership must be preference by group membership. The reason that this false assumption is held is that administrators have not realized that a variety of strategies can be used to consider group membership in a selection process. On this point, Nacoste and Hummels (1994) investigated the influence of beliefs about affirmative action procedures on individuals in a decision-making role. That study showed that individuals who hold to the belief that affirmative action gives an advantage to the target group, and believe that the weight given to group membership is too much, also believe that the target group is generally unqualified. Firmly believing that affirmative action necessarily creates an advantage for one group and that the procedures must necessarily give too much weight to group membership causes administrators to be sure that what they are doing is the best that can be done. I see no other way of explaining how any rational person could argue that the actions of color coding applications by race and using separate evaluation committees by race could be within the boundaries set by the Supreme Court.

References

Adarand Constructors, Inc. v Federico Pena, Secretary of Transportation, et al., 115 S. Ct. 515 (1995).

Cheryl Hopwood, et al. v. University of Texas, et al., 5th Circuit Court of Appeals, #94–50569 (1995).

Cheryl Hopwood, et al. v State of Texas, et al., #A 92 CA 563 SS., United States District Court, W.D. Texas, Austin Division (June 19, 1998).

City of Richmond v. J. A. Croson Co., 109 S. Ct. 706 (1989).

Davis, Abraham L. and Graham, Barbara L. 1995. *The Supreme Court, race, and civil rights.* Thousands Oaks, CA: Sage Publications.

Kravitz, David A., David A. Harrison, Marlene E. Turner, Edward L. Levine, Wanda Chaves, Michael T. Brannick, Donna L. Denning, Craig J., Russell and Maureen A. Conard. 1997. *Affirmative action: A review of psychological and behavioral research.* Monograph. Society for Industrial and Organizational Psychology.

Nacoste, Rupert W. 1989. Affirmative action and self-evaluation, pp. 103–109 in *Affirmative Action in Perspective,* edited by Fletcher A. Blanchard and Faye A. Crosby. New York: Springer-Verlag.

———. 1990. Sources of stigma: Analyzing the psychology of affirmative action. *Law & Policy* 17: 283–293.

———. 1992. Toward a psychological ecology of affirmative action. *Social Justice Research* 5: 269–289.

———. 1994a. If Empowerment is the goal…: Affirmative action and social interaction. *Basic and Applied Social Psychology* 15(1–2)(April): 87–112.

———. 1994b. Policy schemas for affirmative action, pp. 205–221. In *Applications of Heuristics and biases to social issues,* Edited by Linda Heath, et al. New York: Plenum Press.

——— and B. Hummels. 1994. Affirmative action and the behavior of decision makers. *Journal of Applied Social Psychology* 24(7): 595–613.

Regents of the University of California v. Bakke, 438 U.S. 265 (1978).

Skedsvold, Paula R. and Tammy L. Mann. 1996. The affirmative action debate: What's fair in policy and programs? *Journal of Social Issues* 52(4)(Winter)(Entire Issue).

Texas, et al., Petitioners, v. Cheryl Hopwood, et al., #9–1773. Denial of Writ, Supreme Court of the United States (July 1, 1996).

Turner, Marlene E. and Anthony R. Pratkanis. 1994. Affirmative action as help: A review of recipient reactions to preferential selection and affirmative action. *Basic and Applied Social Psychology* 15(1–2): 43–69.

Affirmative Action and International Law: A Test Case

Frank Deale
Associate Professor of Law
City University of New York School of Law

For over twenty-five years, all three branches of the federal government, many of the states, and numerous private and public employers have recognized the validity of affirmative action as an important remedy for systemic racial discrimination.[1] Today, a huge outpouring of resentment, mostly from whites, against "special advantages" provided to women and people of color,[2] fueled by corporate "downsizing," the uncertainties produced by globalisation, and other shake-ups in the domestic economy,[3] have brought about a renewed assault[4] on this attempt to alleviate instances of racial bias. These resentments have resulted in numerous cases being brought before the federal judiciary challenging the use of affirmative action in a number of different contexts.[5]

This article examines four recent cases, which indicate that the anger felt by many Whites toward affirmative action has not gone unnoticed by federal judges. The cases to be discussed include: *Podberesky v. Kirwan*,[6] in which the United States Court of Appeals for the Fourth Circuit declared unconstitutional a University of Maryland scholarship program which provided benefits solely to students of African-American heritage; *Hopwood v. State of Texas*,[7] where the U.S. Court of Appeals for the Fifth Circuit eliminated race as a factor in law school admissions; and *Taxman v. Board of Education of Piscataway*,[8] a decision of the U.S. Court of Appeals for the Third Circuit which held that the Township of Piscataway, New Jersey, acted unlawfully when it utilized race in deciding which of two equally qualified school teachers had to be laid off and ultimately retained the African-American teacher. In addition to these cases, the article discusses Proposition 209, the California Civil Rights Initiative,[9] in which anti-affirmative action California organizers mobilized electors[10] to vote their biases into law via a referendum process. The legality of Proposition 209 was upheld by the United States Court of Appeals for the Ninth Circuit[11] and review was denied by the Supreme Court of the United States.[12]

Viewed collectively, the net effect of the policy changes brought about by the court opinions and Proposition 209 amounts to a broad scale eradication of affirmative action as a remedy for discrimination in two crucial areas of American life: education and employment. Indeed, the extent of the rollback of affirmative action has been such that the time has come to determine whether the International Convention on the Elimination of All Forms of Racial Discrimination,[13] and its provisions regarding affirmative action,[14] should be invoked. The Convention recognizes a fundamental right to be free of racial discrimination and to have an effective remedy against such discrimination when it takes place.[15] Because recent developments threaten to remove the remedy of affirmative action, the enforcement mechanisms of the treaty should be triggered.

Podberesky

For many years, Maryland, like many states, maintained a system of segregated schooling, including higher education. Whites attended various branches of the University of Maryland, while African-Americans received their education at state supported institutions established solely for students of African-American heritage.[16] The first African-American graduate student was admitted to the University of Maryland in 1951;[17] afterwards, the school imposed new admission standards and required standardized testing of all applicants.[18] In addition, the school made no efforts to recruit African-American students.[19] As a consequence, the school's African-American population stayed below 1% of the undergraduate population from 1954 until the end of the 1960's.[20]

In 1964 Congress, as part of the aftermath of *Brown v. Board of Education*[21] enacted Title VI of the Civil Rights Act of 1964, which forbids recipients of federal funds from discriminating on the basis of race, color or national origin.[22] The state of Maryland was notified by the Office of Civil Rights (OCR) in 1969 that its system of higher education was still segregated in violation of Title VI.[23] In 1980, over eleven years later, when the university was still deemed to be maintaining a segregated institution, it adopted, in response, the "Equal Educational Opportunity Plan" for 1980–1985, as part of its effort to comply with Title VI compliance guidelines issued by the OCR in 1978. Under the plan, the school aimed for a freshman class at the College Point campus of between 10% and 12% African-American students by 1985, and 14% by 1989. The University also agreed to use a number of recruitment measures including "outreach strategies, on-campus programs, summer programs, activities to attract prospective Black applicants, recruitment visitors and follow-up procedures."[24]

The Benjamin Banneker Scholarship Program was implemented in 1978 as one of the tools for attracting African-American applicants. Under that program, scholarships not based on need are awarded each year to approximately thirty students. Initially, the program offered two-year scholarships of approximately $1,000 a year. By 1988, the amount of the scholarship was increased to full in-state tuition or out-of-state tuition, plus room, board, and mandatory fees, estimated to be $33,500 over the four years.[25] To compete for a Banneker scholarship, an applicant had to have a 900 score on the Scholastic Achievement Test (S.A.T.), a 3.0 grade point average, and be African-American.

According to the District Court, "it was only...with the advent of the Banneker Program that the UMCP began to take meaningful steps toward integrating its campus."[26] As a result of the scholarship program and other changes over the past 15 years, African-American matriculation rates reached 15% of the freshman class in the fall of 1993. Moreover, the university ranked fourth among predominantly White universities in terms of the number of African-American students receiving degrees.[27]

Daniel Podberesky, a Hispanic male, was admitted to the class of 1989 and applied for a Key scholarship.[28] Although he had an S.A.T. test score of 1340 out of 1600 and a grade point average between 3.56 and 4.0,[29] his scholarship request was denied. He then sought a Banneker scholarship, which was denied him because he was not African-American. Filing suit, he lost twice in the District Court,[30] which upheld the scholarship program, but won twice in Court of Appeals for the Fourth Circuit,[31] which ultimately concluded that the scholarship program was in violation of the Fourteenth Amendment.

To justify continuing the Banneker Scholarship Program as a necessary mechanism for attracting African-American students to the University of Maryland, the university relied upon the following factors: 1) extensive evidence that the university had a poor reputation in the African-American community among parents, high school counselors and prospective students;[32] 2) evidence of underrepresentation in the African-American student body;[33] 3) evidence that African-Americans at UMCP have a disproportionately high attrition rate;[34] 4) evidence of a continuing hostile climate for African-Americans at the University.[35]

The Court of Appeals, hearing the case for the second time, rejected this reasoning, concluding that 1) racial tensions and attitudes are not a sufficient ground for employing race-conscious remedies;[36] 2) that even if the school had high attrition rates and underrepresentation of African-American students, the program was unlawfully designed to "draw only high achieving African-American students to the University...High achievers, whether African-American or not, are not the group against which the University discriminated in the past;"[37] 3) that the Banneker scholarships were available to African-Americans who were not residents of Maryland;[38] 4) that the lower Court's analysis of underrepresentation was flawed because it did not "factor out, to the extent practicable, all non-trivial, non-race based disparities in order to permit an inference that such, if any, racial considerations contributed to the remaining disparity."[39] For these reasons, the Banneker scholarship plan was not narrowly tailored to achieve its purpose. The Court of Appeals also asserted that the university had made no attempt to show that it tried, without success, any race-neutral solutions to the retention problem.[40]

Taxman

In May of 1989, the Board of Education of the Township of Piscataway, New Jersey had to eliminate one of the teaching positions in the business department at the Piscataway High School. The choice of whom to layoff was between two teachers, both of who started work on the same day nine years earlier, and thus were of equal seniority. One of the teachers, Sharon Taxman, was White, the other teacher, Debra Williams, was African-American, and the only minority teacher ever tenured by the department.[41] In preparing to make the layoff decision, the school Board "assessed [the teachers'] classroom performance, evaluations, volunteerism and certifications, and determined that they were teachers of 'equal ability and equal qualifications.'"[42]

The Board chose to layoff Taxman, pursuant to an affirmative action plan adopted in 1975 in accordance with New Jersey State Regulations.[43] The plan was designed to "ensure equal educational opportunity to all persons regardless of race, color, creed, religion, sex, or national origin," to "provide equal educational opportunity for students and equal employment opportunity for employees and prospective employees," and required the Board to "make a concentrated effort to attract...minority personnel for all positions so that their qualifications can be evaluated with other candidates."[44] The plan also stated: "In all cases the most qualified candidate will be recommended for appointment. However, when candidates appear to be of equal qualification, candidates meeting the criteria of the affirmative action plan [members of racial, national origin or gender groups identified as minorities for statistical purposes by the New Jersey State Department of Education] will be recommended."[45] In accordance with the plan, the school chose to retain Williams and layoff Taxman.[46]

Taxman filed a charge of discrimination with the Equal Employment Opportunity Commission. When the Commission failed to resolve the dispute through conciliation, she intervened in a suit filed on her behalf by the United States against the school board, alleging that her layoff violated Title VII of the Civil Rights Act of 1964.[47] The District Court ruled in favor of the plaintiffs,[48] and on appeal, that decision was affirmed by the Third Circuit Court of Appeals.[49]

The majority held that the layoff violated Title VII and Supreme Court precedent because, in its view, affirmative action could only be utilized for the purpose of "eliminating...past discrimination in the workplace."[50] It could not be used to diversify the workplace, even for educational purposes.[51] Since the affirmative action plan was not designed to eliminate the results of past discrimination in the workplace,[52] and African-American teachers were neither "underutilized" nor "underrepresented" in the Piscataway school district workforce, and in fact exceeded their percentage of the available work force, the decision to retain Williams because of the plan could not be justified.[53] The Court suggested that a better way of making the decision would be a "coin toss."[54]

The dissenting judges argued that diversity was a valid goal for educational purposes,[55] that Williams was the only Black teacher ever tenured by the business department,[56] and that under Supreme Court precedents, employers have the discretion[57] to use race as one factor in determining who should be laid off, when all other factors, i.e., seniority and qualifications, were equal.[58]

Hopwood

On March 18, 1996, a three judge panel of the United States Court of Appeals for the Fifth Circuit decided the case of *Hopwood v. State of Texas*, ruling that race may no longer be used as a factor in admissions to the University of Texas School of Law.[59] Two judges, Smith and DeMoss, concluded that "the University of Texas School of Law may not use race as a factor in deciding which applicants to admit in order to achieve a diverse student body, to combat the perceived effects of a hostile environment at the law school, to alleviate the law school's poor reputation in the minority community, or to eliminate any present effects of past discrimination by actors other than the law school."[60] The third judge, Judge Weiner, reached the same conclusion as Judges Smith and DeMoss, that the four plaintiffs were entitled to re-apply for admission to the law school under a revamped admissions process, but did not go so far as to rule out race as a factor to be utilized in that process. Concluding that the panel opinion had gone beyond U.S. Supreme Court precedents, Judge Weiner argued that race could be used in law school admissions for the purpose of "achieving diversity in the student body of a public graduate or professional school."[61]

The Court held that the Texas Law School affirmative action plan was unconstitutional for a number of reasons. First, the University of Texas utilized what the Court of Appeals referred to as a "segregated application evaluation process."[62] As practiced by the law school, all applications were color coded according to race. Those applicants entitled to affirmative action consideration were reviewed by a subcommittee of minority group members, whose decisions regarding minority applicants were considered "virtually final."[63] Moreover, the students who were placed on a wait-list for admission were kept in separate piles, one for those eligible for affirmative action consideration and a separate pile for those who were not eligible.[64]

Second, the groups entitled to affirmative action consideration were limited to African-Americans and Mexican Americans. Native Americans, Asian Americans, and "other Hispanics," (the language of the school application form), were not entitled to preferential consideration.[65] As stated by the Court of Appeals, "benefits are conferred on [African-American and Mexican American] students who attended out of state or private schools for such education,"[66] whereas "Asians, American Indians, Americans from El Salvador and Cuba, and many others did not receive a preference."[67]

Finally, the Court of Appeals saw the plan as placing too much emphasis on race. The school used a "Texas Index" (TI), a composite score of undergraduate grade point average and Law School Aptitude Test scores. The Court concluded that the difference between a TI score for an individual eligible for affirmative action and an ineligible applicant not so entitled was "striking" and "dramatic."[68] From the perspective of the Court, "the purpose of this lowering of standards was to meet an "aspiration" of admitting a class consisting of 10% Mexican Americans and 5% African-Americans, proportions roughly comparable to the percentages of those races graduating from Texas colleges."[69]

On July 1, 1996, the Supreme Court declined to hear the appeal of the University of Texas Law School.[70] The Court's refusal to hear the law school's case means that the law school's policy which was declared unconstitutional[71] cannot lawfully be replicated at the law school or any other public institution of higher education[72] located in the Fifth Federal Judicial Circuit.[73] Moreover, any public institution of higher education outside the Fifth Circuit which maintains a similar plan can expect to face a constitutional challenge. The Fifth Circuit ruling would not be binding authority in such a challenge, but could be persuasive authority for a similar ruling.[74]

Proposition 201

The use of referenda on controversial propositions has assumed importance in many parts of the United States. In the late 1960's, the citizens of Akron,

Ohio protested the adoption of an open housing law by the City Council by holding a referendum to amend the City Charter. The amendment required that all fair housing ordinances be put to a city-wide vote before they could be effectuated. The proponents of the referendum were aware that the result of the referendum would favor those wishing to perpetuate discrimination. The Supreme Court declared the Akron referendum unconstitutional because it singled out an issue of particular interest to racial minorities—racial discrimination in housing—and placed an additional burden on their efforts to enact fair housing legislation, a burden not shared by those seeking other kinds of legislative redress.[75]

In the early 1980's, after a Seattle, Washington school district took steps to establish a mandatory busing plan to promote school desegregation, the voters of the State of Washington passed Initiative 350 which provided that "no school board shall directly or indirectly require any student to attend a school other than the school which is geographically nearest or next nearest the student's place of residence." The purpose of the referendum was to make it extremely difficult for busing to be used as a remedy for segregated schools in the state of Washington. This referendum was also declared unconstitutional by the Supreme Court because it singled out an issue of concern to minorities—racial busing—and imposed special political burdens on those who supported it.[76]

Most recently, the voters in the state of Colorado approved overwhelmingly a constitutional amendment which repealed anti-discrimination ordinances that protected gay men and lesbians. In *Roemer v. Evans*,[77] similar reasoning was used by the Supreme Court to declare the Colorado action unconstitutional.[78] Each of these initiatives was targeted at minority groups within the population, making it harder for them to protect their rights through the political process. Each was subsequently declared unconstitutional.

Proposition 209 has the same intention and effect as the referenda in Akron, Seattle and Colorado. The purpose of the initiative is to end affirmative action in the state of California.[79] A number of organizations[80] brought a lawsuit challenging the proposition, and succeeded in preventing its implementation until there is a final adjudication of its legality.[81] The Court found that the plaintiffs were likely to demonstrate that Proposition 209 violates the equal protection of the law guaranteed by the Fourteenth Amendment and undermines Title VII of the Civil Rights Act.

According to the Court in its interim opinion, Proposition 209 violated equal protection because it "displaces authority with respect to race and gender issues to a new and remote level of government and thus reorders the political process to the detriment of minorities."[82] This is because, as a result of Proposition 209, any future attempts to obtain race or gender conscious remedial programs would first have to secure passage of a constitutional amendment repealing 209 before a governmental entity would be legally enabled to adopt a race or gender conscious remedial program. Before the passage of 209, all one had to do to obtain such a program was to bring a proposal before the relevant governmental entity.[83] As in previous cases raising these issues, Proposition 209 "singles out an issue of special concern to minorities and women: race and gender conscious affirmative action; and alters the political process solely with respect to these issues..."[84] Because of the hurdles erected by the new political process, "members of the plaintiff class are effectively precluded from petitioning local and state policymakers and representatives to adopt, maintain or expand race or gender conscious affirmative action programs."[85] Moreover, the Court concluded that Proposition 209 was probably also unconstitutional because it violated Congressional intent to "protect employer's discretion [to] utilize race and gender conscious affirmative action as a method of complying with their obligations under Title VII."[86] Since Proposition 209 prevents state and local employers from resorting to affirmative action, it conflicts with Title VII in violation of the Supremacy Clause of the Constitution.

The U.S. Court of Appeals for the Ninth Circuit rejected these conclusions.[87] The Court first held that it was unlikely plaintiffs would be able to demonstrate that Proposition 209 violates the Equal Protection Clause since the wording of Proposition 209, consistent with the mandate of the Fourteenth Amendment, prohibits the State from classifying individuals by race or gender.[88] It then went on to hold that 209 did not place political obstacles in the way of minorities and women barring them from protection against discrimination. It merely barred them from obtaining "preferential treatment." As the Court saw the issue, "impediments to preferential treatment do not deny equal protection."[89] Finally, the Court concluded that Proposition 209 was not preempted by Title VII because Title VII was designed to eliminate "discriminatory preference for any group, minority or majority,"[90] consistent with the goals of 209.

Each of these cases primarily concerns the rights of the parties before the various courts. The University of Texas, the University of Maryland, and the Piscataway school district have been deprived of the opportunity to shape the character of their educational institutions.[91] However, the ramifications of the decisions go far beyond the parties before the courts. If the anti-affirmative action arguments in the cases prevail, the material conditions of African-Americans will deteriorate to levels pre-dating the civil rights revolution of the 60's.[92]

Proposition 209 and the case holdings discussed above will lead to a society in which those historically privileged will continue to be the primary beneficiaries of what society offers because they will be able to exercise their privileges unhindered by countervailing considerations.

Indeed, added together, the cases amount to a court ordered imposition of Proposition 209. Students from racially disadvantaged backgrounds will not be able to gain admission to selective institutions of higher education over students whose backgrounds make it easier for them to compete (*Hopwood*). If they do gain access to higher education, they will not be able to get the scholarship assistance they will need because most of it will go to White students, as there are more of them, and many White students will also have serious needs (*Podberesky*). If they succeed in getting admitted to a selective institution, pay their way through school, and get a job, they can be laid off, although they may have obtained as much seniority as White workers and have attained equivalent qualifications (*Taxman*). Finally, if they seek to challenge the regime which has placed so much hardship upon them, they have to assume additional burdens in using the political process, because they belong to groups which have been historically subject to discrimination because of immutable group characteristics (Proposition 209).

These cases demonstrate the development of a substantial body of recent federal law that fails to recognize the historical justifications for affirmative action—a situation which clearly calls for new thinking by those committed to the proposition that the federal and state governments are obligated to provide and retain effective remedies for systematic discrimination based upon race.

Convention on the Elimination of Racial Discrimination

The United States has ratified a number of international instruments which outlaw discrimination and provide for equal protection of the law.[93] One of these instruments, the recently ratified International Convention of the Elimination of All Forms of Racial Discrimination (ICERD),[94] specifically authorizes the use of race-based affirmative action.[95] In perhaps grandiose terms, the Convention has been referred to as "the international community's only tool for combating racial discrimination which is at one and the same time universal in reach, comprehensive in scope, legally binding in character and equipped with built in measures of implementation."[96] The Convention was ratified by the United States Senate in 1994.[97]

Under the terms of the Convention, enforcement is delegated in the first instance to an 18 person Committee on the Elimination of Racial Discrimination. This Committee is established to hear complaints from state-parties[98] that accuse other state-parties of not abiding by the provisions of the Convention.[99] The state-party against which a complaint has been made then has the opportunity to explain the situation to the Committee. If such explanation does not resolve the matter, the issues are referred back to the Committee which will then, upon assuring that "all domestic remedies have been invoked and exhausted in the case in conformity with the generally recognized principles of international law," report the matter to an "Ad-Hoc Conciliation Commission."[100] Upon consideration of the matter, the Commission submits to the Chair of the full Committee a report and recommendations which the disputing parties may accept or reject.[101] After three months, the Chair of the Committee "shall communicate the report of the Commission and the declarations of the states parties concerned to the other parties to the convention."[102]

The failure of the Supreme Court to hear the cases discussed above, requires resort to federal litigation and the complaint procedure of the Convention on the Elimination of All Forms of Racial Discrimination by advocates of affirmative action in the United States. Although well settled doctrine bars litigation under human rights instruments unless such instruments have either self-executing language, or Congressional validation,[103] a number of U.S. domestic laws are currently in place which authorize affirmative action remedies,[104] as well as numerous Executive Orders promulgated by the Executive Branch of the United States Government.[105] The question is whether such legislation can be construed and/or eliminated by courts and other agencies of government because of a popular perception that there has been "enough" affirmative action, or, in the words of the Convention, "that...such measures [have been] continued after the objectives for which they have been taken have been achieved."[106]

Conclusion

One cannot be optimistic about the outcome of such litigation in the federal courts of the United States. On the other hand, primarily because of the devastating effect that the anti-affirmative action decisions discussed in the text have already brought about, we have seen some slight changes in the public perception of affirmative action which may indicate that better times for the opponents of race discrimination may lie in the future.[107]

• CHAPTER EIGHT •

International Human Rights Instruments and Racial Discrimination in the United States

WALTER W. STAFFORD
Professor, Wagner Graduate School of Public Service
New York University

In a period in which affirmative action laws are being weakened in the United States, it is important to assess how these policies and practices resonate with broader conceptions of racial discrimination and human rights. This article looks at two international human rights instruments recently ratified by the United States and the path they open for broader views of racial injustice. It is important for blacks, Latinos and Native Americans, whose relative status on some international indicators of social and economic well-being is lower than that of citizens of developing countries, to review and utilize instruments that can reduce structural discrimination in the institutions and marketplace of the U.S. (World Bank 1993).

Shortly before the United Nations' 50th birthday in 1995 the United States joined the member states that had ratified the International Covenant on Civil and Political Rights (ICCPR) and the International Convention Against All Forms of Racial Discrimination (ICERD). ICCPR was ratified in 1992 and ICERD in 1994. Under the requirements of ICCPR the U.S. also submitted to the United Nations its first report on human rights in the United States, *Civil and Political Rights in the United States* (Washington 1994).

Even though in 1995 the press was carrying banner stories about human rights problems in the other countries, there were few papers that mentioned the ratification of these instruments or the publication of the U.S. human rights report. Moreover, the State Department published and circulated only a limited number of copies of the report for domestic review.

Despite the limited coverage by the press, the ratification of the Covenant and the Convention and the publication of the report were important milestones. The Covenant on Civil and Political Rights (ICCPR) is one of two international instruments that elaborate and give legal grounding to the broad commitments required of each nation under the U.N. Charter (1948). The other instrument is the International Covenant on Economic, Social and Cultural Rights which the United States has not ratified. Both Covenants were adopted by the United Nations in 1966 and were given force a decade later. The International Convention Against All Forms of Racial Discrimination was adopted in 1965 and entered into force in 1969.

Historically, the United States had refrained from ratifying the Covenants and the Convention because they went beyond the American concept of rights. The American conception of rights grew out of a commitment to government for limited purposes. This concept of "negative rights," often referred to as the first generation of human rights, has emphasized civil and political rights that government activities must not violate. However, as Louis Henkin (1984) notes, most international human rights were recognized after the establishment and proliferation of socialist states, and after commitment to welfare economics and the welfare state was nearly universal. Referred to as "positive rights," they require active intervention of governments and cannot be realized without such intervention (Alston and Quinn 1987). The Covenant on Economic, Social and Cultural Rights is the cornerstone of this recognition of a second generation of human rights.

When the Declaration was adopted in 1948, most of the world's population, including blacks in the United States, lived under systems that systematically denied their rights. In shaping new nation-states and ideas for their own self-determination, the peoples who emerged from colonization, segregation, and most recently apartheid turned to the Declaration. But they also expanded on the second generation of human rights to meet their needs for developing and protecting their cultures and resources. Concepts of the right to development and the right to a clean environment are now framing what is being called the third generation of human rights.

Before its decision to ratify the Covenant (ICCPR) in 1992 and the Convention (ICERD) in 1994, the United States had the dubious distinction of being the only non-communist state other than South Africa that had not ratified the International Covenant on Civil and Political Rights or the International Convention Against All Forms of Racial Discrimination. The United States remains one of the few member states that have not ratified the International Covenant on Economic, Social and Cultural Rights (United Nations 1995).

The United States' decision to ratify the Convention came in part from its concern about the way member states and nongovernmental organizations

(NGOs) were expanding positive rights, including the definition of racial discrimination. By the 1990s, there was considerable global activity among NGOs representing minorities, women, and indigenous peoples to get member states to ratify instruments protecting and respecting their individual and collective rights. The Vienna Declaration, growing out of the World Conference on Human Rights in 1994, called for member states to ratify the Convention on the Rights of the Child by 1995, and encouraged states to ratify the Convention on the Elimination of All Forms of Discrimination Against Women by the year 2000. Moreover, the United Nations, UNESCO, and the International Labor Organization (ILO) had developed extensive reviews, reports, and resolutions on racial discrimination. Indeed, by 1993 the General Assembly had proclaimed the Third Decade to Combat Racism and Racial Discrimination (United Nations 1995).

The starting point of many of the international activities against discrimination is Article 1 of the Convention which defines the term "racial discrimination" as meaning:

> "any distinction, exclusion, restriction or preference based on race, colour, descent or national or ethnic origin which has the purpose or effect of nullifying or impairing the recognition, enjoyment or exercise on an equal footing, of human rights and fundamental freedom in the political, economic, social, cultural or any other field of public life."

This broad definition of discrimination is not elaborated in the United Nations Charter, and discrimination is defined only briefly in the Civil Rights Amendments to the United States Constitution (Ginger 1993). The U.N. definition essentially undermines the individualistic-assimilationist framework that the United States had promoted based on its dealings with Native Americans, blacks, Puerto Ricans and other groups of color.

John Shattuck, Assistant Secretary of State for Democracy, Human Rights and Labor, recognized the problems and growing influence of post-colonial states and NGOs, in their attempts to reconcile the need for self determination by various national minorities as well as the growing restlessness of indigenous peoples and other minorities within the United States. In 1994, Shattuck warned the Senate Committee on Foreign Relations:

> "If we are not fully and actively engaged in this debate, then others will be setting the international community's agenda on race discrimination." (Shattuck 1994)

Shattuck also revealed his sensitivity to the growing influence of international concerns for Native Americans. In his introduction to *Civil and Political Rights in the United States* Shattuck wrote:

> "Native Americans have suffered a fate similar to that of many indigenous civilizations: destruction and displacement of their cultures and societies. The lessons

of those injustices, and the responsibilities the people of the United States are charged with as a result, are also central legacies of American history."

In his analysis of the effect of discrimination against blacks in the context of the United States' interpretation of the International Covenant on Civil and Political Rights he was more reserved. He had noted that the injustices of slavery and the heroic leadership of the civil rights movement helped shape constitutional law so that human rights could be respected. He asserted that other nations could learn from America's battle with racial discrimination. Nevertheless, he avoided any discussion of how, in the U.S., African civilization and black culture had been undermined.

Human rights groups criticized the report for failing to deal adequately with the many problems of racial discrimination in the United States, including disproportionate incarceration of blacks, police violence, and poverty.

The Human Rights Committee of the United Nations, to whom the report was submitted, also raised significant questions about the U.S. report. While the committee praised the high quality of the report and the participation of important members of the U.S. government at its hearings, the committee identified 14 areas of concern. Six of the areas of concern which strongly implicate racial discrimination are: the excessive number of offenses punishable by the death penalty; the large number of persons killed or wounded by, or ill-treated by the police; the deprivation of liberty of persons in detention; the high financial costs required to participate in elections; the potential abrogation of the rights of Native Americans by Congress; and the high poverty rates of groups of color (United Nations 1995).

As a final recommendation regarding the U.S. report on human rights, the Human Rights Committee noted that measures should be taken to ensure greater awareness of the International Covenant on Civil and Political Rights by the public at large and by the legal profession. To date little has been done to inform the public. Editorials in the major press are often cynical about the United Nations and undermine the credibility of the institution. Few schools or universities incorporate human rights into their curricula. Nevertheless, advocacy for and monitoring of human rights in the U.S. is increasing, and groups are preparing to see how the U.S. will respond to the United Nations on issues of racial discrimination as required by its recent ratification of the International Convention Against All Forms of Racial Discrimination.

References

Alston, Philip and Gerard Quinn. 1987. The nature and scope of states parties obligations under the International Covenant on Economic, Social and Cultural Rights. *Human Rights Quarterly* 9(2): 156–230.

Center for the Study of Human Rights. 1994. *Twenty-Five human rights documents*. New York: Columbia University.

Ginger, Ann Fagan. 1993. The energizing effect of enforcing a human rights treaty. *DePaul Law Review* 42(134): 1342–1401.

Henkin, Louis. International human rights and rights in the United States," pp. 25–67. In *Human rights in international law*, edited by Theodore Meron. New York: Oxford.

Shattuck, John. 1994. *Statement to the Committee on Foreign Relations, United States Senate.* Hearings on the International Convention on the Elimination of All Forms of Racial Discrimination. Washington: Government Printing Office, 7–8.

———. 1994. Introduction, pp. 1–vi. In *Civil and political rights in the United States.* Washington: State Department.

United Nations. 1995. *The United Nations and human rights 1945–1995*. New York: United Nations.

———. 1994. *United Nations action in the field of human rights*. New York: United Nations.

———. Human Rights Committee. April 7, 1995. *Consideration of reports by states parties under Article 40 of the Covenant*, Comments of the Human Rights Committee. New York: United Nations.

United States Department of State. 1994. *Civil and political rights in the United States: Initial report of the United States of America to the U.N. Human Rights Committee under the International Covenant on Civil and Political Rights*. Washington: Department of State.

World Bank. *Human development report*. New York: Oxford University Press.

• CHAPTER NINE •

An Indigeneous Australian University

ELEANOR BOURKE
Adjunct Professor
Centre for Australian Indigenous Studies
Monash University, Australia

COLIN BOURKE
Adjunct Professor
Centre for Australian Indigenous Studies
Monash University, Australia

Australia has two groups of Indigenous Australians: Aborigines and Torres Strait Islanders. Aboriginal people have occupied mainland Australia for more than 60,000 years while Torres Strait Islanders, a Melanesian people, have occupied the Torres Strait beginning many centuries before European settlement in 1788. This paper is written by Aboriginal authors and represents one Aboriginal perspective. The accepted Australian definition of an Aboriginal person is one who is of Aboriginal descent, identifies as being Aboriginal, and is recognised by his or her community as being an Aboriginal person.

The 1996 Census revealed that there were some 386,000 Indigenous people in Australia, some 2% of the total population with New South Wales and Queensland having more than fifty percent of the total Indigenous population. In Western Australia and the Northern Territory the Indigenous population comprises a significant proportion of their relatively smaller populations.

In Australia today the extremities of Indigenous life exist side by side. The positives are the developments of the past 30 years: the increased participation of Indigenous Australians in education, broadcasting and public affairs;

the growing interest in Indigenous cultures and art forms; and a pride in Aboriginal identity.

The negatives are the often quoted social indicators: health, housing, employment and statistics on incarceration and contact with the law, all of which show a continuing negative disparity between Indigenous Australians and others. Indeed in some respects statistics are getting worse. Complex social processes are at work. Improvements in one area are often undermined by negative factors in another.

Education has long been an area of concern because of low achievement by Indigenous Australians and negative attitudes of other Australians. In 1994 the Australian Council for Educational Research (ACER) found that forty-five percent of Indigenous primary school children have significantly lower literacy and numeracy achievement, i.e., one standard deviation or more below the Australian mean compared with 16 percent of other Australian students. Even though national statistics indicate the school system is failing Indigenous Australians there has been considerable improvement in apparent retention rates over recent years. Despite this improvement, in 1993 while 75 percent of other Australians studied at year 12 just 25 percent of Indigenous Australian achieved the same level.

Indigenous Australians and Higher Education

Over the past quarter of a century Indigenous Australians have had a significant impact on the higher education sector in Australia. In 1975 the Aboriginal Consultative Group to the Commonwealth Schools Commission reported that they had identified some 55 Indigenous people enrolled in universities to 1974. By 1999 the Department for Education, Training and Youth Affairs (DETYA) reported an enrollment of some 8,000 in post-secondary education.

While participation rates have increased dramatically, the academic and cultural outcomes provide a less positive picture. The choice of study for Indigenous students is skewed toward the humanities (80%) while the sciences are underrepresented (20%) compared with other Australian students at about 40 percent. Graduation rates are a concern, as attrition appears to be high. In 1992 just 646 Indigenous students had graduated although the enrollments in the three previous years were at 3,307, 3,609 and 4,807. With most university courses being three years in length, an overall attrition rate of at least 40 percent is suggested. This is double the attrition rate of other Australian students.

Indigenous students are enrolled in all Australian universities with the majority participating in mainstream courses. The largest enrollments have shifted in recent years from the University of South Australia to James Cook

University of Northern Queensland and Edith Cowan University in Western Australia.

If one examines the cultural content of university courses in Australia it is obvious that even though Aboriginal studies programs are now available in some universities, most offer little in Indigenous content and even fewer are taught by Indigenous people. For example, for a long time the University of South Australia was the only university to teach an Indigenous language. Now three or four do so. Indigenous education programs in most universities are academic support programs intended to assist Indigenous students enrolled in a predominantly Anglo Saxon-designed and oriented, middle class education system. The courses offered do not provide Indigenous students an education framed within an Indigenous cultural context. Indigenous staff of Australian universities have begun to form an Indigenous Higher Education network to promote and advance Indigenous education in Australian universities and to liaise with government on policy matters.

An Indigenous Australian University

Over the past two decades the world's Indigenous peoples have endeavoured to get out from under the yoke of fourth world colonial status (Barnhardt 1993). Indigenous people in the United States (Native Americans, Native Hawaiians and Yupik), Canada (First Nations and Inuit), New Zealand (Maori) Australia (Aborigines and Torres Strait Islanders) Greenland (Inuit), Scandinavia (Saami) and elsewhere have sought to establish and control their own versions of institutions offering programs of post-schooling education.

The attributes, qualities, character, and intent of these innovations have varied greatly due to the circumstances in which they were conceived. All have, however, been distinguished from their mainstream counterparts in that they have endeavoured to meet the particular social, cultural, political, and economic interests of the Indigenous people they were designed to serve. Each has had a cultural focus and has endeavoured to include Indigenous perspectives, philosophies, principles and practices.

As Ray Barnhardt found in his study of higher education in the fourth world, these institutions/programs have ranged from small local initiatives to larger full-scale national institutions. Some have incorporated Indigenous perspectives in their design while others have been adaptations of non-Indigenous institutions and programs.

Some programs of higher education for indigenous populations involve independently administered and accredited institutions. Independent institutions include the Indian Tribal Colleges, Heritage College in Tappernish, Washington and Te Wangae o Rankawa in New Zealand. Government-established institutions in areas where the majority of the population is Indigenous include the University of Greenland and the Saami College of Education in Norway.

Some programs have been established as institutions affiliated with mainstream institutions. Affiliated institutions which are run under the academic review and accreditation umbrella of the co-operating institution include the Saskatchewan Indian Federated College under the aegis of the University of Regina in Canada.

In other instances, programs have simply been integrated into established institutions. Integrated programs and units which are contained wholly within, and administered by existing mainstream institutions, included models like the former Faculties of Aboriginal and Islander Studies in the University of South Australia and the Northern Territory University. The most mature models in Australia today equate to schools or departments of their institutions.

All of these structures have advantages and disadvantages for Indigenous peoples. Independent structures, although in danger of becoming isolated, are more responsive to the needs of Indigenous people and can be more flexible in the search for services and resources than those operating within large cumbersome university structures. Affiliated structures have access to existing resources and can exercise some control over program content and services. There are some economies of scale, along with increased credibility and status. In addition integrated structures enable Indigenous perspectives to be brought to bear on the university as the Indigenous network has increasing influence on university administrations and particularly on their presidents. In such cases universities gain credibility and status in their reporting on Indigenous and equity issues. However the control and decision making authority resides firmly within the senior management of the institution. In the long term this may even constitute a threat to the idea of an Indigenous university.

The most crucial aspect of self-determination in education, according to Josephson (1986), is the choice between two alternatives: whether to allow English language to continue to be the primary instrument through which the ethnic-majority values are gradually assimilated into the Western-White cultural monolith (the Nigerian Hausa option); or whether to begin to insist that English be used only as a means of communication, stripped of its cultural biases (the Saudi Arabian option).

Josephson believes the lesson is clear. Mainstream education can turn Indigenous people into imitations of the colonisers. For this reason Josephson believes that Afro-Americans have lost their revolution, which has been defused by token Black Studies courses offered by, and controlled by, the western White academic establishment. If Indigenous people want the same thing to happen to their values then they need only remain content with having some Indigenous studies courses, and having the opportunity to access and participate in some mainstream courses in existing universities.

Professor Errol West, former chairperson of the National Aboriginal Education Committee (NAEC) proposed in 1993 an illustrative mode for an Australian First Nations University (AFNU) which would involve the ...*Amalgamation of all existing Aboriginal education units/centres in all 37 university campuses across Australia.*

This model intended to centralise the government funding for Indigenous Higher education which is presently distributed between 37 universities. The model required that AFNU be recognised as a bona fide university under the Federal Higher Education Act with a standard university management infrastructure and an appropriate administrative and academic structure.

Eric Willmot, a former Principal of the Australian Institute of Aboriginal and Torres Strait Islander Studies (AIATSIS) put forward three models for an Indigenous university:

1. "Custodial/definitional"
2. An Indigenous controlled Australian university
3. A dedicated Indigenous multi-functional tertiary and higher education institution

Willmot also espoused the idea of an amalgamation of all three models into a Pan Australian constellation model. In 1995 however, he favoured the custodial and definitional model which he believed is the purest form of university. In this model, the university would take the major responsibility for being the keeping place or the custodial body which holds and protects the accumulated knowledge about Aboriginal and Torres Strait Islander peoples. Such a university would also promote scholarship and carry out research aimed specifically at extending that knowledge. As Willmot envisions it, the university would be primarily involved in passing this knowledge on to Indigenous Australian students and in some limited part to other Australians.

The custodial/definitional model could expand knowledge on the existing Australian Institute of Aboriginal and Torres Strait Islander Studies located in Canberra and be co-located with the National Museum of Australia. The institute has a staff of approximately 50 and the largest collection of print, audio and visual, reference material on Indigenous Australians in existence. Willmot sees this as the simplest and most effective way to establish and operate the university. He believes that AIATSIS would serve as an exceptional foundation—in terms of administrative as well as subject matter resources—for the new institution. Attracting additional funds and the best modern Aboriginal and Torres Strait Islander scholars and Indigenous students would transform AIATSIS into the new Indigenous university. Management by an

Indigenous Council with Indigenous senior management would complete Willmot's custodial and definitional model.

These two models have some difficulties which need further consideration. Neither takes into account Josephson's concerns about curriculum, literature, and reference materials currently available to undergraduate students. Most university reading materials recommended for Aboriginal studies courses are written by non-Aboriginals and therefore, according to Josephson, teach—directly and indirectly—the values of mainstream culture to the detriment of Indigenous cultures. The First Nations model does not take account of the fact that most of the existing programs are student support programs rather than subject matter teaching and research units. As university life is about teaching and research, continuing to include non-teaching programs in an Indigeneous University model would keep it firmly anchored into the mainstream institutions it would be servicing. Willmot's preferred model while being an independent institution would be in direct opposition to the existing Aboriginal studies undergraduate programs in Australian universities.

The Willmot model, nevertheless, gets to the nub of what an Indigenous university must do. His concept is in harmony with Josephson's beliefs that the University would be the holder and creator of specific knowledge as well as being under Indigenous control. Its teaching and research would be specifically focused and associated with the knowledge systems of Indigenous Australians, and would generally not be involved in most areas of professional preparation for mainstream society. Some traditionalists may question the aims of so focused a curriculum. However, the model here supposes that an Indigenous Australian University offering an Indigenous curriculum should not even try to compete with the usual mainstream offerings in other fields of knowledge.

The Australian First Nations model proposes the existing undergraduate programs in Aboriginal Studies as discrete programs leading to an AFNU degree, diploma or certificate. This model promotes reconciliation to a greater degree than the Indigenous university model, because it promotes the serious study, by non-Indigenous as well as Indigenous students of the complex cultures and aspirations of Indigenous Australian peoples. It too would propose to concentrate on its efforts in undergraduate Aboriginal studies courses.

The Australian National University (ANU) based in Canberra has shown that universities need not have undergraduate programs before establishing postgraduate and advanced degree courses. In 1946 the ANU was founded by an Act of the Commonwealth Parliament which laid down its function to encourage and provide facilities for postgraduate study and research, both generally and in subjects of national importance to Australia. It was also to provide a university education for persons who elected to avail themselves of those facilities and were eligible to do so. It was also seen as providing specialised training for the Australian Public Service. The Act provided for the ANU's incorporation into the Canberra University College, an offshoot of the University of Melbourne.

The ANU model of university organisation differs from others in Australia (Macmillan 1968). Its emphasis on postgraduate work and research activity, and its relationship with other Australian universities more closely resembles Cambridge and Oxford in the United Kingdom (though lacking their undergraduate teaching programs). As a research oriented university it has conducted research at the very frontiers of knowledge and provided graduate training to scholars of exceptional ability and distinction. This unique character changed somewhat when, in 1960, undergraduate teaching was added through ANU's amalgamation with the Canberra University College. The ANU's five research schools continued their work within Canberra's Institute of Advanced Studies, and the College became the School of General Studies leading eventually to the Faculties of Arts, Economics, Law, Oriental Studies and Science. The Institute is generally responsible for the doctoral degrees and the Faculties for other degrees. ANU continues to lead in Asian studies and scientific research, and the Faculty of Science is the main provider of forestry training in Australia.

The ANU then offers a different model to those already proposed. The proponents of an Australian Indigenous University could well adapt features of this model to the contemporary setting to ascertain their applicability to an Indigenous University. Since 1946, modes of study have change significantly. Part time, off campus, distance education and online courses—in addition to the traditional on campus study mode—are all possible choices for students today.

An Australian Indigenous University has the opportunity to launch its research activities and postgraduate studies using today's communication technologies, such as post-audio, video broadcasting taping, telephone, facsimile and internet communications to deliver the courses and provide interactivity. It could offer a unique curriculum, with flexible approaches to teaching, learning, supervision and collaboration.

Most universities in Australia have opened their programs so that their research students can pursue their studies at home or in the workplace. Many are now offering good quality research degrees which are conducted off campus with supervision mediated using forms of communication technology (Evans 1995). While the university would need an administration and communications epicentre, the Indigenous University could venture into open educational space unconfined by institutional walls, free to address and overcome other constraints: language, culture, finance, time and imagination.

The challenges for the Indigenous University in Australia are: to break out of existing comfort zones and actually make the decision to control and preserve Australian Indigenous culture; and to develop appropriate programs and supervision practices which relate to the context of its students and mission. Australia's Monash University has already taken up this same challenge in South Africa, with the aim of developing practices framed by a dialogue which reflects the personal autonomy of the student as researcher-learner yet enable the attainment of international standards of scholarship within that University's framework.

The ANU's experience and the existence of the AIATSIS suggest that an Indigenous University could be developed, offering research degrees at masters and doctoral levels. The Willmot model for incorporating AIATSIS in the new university is a viable option because AIATSIS is already funded and has international research activity. It needs leadership, vision and the will to make it happen. The postgraduate activity and research outcomes could provide much of the reference resource base for undergraduate studies in the future. This would mean Indigenous undergraduates would not only be taught by Indigenous faculty, they would be able to study texts and scholarly work produced by Indigenous scholars. Indigenous Australians would then receive an authentic Indigenous education. Or is the alternative to develop a virtual Indigenous university like the Virtual Jewish University, The Bar-Ilan University at http://www.biu.ac.il/index_eng.shtml

References

Australian Bureau of Statistics. 1996. *1996 Census.*

Barnhardt, Ray. 1993. College of rural Alaska. *Canadian Journal of Native Education* 18(2).

Butlin, R. 1993. *Economics and the Dreamtime.* Melbourne: Cambridge University Press.

Department of Education, Training and Youth Affairs. 1999. *Students 1999: Selected higher education statistics.*

Evans, T. 1995. *Post graduate research supervision in the emerging open universities.* The Australian Universities Review.

Josephson, J. 1986. TEFL and the case for Indian universities. *Canadian Journal of Native Education* 13(2).

The Report of the Aboriginal Consultative Group to the Commonwealth Schools Commission. 1975. Canberra.

Macmillan, D. 1968. A *descriptive sketch.* The Australian Universities Review. Sydney University Press.

West, E. 1993. *Australian First Nations Universities: A discussion on the establishment of an Aboriginal University.* James Cook University.

Willmot, E. 1995. *An Indigenous University: To be or what to be?* National Aboriginal Higher Education Conference http://www.biu.ac.il/index_eng.shtml

• CHAPTER TEN •

Unequal Opportunities in Education and Labour Market in India

AUTAR S. DHESI
Professor, Honorable Research Fellow
Coventry Business School, Coventry University, Coventry, U.K.
Formerly Professor and Chairman
Punjab School of Economics, Grur Nanak University, Amritsar, India

Indian Situation

India is ethnically and religiously heterogeneous. Its predominant religious tradition sanctifies the concept of homohierarchicus (Dumont 1970; Stern 1993). The referent ideology of Hinduism is *Varnashram dharma*, according to which mankind is divided into four categories *(varnas)*. All men are born unequal, with unequal capacities, in order to perform functions of unequal importance to Him. The individuals are placed hierarchically with prescribed sacred duties and functions in accordance with one's past deeds. The rewards of performing one's sacred duty are to be reaped after death or in the next life. The social order is maintained if everyone performs one's "prescribed" sacred duty.

This sums up the inegalitarian "caste ideology" of Hinduism. The social groups, numbering in thousands that subscribe to this ideology, are accordingly hierarchically placed. Caste is the most pervasive parameter differentiating Indian society. Though caste is an institution of Hindu inegalitarianism, its imprint on other religious groups is real and discernible. The influence of some other Indian religious traditions like Jainism, Buddhism, and the most recent one, Sikhism, which strongly reject the inegalitarian institution of caste, has remained marginal in India. While caste is determined on the basis of birth, it, in turn, traditionally determines the distribution of human and physical capital, occupation, social status, and power. Class differentiation is still weak and tends to overlap caste.

Since Indians are very religious people, this ideology is deeply embedded in their collective consciousness, considerably influencing their behaviour. The secular constitutional government notwithstanding, this "sacral tradition" still has a strong hold over the minds and lives of Indians. Their adjustment to a secular value system is taking place but very slowly. The secular ideology of capitalist development and parliamentary democracy are acting on the traditional social order. A wide range of new opportunities for social mobility is emerging, in which India's "superbrahmins" are the westernized, educated elite—though still largely dominated by the upper castes. In theory, everyone having the will and enterprise can join them. The reality, however, is much more complex. "The new has not so much challenged the old as been accommodated by it" (Stern 1993, 70). The caste/religious groups have largely metamorphosed into interest groups that operate as such in different spheres of life. The emerging class relations are mediated by different caste-religious categories. Because of their sacral ideological base, longevity and reliability, castes have emerged as primary mediators of their members' class interests. Under democratic dispensation, disadvantaged groups are organized and knocking hard at the citadel of privilege of dominant castes which, in turn, seek new ways to protect it. No wonder, Indian society is in turmoil. The final outcome shall depend on the Indian elite's philosophy of social justice and its commitment to translate it effectively into societal norms and methods of management.

Modern India officially abolished untouchability and introduced compensatory positive discrimination in education and employment for Scheduled Castes and scheduled tribes (considered lowest in the sacral hierarchy) who have suffered cumulative social and economic disabilities. Recently, these benefits have been extended to other lower castes in response to their organised political assertions. However, the designation of social categories for extending compensatory benefits is broadly drawn and fails to encompass their heterogeneity and internal stratification. The benefits of affirmative action have therefore gone to the upper crust within each broad social category rather than raising the general socio-economic level. Further, it is a patron-client relationship—largely reflecting traditional high caste-low caste social hierarchy—which is the basis for political mobilization, and the caste/religious groups have shown a marked tendency to over-represent the interests of dominant social categories, and over-represent the interests of articulate well-to-do sections across all social categories. So it seems that "divinely ordained" social inequities persist in secular garb, though possibly with a little less inhumanity.

The priorities of development have been anchored in the philosophy of centrally controlled management of societal transformation, and have the reflected perceptions and class interests of the dominant elite-urban, westernized, educated segments of society, mainly from upper castes, which took over the reins of power from the British. The development strategy put excessive emphasis on the development of highly capital-intensive, urban-based modern industries in a protected environment. The agriculture and traditional industrial sectors were deliberately neglected and were subordinated to the rapid development of the modern sector. The technological backwardness of the traditional sectors, the underdevelopment and underutilisation of India's abundant human resources, the high incidence of poverty, and the low quality, high cost industrial output are some of the adverse consequences of that development strategy (Dhesi 1986; 1995; 1996). Rhetoric notwithstanding advanced education got priority over literacy for the masses. As a result, the absolute number of illiterates has been increasingly rapidly since independence. Most of them are poor and belong to the traditionally disadvantaged sections of society. As observed earlier, the compensatory discrimination in education and employment has benefited only the well-off sections of the "disadvantaged" groups. The intended trickle-down of benefits as perceived in the centralised planned development did not materialise.

Unequal Opportunities

There is sufficient empirical evidence to suggest that discrimination, defined as absence of equal opportunities, exists before the market as well as in the market against certain social categories in India.

Education

In the context of planned development, mass literacy and the generation of skills of various types and levels were considered priority areas in education. However, the development strategy's excessive emphasis on modern industries had an inbuilt bias for investment in higher education. The most comprehensive recently compiled empirical evidence which suggests that Indian educational policy favours higher education is in Jan and Mingat's (1992) *Education in Asia*. Three complementary pieces of data are used to identify the priorities of the education system: resource intensity (measured by unit costs), coverage, and extent of government subsidization. Resource intensity reveals the relative concentration of resources per pupil by stage of education. Data on the total operating costs per pupil, regardless of funding source, are used to assess the relative resource intensity and implicit priority given to the various stages of education. The deviation of unit costs from the Asian regional mean at each level of education is the basis for assessing the priorities of the system. In India, unit costs in primary education are 41 percent below the corresponding regional mean but in higher education the unit costs are 51 percent above the regional mean. These patterns suggest that resources in India, on average, are more heavily concentrated in higher education compared with the situation in the neighbouring countries.

A second indicator of bias toward higher education is the structure of coverage across levels of education as reflected in enrolment ratios. Recognizing that coverage and income levels are positively correlated, the actual enrolment ratios are compared with those predicted on the basis of a country's per capita income. The deviations of actual from predicted ratios at three levels of education are used as a rough indication of the bias in coverage. India's actual ratios at three levels of education are higher than those predicted. However, the actual gross enrolment ratio of 92 percent in primary education is only marginally higher than the predicted ratio of 82 percent. In contrast, the 9 percent actual enrolment ratio in higher education is 172 percent of the predicted 5.8 percent enrolment ratio. These patterns suggest a bias in coverage favouring higher education.

The extent of private financing in higher education is extremely limited (7.1 percent) compared with that in the Asian region (33.7 percent) as a whole. The structure of enrolments and financing arrangements result in a distribution of public spending that is skewed toward the privileged. The cumulative government subsidies per higher education graduate amount to 836 percent of per capita GNP; that is, 26 percent of per capita GNP in the primary cycle, 116 percent in the secondary cycle, and 720 percent in higher education. The social implications of these patterns become clear when we note that the majority of the students in higher education belong to the better off sections of the society (World Bank 1995; Dhesi 1992).

There is compelling evidence to suggest that both from an efficiency and equity point of view primary education should have received a higher priority. According to the 1991 Census, the literacy rate of the general population (51 percent) is significantly higher than the literacy rates of Tribals (24 percent) and Scheduled Castes (30 percent). The respective female literacy rates of the general population, Tribals, and Scheduled Castes are 39.29 percent, 14.5 percent, and 19.03 percent. However, since the two disadvantaged groups are also included in the general population, levels of their disadvantage are underestimated. According to Krishna and Akila (1993), underestimation could be as high as 6 percentage points. If other disadvantaged groups, Muslims, and lower castes are also excluded from the general population for purposes of comparison, the gap in the literacy rates between the privileged and disadvantaged social categories would widen further. Some additional empirical evidence in support of this contention has been observed from a fairly large sample of the Delhi population (Dhesi and Singh 1989). Excluding low castes, Scheduled Castes, and Muslims, 90 percent of the sample population has been found to be literate with even higher rates of literacy among Brahmins (92 percent) and the other high castes excluding Brahmins (97 percent). The respective literacy rates of Scheduled Castes, Muslims, and low castes are 39 percent, 48 percent, and 57 percent. Data further suggest that a very large proportion of the educated belonging to the disadvantaged social categories, especially Scheduled Castes, do not go beyond the primary stage. The gap between the two top social categories—Brahmins and high castes—and the remaining categories tends to increase significantly as we move along the higher stages of education. Highly subsidised higher education is almost monopolised by the top two social categories.

The access to schooling also has a class character. The disadvantaged groups are not only poor, they disproportionately live in rural areas with poor educational facilities (Singh 1993). They not only have poor education opportunity but also lack capacity to act on whatever is available. The drop-out rate, reflecting poor education quality as well as poor economic conditions of affected pupils, is relatively much higher among the disadvantaged groups (Singh 1993).

To assess the economic rationality of the allocation of public resources across levels of education, the rates of return for education are compared (Jan and Mingat 1992). The rates of return are high among all levels of society in all regions of the world, but they decline with ascending levels of education. In the case of India, social rates of return at secondary and higher levels are significantly lower as compared to those for Asia as a whole and for LDCs as a group. However, the social rate of return at the primary level is highest in India. These patterns suggest that primary education deserves top priority in the allocation of education resources. But in allocating 27 percent of its educational resources to primary education, India comes out poorly compared to the Asian regional average of 48 percent (Jan and Mingat 1992, 27).

Literacy is the main reason for high rates of return to investment in primary education. However, simply expanding coverage does not maximize the achievement of literacy in the population. The early dropout of pupils may result in their either not attaining literacy or their lapsing back into illiteracy. The completion rate in India is only 37 percent at the primary level as compared to Asia's 61 percent.[1] The completion rate among disadvantaged groups is much lower than the average (Singh 1993). This is yet another reason for resetting priorities in education in favour of primary education.

In sum, education policy has favoured highly subsidised higher education which primarily benefits the higher castes. Primary education—so necessary for creating mass literacy and alleviating poverty, and therefore benefiting disadvantaged castes—has received low priority. Findings clearly suggest that there are unequal opportunities in education for different social categories.

Labour Market

The various social categories may also face different employment opportunities due to labor market differences as well as differences in levels and quality of educational attainment. Inequalities between different social categories in access to education and in the market reinforce each other. First, unequal educational attainments are reflected in dissimilar occupational profiles for different social categories, with the disadvantaged categories concentrated in low-income occupations. In addition, their comparative wages may be lower than those of the privileged categories due to discrimination and/or inferior quality of schooling. So the disadvantaged categories may invest less due to lack of capacity as well as to discouraging signals from the labour market. Thus disadvantages become cumulative, and unequal opportunities because of caste and class tend to reinforce each other.

The available empirical evidence, based on a fairly large sample of the Delhi population cited above, suggests that the educationally most disadvantaged categories like Scheduled Castes and Muslims, in comparison to the remaining social categories, also suffer severe disadvantage in employment. Their employment is concentrated in blue-collar jobs, with those jobs representing 89 percent of Scheduled Caste employment, 73 percent of low caste employment, and 72 percent of Muslim employment. Among the remaining social categories, blue collar work represents only 47 percent of their employment. The underrepresentation of the disadvantaged groups tends to increase with the level of occupation. This occupational inequality is, in turn, reflected in earnings inequality. There is considerable variation in average earnings among different social categories. The ratio of the other social categories to high caste earnings ranges from 0.950 for Brahmins to 0.367 for the Scheduled Castes. The average earnings of low castes, middle castes, and Muslims are about 50 percent of those of the high castes other than Brahmins.

The earlier analysis based on the same Delhi sample data indicates the existence of labour market discrimination against certain social categories (Dhesi and Singh 1989). The analysis suggests that the impact of human capital variables, socio-economic background variables and job-related variables on earnings vary across social categories. The results suggest that high caste employees earn more than employees of all other social categories because of their superior characteristics (education, father's education, occupation, age, duration of stay in urban areas, organization where engaged, and duration of stay at the present job). However, the impact of these "positive" characteristics varies across the various social categories. In the case of Brahmins, earnings differential would have been larger but for their favourable earnings function. The latter reduced the impact of differences in observed characteristics by 60.42 percent. The positive residual portion of the earnings differential for the remaining categories suggests that the earnings function is less favourable to these categories than to Brahmins and high castes. Simply, the former social categories face discrimination in the market. In the case of Sikhs, 81.55 percent of the earnings differential is due to unfavourable earnings function and only 18.45 percent of the differential is explained by differences in observed characteristics.

One possible explanation of this unexpected finding is that caste factor, though relatively less important but not completely absent, has not been used to differentiate the community. However, the relatively low level of disadvantage in market suffered by lower castes suggests that disadvantage suffered by Sikhs still would have been significantly higher than that for other disadvantaged categories. The percentage of earnings differential attributed to discrimination and other factors excluded from the earnings function in the case of Muslims (40 percent) and other religious categories-Christians, Buddhists, Parsees, etc. (30 percent) is also quite high. However, in the case of Hindu middle castes, low caste and Scheduled Castes, this percentage varies from 5.69 percent to 23.19.

Summary and Conclusion

The results clearly suggest that labour market opportunities vary across social categories. There is sufficient empirical evidence to suggest that discrimination, defined as absence of equal opportunities, exists before the market as well as in the market against certain social categories in India. Inequality in access to sources of human capital acquisition reinforces inequality in the labour market and vice versa. Apparently, caste/religious discrimination and class discrimination overlap. However, in the case of socially deprived lower castes and minorities, especially Muslims, caste/religious discrimination seems to accentuate class discrimination. The impact of secular ideologies and institutions of modernity notwithstanding, the inegalitarian sacred tradition of caste still has strong hold over the minds and lives of Indians.

The social change that is taking place as a result of economic development and democratic policy has a dual nature. On the one hand, caste, community, and identity consciousness has increased; on the other, there is emergence of a non-brahmanical pragmatic cultural ethos.

The logical consequence of the first aspect of change is that different social categories have metamorphosed into interest groups operating in different spheres of life. With patron-client relationships as the basis for political mobilization, development policies have favoured the dominant social categories as well as the better-off, articulate sections across all social categories. So it seems that divinely ordained social inequalities persist in secular garb, though with reduced inhumanity.

The second aspect of the social change is more positive. With increasing political assertion by the lower social categories, and increased opportunities for social mobility created by economic development and parliamentary democracy, hegemony of the dominant social categories is likely to decline. In turn, this change in the composition of elite should foster a non-brahmanical, pragmatic cultural ethos conducive to social mobility and development (Dhesi 1982). The transparent policies designed to promote equal opportunities taking into account specificities of different social categories shall speed up the process of socio-economic change.

References

Darity, Jr., William, A. 1996. Private communication. May 20.

Dhesi, Autar S. 1982. The role of social mobility in Punjab's development, Anvesak. *Journal of Sardar Patel Institute of Economic and Social Research, Ahmedabad* XII(1): 127–38.

———. 1986. Development strategy, human capital and technological development: India's experience. *Asian Thought & Society* XI: 32–33, 138–49.

——— and H. Singh. 1989. Education, labour market distortions and relative earnings of different religion-caste categories in India. *Canadian Journal of Development Studies* X(1): 75–89.

———. 1996. Review of A.S. Bhalla and K.N. Reddy, (Eds.): The technological transformation of rural India. *Kyklos* 49(1): 71–73.

———. 1996. From Centralised to decentralised development in India: The communitarian perspective. *Community Development* 31: 201–213.

Dumont, Louis. 1970. *Homo Hierarchicus: The Caste System and its implications.* Chicago: University of Chicago Press.

Jan, Jee-Peng and Alain Mingat. 1992. *Education in Asia.* Washington D.C.: The World Bank.

Singh, Amar Kumar. 1993. Status of the Tribals in India. *Social Change* 23(2–3): 3–13.

Stern, Robert W. 1993. *Changing India.* Cambridge, England: Cambridge University Press.

• CHAPTER ELEVEN •

Programs for Empowerment and Reducing Equality: A Long Way to Go for Untouchables

SUKHADEO THORAT
Professor of Economics, Centre for the Study of Regional Development
School of Social Sciences, Jawaharlal Nehru University, New Delhi, India

Introduction

Untouchables constitute nearly one-fifth of India's population and they present a complex case which differs from that of other deprived groups in Indian society.[1] The discrimination and deprivation arising out of the caste system has affected them far more adversely than any other group in Indian society. Their problems differ from those of other deprived groups in a distinct way. Firstly, for historical reasons, the incidence of social and economic deprivation measured by any indicators of human development is far more intense in their case (Thorat 1996). They are far behind other identical groups of Indian society with respect to access to sources of income such as agricultural land, capital assets, employment, education and social services. Secondly, and more importantly, discrimination based on untouchability continues today and, as a result, their efforts for upward mobility are often frustrated by actions of the upper castes in India.

The incidence of economic discrimination against untouchables has been well recognized by policymakers. The Indian Government has developed a fairly comprehensive package of policy instruments, particularly in public employment and education, to protect them from discrimination. These affirmative action measures, which are popularly known as "Reservation Policy," are however confined to the government or public sector jobs and services. Due to the small size of the government and public sector, the jobs under the reservation category account for only 3 percent of the total employment of the Scheduled Caste workers.

The remaining 97 percent of Scheduled Caste workers are self-employed and wage or salaried workers in private agriculture and in the organized and unorganized manufacturing and service sectors. These private employers have no reservation policy because there is no legislation requiring it.

Because there is no legal provision for private sector reservation policy the Government of India has resorted to an alternative set of measures, although not obligatory to facilitate Scheduled Caste participation in various private economic, social and educational activities. These government programs operate in the agricultural, organized and unorganized manufacturing and services sectors. The programs also include schemes for educational development and improvement in access to social services like housing, electricity, and drinking water.

Over time a number of economic, educational and social development programs for Scheduled Castes have been developed through both plan and non-plan channels, but the schemes operating through the regular five years plans are the major ones. From 1951–2000 the policy towards Scheduled Castes has undergone a change over successive five-year plans. In the first Five-Year Plan schemes were largely confined to education and allotment of agricultural land. The same policy continued in the second Five-Year Plan. In the third Five-Year Plan education received high priority with additional emphasis placed on technical and vocational education and training. One of the schemes for economic development emphasized the allotment of agricultural land as well as special financial support to Scheduled Caste farmers, village artisans, traditional craft and small-scale industries. In the fourth Five-Year Plan, the emphasis on economic and educational programs continued. In the sphere of economic development, programs were initiated to provide support to individual cultivators to purchase agricultural equipment, inputs and land reclamation. It was expected that with these supportive schemes the Scheduled Castes would be able to benefit from general economic development.

In the sixth Five-Year Plan a significant modification was made in the strategy and methodology for addressing the problems of Scheduled Castes. The "Special Component Plan for Scheduled Castes" (SCP) was adopted in 1978–79 with a specific purpose to quantify the flow of funds and benefits of various schemes to the Scheduled Castes. There was also a shift in the emphasis towards beneficiary-oriented development programs. Under these programs specific target groups from within the Scheduled Castes were identified for special supports. For the first time, the plan set a specific goal, which was to assist 50 percent of the Scheduled Caste families across the poverty line.

On the economic side an organization called the "National Scheduled Caste Finance Corporation," with branches in several states, was set up as catalyst for financing Scheduled Caste development programs. Previously financial support for programs aimed at Scheduled Castes was drawn from the general fund with some provision for quotas and preferences. The assumption was that, along with some special schemes for the poor, the benefit from general economic development would trickle down to the Scheduled Castes. However an assessment by mid-1970 (beginning of the Sixth Plan) revealed that despite programs targeting the poor in general and the Scheduled Castes in particular, the benefits of general development did not trickle down to Scheduled Caste to any significant degree. Among other reasons, the practice of discrimination against Scheduled Castes was thought to one of the important reasons for the failure of the programs. The Special Component Plan for Scheduled Castes was therefore developed under which special allocation of funds was to be made on schemes meant for the Scheduled Castes. Wherever the general schemes were divisible they were made apart of the Special Component Plan. In the case of non-divisible schemes (such as road, electricity, etc.) it was hoped that gains would trickle down to the Scheduled Castes. Further, time-bound targets of achievements were set and assessments were made at end of the period.

In the seventh and eighth Five-Year Plans the emphasis remained on beneficiary-oriented programs for socio-economic development. In the ninth Five-Year Plan, in addition to the ongoing programs, the plan placed emphasis on empowering every landless rural Scheduled Caste family with a minimum piece of land, preservation and restoration of land ownership rights and implementation of existing legislation to protect the ownership of land.

Nature of Programs

Since the early 1950s a set of targeted programs have been developed to improve access by Scheduled Castes to agricultural land, financial and other capital assets, and general and vocational education so that they could participate in the private agriculture, manufacturing and service sector economies. These measures are intended to provide some source of income and also to build the human resource capabilities of Scheduled Caste persons. The programs, which have evolved over time, can be classified as follows:

1. Programs to provide a supplementary wage employment in rural areas. The main purpose of these programs is to provide minimum wage employment and income to wage labour, particularly to those belonging to the Scheduled Castes.
2. Programs to provide agricultural land, either private land acquired through ceiling on agricultural land or government land, as well as credit to buy agricultural inputs and land and irrigation improvement.
3. Programs to provide credit for self-employment.

4. Programs to provide education and vocational training to undertake wage/salaried employment and self-employment; and finally,
5. Programs to protect Scheduled Castes from discrimination in public employment, through the instrument of reservation policy, and preferences.

The programs which assured minimum income to wage labor include employment programs like Jawahar Employment Programme (JEP) and Employment Assurance Scheme (EAS). The objective of JEP is to provide supplementary employment to the unemployed and underemployed in rural areas. These programs also aim at strengthening capital (land and irrigation) assets of the poor people. Persons below the poverty line constituted the target group and preference was given to Scheduled Castes in proportion to their share among poor households.

As a part of the JEP the development of private agricultural land (under the Land Development Scheme) irrigation (under "Million Wells Schemes") and irrigation facilities for marginal and small farmers was also undertaken. In both the schemes, the small and marginal farmers, particularly those belonging to Scheduled Castes, were given priority.

In addition to JEP, a new scheme known as the Employment Assurance Scheme (EAS) was launched in 1993. EAS now covers 2446 blocks in over 261 districts situated in drought-prone, desert, tribal and hill areas. The scheme aims at providing assured employment of 100 days of unskilled work to the rural poor in the 18–60 age group. The Nehru Employment scheme introduced in 1992 is now extended to the urban poor.

The Integrated Rural Development Programs (IRDP) also falls into this category. The IRDP was launched as a credit-linked program for self-employment as a strategy to alleviate poverty. The objective is to enable targeted rural poor families to augment their income and cross the poverty line by acquiring productive assets through credit. The target groups are small and marginal farmers and artisans below the poverty line, with 50 percent of the assisted families being from the Scheduled Castes and Scheduled Tribes. Similar schemes for self-employment were introduced for the urban poor under the Nehru Employment scheme as well as a separate Scheme of Urban Micro-Enterprise. In addition, training for rural and urban youth from families below the poverty line was initiated to provide basic technical and managerial skills for self employment or employment in agricultural and non-agricultural sectors.

Economic Impact of the Programs: An Assessment

In this section we try to assess the impact of these programs on the levels of living of the Scheduled Castes at the macro level. In order to assess the changes in the level of living we use various indicators such as occupational patterns, employment/unemployment levels and the level of poverty among Scheduled Castes vis-a-vis other groups in Indian society. What kinds of changes are likely to occur in the occupational patterns, employment, and poverty of individuals in the Scheduled Castes? Based on the design of the self-employment, wage employment and other programs we expect the following changes to occur (see Panel 1).

- Firstly, it is expected that the proportion of land-owning self-employed cultivators should increase. Priority distribution of surplus land under land ceiling laws, government land and other land should bring a shift in the occupational status from wage-labour to self-employed cultivating households in the Scheduled Castes. Further, the improvement in private agricultural land (through leveling, drainage, and irrigation) should also make marginal and small farmers viable cultivators.
- Similarly the proportion of self-employed households/persons in the rural non-farm sector and in urban areas should improve due to self-employment programs under IRDP.
- With the expected increase in the proportion of self-employed, there should be a corresponding decline in the proportion of wage-labour households.
- It is also expected that wage and self-employment programs should reduce unemployment among Scheduled Caste workers in rural and urban areas.
- Reservation in government jobs and services should increase the percentage of salaried worker among the Scheduled Castes.
- With an improvement in the levels of self-employment, wage employment and salaried employment it is expected that the incidence of poverty among rural and urban Scheduled Caste households/persons should decrease.
- In relative terms, the gap between the Scheduled Castes and other segments of India society should be reduced.

Panel I

Expected Impact of Anti-poverty Programs on Occupational Pattern, Employment and Poverty of Scheduled Caste

Programs	Impact on Occupational Status	Impact on Employment and Poverty
Self-Employment Programs		
(a) Land distribution for agriculture	Switch over to self-employment status	Reduce wage employment, and increase self-employment, consumption and reduce poverty
(b) Improvement in land and irrigation through private agricultural land development programs and irrigation through millions wells scheme	Improve and strengthen productivity of marginal and small farmer self-employment status	Become viable farmer, acquires self-employed status, increase income and reduces poverty
(c) Capital assets through credit for non-farm activities	Achieve self-employed status	Reduce wage employment increase self-employment, income increases, poverty declines
(d) Vocational training in skill formation	Achieve self-employed status or skilled wage employment	Self-employment increase, income rise, poverty decline
Wage Employment Programs		
(e) Wage employment programs	Obtain supplementary wage employment	Increase wage employment and income rises and reduce poverty
(f) Education programs and reservation in government jobs	Increase percentage of salaried persons	Increase income and reduce poverty

Changes in Status

Changes in Land Ownership

About three-fourths of the Scheduled Caste population live in rural areas where the main source of income is either cultivation of agricultural land (as self-employed farmers), wage labour or some type of non-farm self or wage employment. Surplus land acquired through private agricultural land ceilings, government land and other lands are to be distributed to landless Scheduled Caste families. As of September 30, 1996, about 5.2 million acres were distributed at the all-India level. Of these, about 1.8 million acres was distributed to Scheduled Caste families, and 2.6 million acres to other groups. Of the total 5.1 million program beneficiaries, 1.8 million were Scheduled Caste families, and 2.5 million were from other groups (Table 1). The land distributed comes to .0977 acre per Scheduled Caste beneficiary, less than the 1.047 acre per beneficiary in other groups. Of the land distributed to Scheduled Caste households, West Bengal accounted for about 20 percent of the land distribution, followed by Uttar Pradesh. In terms of beneficiaries West Bengal accounted for nearly 43 percent of total beneficiaries, followed by Uttar Pradesh (13 percent), Andhra Pradesh (12 percent) and Bihar (12.4 percent).

Table 2 presents the situation of Scheduled Caste families with respect to ownership of agricultural land for 1981 and 1991 (land ownership data for Scheduled Castes is not available for earlier years). These data are helpful in assessing the effects of land reform measures on land ownership status among Scheduled Caste families. In 1991 about 13.34 percent of the Scheduled Caste families in India were landless, higher than the 10.54 landless rate for other groups. At the state level, 13 out of 17 states show a higher incidence of landlessness among Scheduled Caste families in 1991. The percentage of landless households among the Scheduled Castes was relatively high in Maharastra (24.31 percent), Madhya Pradesh (20.53 percent Scheduled Castes) and 6.0 percent for other), Haryana (9.0 percent Scheduled Castes and 1.81 percent other), Kerala (14.33 percent Scheduled Castes and 7.67 percent others), and Madhya Pradesh (20.53 percent Scheduled Castes and 12.57 percent other).

Despite the distribution of agricultural land under ceiling to about 1.8 million Scheduled Caste beneficiaries, the percentage of landless households among Scheduled Castes has increased from 12.62 percent in 1981 to 13.34 percent 1991, while the rate has remained constant at around 10 percent for others group. The increase in the percentage of landless Scheduled Caste households occurred in the states of Himachal Pradesh, Madhya Pradesh, Jammu and Kashmir, Punjab, Kerala, Orissa and Tamil Nadu (Table 2). In the rest of the states the percentage of landless household, among the Scheduled Castes declined during 1981–91.

With respect to the 87 percent of Scheduled Caste households who owned land in 1991, nearly 72 percent were marginal holdings of less than 5 acres of land. This ratio was much higher than the 55 percent marginal holdings for other groups. Between 1981 and 1991 the ratio of marginal farmers remained constant at around 72 percent but there has been some improvement in the area owned by them from 22.62 percent in 1981 to around 30 percent in 1991.

Table 2 presents a more detailed picture about the percentage of households owning no land, (i.e., landless), and those owning less than 0.50 acres and between 0.50 and one acre. At all-India level in 1991 nearly 56.00 percent of Scheduled Caste households owned less than one acre and of them nearly 47.50 percent owned less than half acre. The landless and near landless (i.e., those owning less than one acre) put together accounted for nearly 70 percent of the total Scheduled Caste households. The proportion of landless and near landless household among Scheduled Castes was astonishingly high at 93 percent in Punjab and Kerala, followed by 88 percent in Bihar, and 86 percent in Tamil Nadu, 84 percent in Haryana and around 70 percent in West Bengal, Orissa, Andhra Pradesh and Uttar Pradesh. The incidence was relatively low in low rainfall or dry farming states in India.

Between 1981 and 1991 the proportion of landless households increased marginally at the all India level, mainly due to increases in Himachal Pradesh, Jammu and Kashmir, Madhya Pradesh, Orissa and Tamil Nadu. The increase was quite prominent in Orissa. The remaining states showed decline in various magnitudes.

The percentage of those owning less than half an acre remained constant at around 48 percent during 1981 and 1991. But it has increased in Andhra Pradesh, Rajasthan, Uttar Pradesh and West Bengal, and declined in other states. Taking the ratio of landless and near landless household (i.e., those owing less than one acre) it is observed that while the rates remained stable at all-India level, the ratio increased in Andhra Pradesh, Orissa, Rajasthan, Tamil Nadu and Uttar Pradesh and declined in nine other states.

Trends in Self-Employed Household in Farm and (Rural) Non-Farm Sector

Although nearly 87 percent of Scheduled Caste households own some land, most of them are marginal owners and so their capacity to pursue cultivation as a viable independent economic activity is extremely limited. It is precisely because of the vulnerability of marginal holdings that IRDP and JEP programs have attempted to improve the productive capacity of Scheduled Caste

Table 1: Distribution of Surplus Land to Scheduled Castes September 1996

	Total Area and Beneficiaries			Area Distributed and No. of Scheduled Caste Beneficiaries					
State	Area Distribution	Total No. Beneficiaries	Area Distributed	No. Of Beneficiaries	% Share in Area	% Share in Beneficiaries	% Share in All India Area	% Share in All India No. Beneficiaries	Average Area Distributed
Andhra Pradesh	594352	521563	226890	216537	38.17	41.51	12.55	11.71	10.4
Assam	479878	441804	45746	43406	9.53	9.82	2.53	2.34	1.05
Bihar	303217	372529	179161	229832	59.08	61.69	9.91	12.43	0.779
Gujarat	133999	31376	83247	14584	62.12	46.48	4.60	0.78	5.20
Haryana	87259	27392	37623	11753	43.11	42.90	2.08	0.63	3.20
Himachal Pracesh	3340	4400	2305	2934	69.01	66.68	0.12	0.15	0.785
Jammu & Kashmir	45000	450000	0	0	0	0	0	0	0
Karnataka	117147	31415	71133	18953	60.72	60.33	3.93	1.02	3.75
Kerala	64283	145106	25197	62174	39.01	42.84	1.39	3.36	0.40
Madhya Pradesh	185313	72131	49433	21528	26.67	29.84	2.73	1.16	2.29
Maharashtra	554870	14580	161715	41945	29.14	29.83	8.94	2.26	3.85
Orissa	154298	135219	49075	45561	31.80	33.69	2.71	2.46	1.077
Punjab	103487	28287	44015	11301	42.53	39.95	2.43	0.61	3.89
Rajasthan	452176	77899	145317	28453	32.13	36.52	8.03	1.53	5.10
Tamilnadu	162369	135269	62096	59729	38.24	44.15	3.43	3.23	1.03
Uttar Pradesh	390501	346209	263815	236599	67.55	68.33	14.59	12.79	1.11
West Bengal	965293	2151632	359519	800870	37.24	37.22	19.88	43.31	0.44
TOTAL	5213328	5120859	1807575	1848833	34.67	36.10	100.00	100.00	0.97

Source: Report of the Commission for SC/ST, 1995–1996 Delhi.

Table 2: Percentage of Landless and Near Landless Scheduled Castes Households (% to Total Rural Households)

State	1982 Landless	1982 Less than Half Acre	1982 Between Half and One Acre	1982 Up to One Acre	1982 Landless and Up to One Acre	1992 Landless	1992 Less than Half Acre	1992 Between Half and One Acre	1992 Up to One Acre	1992 Landless and Up to one Acre
Andhra Pradesh	13.58	44.34	7.95	52.29	65.87	12.49	49.95	9.91	59.86	72.35
Assam	5.02	36.98	17.27	54.25	59.27	5.52	37.10	7.94	45.04	50.56
Bihar	35.58	69.78	9.76	79.54	89.24	19.73	62.62	6.15	68.77	88.50
Gujarat	23.86	44.69	6.38	51.22	75.06	18.09	34.11	4.22	38.88	56.42
Haryana	10.09	87.52	0.97	88.49	98.58	7.95	73.10	3.63	76.73	84.68
Himachal Pracesh	6.01	34.71	9.96	44.67	50.73	7.09	22.67	5.37	28.04	35.13
Jammu and Kashmir	0.66	41.56	3.58	45.14	45.80	4.00	34.37	7.91	42.28	46.28
Karnataka	14.52	38.41	8.51	46.92	61.44	10.69	32.60	2.67	35.27	45.96
Kerala	16.56	77.33	5.35	82.68	99.24	14.33	79.32	-	79.32	93.65
Madhya Pradesh	18.11	24.21	2.55	26.76	44.87	20.53	19.04	3.17	22.21	42.74
Maharashtra	26.39	33.42	3.38	36.80	63.19	24.31	32.13	2.99	35.12	59.43
Orissa	7.2	47.78	6.70	54.18	61.38	11.19	49.82	9.78	59.60	70.79
Punjab	6.01	56.84	2.96	89.50	95.81	6.7	85.57	1.43	87.00	93.78
Rajasthan	12.91	18.10	2.40	20.50	33.41	76.11	29.10	6.18	35.28	43.04
Tamilnadu	14.5	61.66	7.48	69.14	83.64	19.21	57.4	9.82	67.03	86.24
Uttar Pradesh	7.18	40.88	18.33	59.21	66.39	6.15	45.98	16.08	62.06	68.21
West Bengal	19.13	42.74	11.05	53.79	72.92	12.02	47.66	11.64	59.30	71.32
TOTAL	12.62	47.97	9.53	57.50	70.12	13.34	47.50	8.89	56.39	69.73

Source: NSS Land Holding Survey 1982 and 1992

marginal and small farmers through improvement of land (under private land development programs) and irrigation (under the Million Wells Scheme). Along with supplying inputs at subsidized rate, the improvement in land and irrigation is expected to improve land productivity and make the marginal and small farmers viable and hence self-employed cultivators.

Table 3A shows the percentage of self-employed households for 1987–88 and 1993–94. At the all-India level in the early 1990's (i.e., 1991), the percentage of land-owning households among the Scheduled Caste households was about 87 percent. But NSS data for 1993–94 shows that only 19.12 percent were self-employed cultivators. This ratio was about the same during 1987–88. In contrast, the percentage of self-employed cultivating household among other groups was more than double that of the Special Castes for 1987–88 (43.3 percent) as well as 1993–94 (42.22 percent).

It is important to note that the proportion of Scheduled Caste self-employed cultivating households in rural areas was lowest in Punjab (4.31 percent), closely followed by Kerala (5.97 percent), Tamil Nadu (6.99 percent), Haryana (8.64 percent), Maharastra (8.37 percent), Gujarat (7.43 percent), Andhra Pradesh (8.4 percent) and Bihar (10.08 percent). The situation in Punjab and Haryana is obviously quite disturbing because it was expected that the new agricultural technology would make the Scheduled Caste marginal and small farmers viable. However the reasons for this failed expectation are quite obvious. In Punjab and Haryana the proportion of Scheduled Castes who owned less than half an acre of land is astonishingly high; i.e., 86.84 percent in Punjab and 87.52 percent in Haryana in the year 1982, and 85.57 percent in Punjab, and 73.10 percent in Haryana in 1992. Even government supported high-yield technology could not convert such mini holdings into viable units. A similar situation was the case in Kerala. In this state the proportion of those owning less than a half-acre was 77 percent in 1982 and 79.72 percent in 1992. The ratio of self-employed households was, however, relatively higher in Himachal Pradesh, Assam, Rajasthan, Uttar Pradesh and West Bengal. In these states the ratio varied between 31.07 percent in Uttar Pradesh to 48.3 percent in Himachal Pradesh. Thus, it is clear that because of the non-viable character of marginal land holdings a very small proportion of Scheduled Caste landowners in the end turned out to be self-employed cultivators. Thus the various schemes of land and irrigation improvement, credit support and subsidised input have benefited these households only marginally.

In about eight states the proportion of Scheduled Caste self-employed households in the rural non-farm sector was lower than that of other groups. On the other hand in a few states like Assam, Himachal Pradesh, and Orissa, the ratio of Scheduled Caste self-employed households was higher than for other groups. In the remaining states the percentage of self-employed non-farm rural households was more or less the same for the Scheduled Castes and

Table 3A: Percentage of Self-employed Among Scheduled Castes and Other Households (% to Total Rural Households)

	STATE	SEA (R)		SENA (R)		SEA (R)		SENA (R)		SE (U)		SE (U)	
		1987–88		1987–88		1993–94		1993–94		1993–94		1987–88	
		SC	OT	SC	OT	SC	OT	SC	OT	SC	OT	SC	OT
1.	Andhra Pradesh	8.8	31.2	7.1	15.6	8.4	27.79	4.98	15.43	15.2	35.0	17.06	31.62
2.	Assam	44.47	44.5	17.1	12.2	32.49	39.88	19.47	11.84	30.7	37.7	37.82	35.4
3.	Bihar	9.9	39.8	7.2	14.4	10.68	45.45	6.83	13.11	24.4	38.1	31.71	36.83
4.	Gujarat	10.1	38.2	4.3	10.0	7.43	34.16	7.77	10.17	14.3	35.0	31.71	36.83
5.	Haryana	5.88	56.0	17.4	14.50	8.64	50.90	15.20	17.09	31.1	42.0	14.20	30.16
6.	Himachal Pracesh	50.6	70.5	15.5	6.3	48.3	65.07	14.59	8.32	33.9	26.7	13.79	20.25
7.	Jammu and Kashmir	39.5	54.0	9.5	12.8	40.19	62.77	10.62	9.85	28.4	33.40	36.23	34.81
8.	Karnataka	12.4	41.0	6.9	11.6	15.94	44.81	9.27	13.78	14.33	33.0	18.75	33.95
9.	Kerala	4.8	27.0	8.6	16.8	5.97	23.0	4.87	14.72	11.7	33.6	10.17	33.00
10.	Madhya Pradesh	30.5	55.5	11.4	9.9	31.92	54.47	5.89	7.9	29.2	35.2	21.76	35.39
11.	Maharashtra	11.3	40.2	13.8	8.8	8.37	31.07	7.90	8.03	16.3	27.4	13.55	30.95
12.	Orissa	8.9	NA	4.4	NA	20.93	39.42	17.7	15.98	36.7	36.6	38.68	28.0
13.	Punjab	4.9	51.7	11.9	19.1	4.31	54.64	16.70	15.42	34.2	47.9	31.61	45.89
14.	Rajasthan	27.4	53.5	15.0	14.3	32.97	64.46	12.92	11.26	30.8	41.3	40.17	40.82
15.	Tamilnadu	6.9	27.7	5.9	16.0	6.99	25.08	4.07	16.20	17.4	30.4	17.03	29.89
16.	Uttar Pradesh	30.9	62.5	11.3	13.2	31.67	61.29	11.26	13.90	44.9	46.0	33.87	48.55
17.	West Bengal	23.2	32.1	15.4	17.8	22.92	30.96	17.77	23.55	32.9	29.7	26.87	32.09
	India	18.9	43.3	11.0	13.8	19.12	42.42	13.89	10.32	13.89	26.0	35.2	24.08
		18.8		5.5									

Note: SEA (R) = Self employed in agri-rural; SENA (R) = Self-employed in (rural) non-agri; SE(U) = Self-employed in urban sector; SC = Scheduled Caste; OT = non SC/ST other groups. The lower proportion of self-employed households in the rural non-farm sector in several states despite IRDP self-employment programs reveals the weakness of the schemes with respect to Scheduled Castes.

Self-employment in Urban Areas

Disparities in access to financial and physical capital assets are far more glaring in urban areas. In 1993–94 the proportion of Scheduled Caste households depending on self-employment was 24 percent, 11 percent lower than other groups (35.05 percent). With the exception of Assam, Jammu and Kashmir, Orissa and Punjab the percentage of Scheduled Caste self-employed households in urban areas was quite low compared to other groups. Orissa is the only state where the ratio of self employed Scheduled Caste households was higher than other households by a substantial margin.

Magnitude of Wage Labour in Rural Areas

The high incidence of landless and near landless households among the Scheduled Castes obviously has created an enormously high level of manual wage labourers among them. The statistics on the magnitude of rural wage labor regularly generated by the Population Census, National Sample Survey and Rural Labour Enquiries bring out this fact quite clearly (Table 3B).

According to the Population Census of 1991, the percentage of agricultural labour among the Scheduled Castes was 55.37, which was double the ratio of other households (25 percent). In fact, Scheduled Caste agricultural labour accounts for 35 percent of the agricultural labour in the country, although their share in total rural population was only 17 percent. Over time, the proportion of Scheduled Caste agricultural labour has also increased from 53.37 percent in 1981 to 55.12 percent in 1991.

The disparities in the incidence of agricultural labour between Scheduled Castes and other populations were fairly widespread across the states. The proportion of wage labour was more than double the ratio for other groups in several states. For instance, the proportion of agricultural labour among the Scheduled Castes was 77.48 percent in Andhra Pradesh, 75.64 percent in Bihar, 75 percent in Tamil Nadu, 63.18 percent in Haryana, 69.71 percent in Punjab, and 62 percent in Karnataka. The disparity indeed was quite large in the states of Punjab, Haryana, Andhra Pradesh, Tamil Nadu and Rajasthan. In the "Green Revolution States" of Punjab and Haryana the ratio of wage labour among the Scheduled Castes was more than five times the ratio for other households.

The information generated by successive NSS and Rural Labour Inquiries throw additional light on the incidence of wage labour households across social groups. Table 3B presents the percentage of wage labour households

Table 3B: Magnitude of Wage Labour among Scheduled Castes: Rural
(% of Rural Labor Households to Rural Labor Households)

	1974-75		1983-84		1987-88		1993-94		1981 *AL		1991 *AL	
State	SC	OT	SC	OT	SC	OT	SC	OT	SC	OT	SC	OT
Andhra Pradesh	72.87	32.56	79.29	39.2	75.90	42.34	66.6	37.0	72.68	33.72	77.40	39.17
Assam	37.08	21.57	25.97	31.98	29.29	31.55	38.16	38.16				
Bihar	78.73	27.06	75.65	29.69	77.35	32.69	76.82	30.20	76.51	31.06	75.64	33.39
Gujarat	74.67	20.73	57.05	30.18	73.33	38.82	59.19	31.52	58.95	23.26	57.88	24.64
Haryana	58.41	7.77	72.84	15.65	67.50	10.36	64.64	16.57	5.72	9.21	63.18	12.40
Himachal Pradesh	11.45	1.73	17.24	3.65	27.16	9.79	27.98	10.82	NA	2.05	5.65	2.72
Jammu and Kashmir	13.16	3.89	27.59	16.04	36.04	16.83	29.87	8.25	NA	NA	NA	NA
Karnataka	69.24	30.04	75.27	35.25	74.78	38.29	68.62	31.92	51.72	26.70	56.70	29.81
Kerala	84.59	36.86	81.48	44.75	78.08	42.74	73.04	38.8	60.95	26.82	57.80	25.25
Madhya Pradesh	39.20	16.72	48.94	25.74	52.35	26.23	57.7	29.90	43.03	20.55	43.57	20.72
Maharashtra	68.18	32.03	64.10	40.08	66.90	39.03	59.3	33.85	58.30	30.47	62.30	29.79
Orissa	60.77	16.51	54.58	31.03	60.17	31.25	53.61	30.28	50.28	20.27	49.45	21.20
Punjab	67.96	6.52	69.71	13.34	72.83	14.17	64.01	14.52	69.49	10.96	69.71	12.62
Rajasthan	18.99	2.78	42.28	9.79	53.23	22.55	46.18	14.39	19.25	4.96	24.33	7.43
Tamil Nadu	77.36	34.31	82.58	42.93	80.57	44.07	82.62	44.04	68.88	30.75	71.77	35.52
Uttar Pradesh	45.51	10.42	48.78	13.62	51.86	15.65	51.76	15.92	37.09	11.58	41.34	14.83
West Bengal	49.66	59.74	59.33	37.59	53.96	36.33	52.92	33.25	46.94	24.64	46.06	22.48

SC = Scheduled Caste; OT = non SC/ST; * = Population Census; AL = Agricultural Labour

Sources: 1. Rural Labour Enquiry Reports 1974–75, 1983, 1987–88, 1993–94, Simla. 2. Population of India, 1981 and 1991.

among the Scheduled Castes and other households in rural areas during 1974–75, 1983–84, 1987–88 and 1993–94.

In 1993–94, of the total Scheduled Caste rural households, 61 percent were wage labour households. This ratio was very high compared to 36.26 percent for other groups. Similar levels prevailed during 1987–88 and earlier years (i.e., 1974–75, 1983–84 and 1987–88). For example, the ratio of rural labour households for Scheduled Castes stood at 57.41 in 1974–75, 63.18 in 1977–78, 62.55 in 1983, and 63.10 percent in 1987–88. In all years, the level of wage labour households among the Schedule Castes was twice that of other groups.

At the state level, in 1993–94 the percentage of rural labour households was 82.76 percent in Tamil Nadu, 76 percent in Bihar, 73 percent in Kerala, 68 percent in Karnataka, 66.6 percent in Andhra Pradesh, and 64 percent each in Punjab and Haryana. These ratios were far higher than those of other groups. i.e., 44.04 percent in Tamil Nadu, 30.20 percent in Bihar, 38.8 percent in Kerala, 31.92 percent in Karnataka, 37 percent in Andhra Pradesh and around 15 percent in Punjab and Haryana.

A comparison of the percentage of wage labour households across states for the earlier years indicates that in 1974–75, 1983–84 and 1987–88 and 1993, with the exception of Assam, the incidence of wage labour among Scheduled Castes was higher than that of other households. In 1987–88 in most of the states, the level of wage labour households was twice the level of other households. The disparity across social groups was quite high in Haryana, Punjab, Uttar Pradesh and Himachal Pradesh. In fact, in Punjab and Haryana the level was higher by seven and five times respectively, while it is exceeded by about three times in Uttar Pradesh and Himachal Pradesh. In 1983–84, in all the states the difference between Scheduled Castes and other households in the level of wage labour was more than double. The disparities were much greater again in Haryana, Himachal Pradesh, Punjab, Rajasthan and Uttar Pradesh.

Another way to look at the disparities in the incidence of wage labour between the Scheduled Caste and other households is to see the gap in the respective shares of all rural households. In 1983–84 and 1987–88, respectively, the Scheduled Castes constituted 23 percent and 20.54 percent of the total rural households in the country but comprised 32.64 percent and 35 percent of the labour households in the country. Scheduled Caste share in labour households therefore excluded their representation among rural households by about 12 percent. In all the states the share of the Scheduled Caste labor households exceeds their share of rural households. The difference in the relative share, however, differs considerably across the states. The
relative share in labour households was indeed quite high in states like Haryana, Himachal Pradesh, Jammu and Kashmir, Punjab, and Tamil Nadu. In

fact in Haryana, Himachal Pradesh, Punjab, Tamil Nadu, and Uttar Pradesh the Scheduled Caste households account for 68.97 percent, 50 percent, 74.3 percent, 79.42 and 52 percent of total labour households respectively, although their share in the total rural households worked out to be 27.42, 17.36, 36.50, 25.30, 26 and 30.80 percent respectively. The segregation of the Scheduled Castes into manual labour was thus quite clear.It is important to recognize that not all wage labourers belong to landless households. A substantial portion of them own some land, but since their land holdings are very small, many of them have to resort to wage labour. In 1987–88 about 76 percent of the labour households owned some land. This ratio was very high in Assam (93.55 percent), Haryana (84 percent), Himachal Pradesh (84.20 percent), Jammu and Kashmir (87.37 percent), Karnataka (86 percent), Kerala (95 percent), Orissa (90.33 percent), Rajasthan (82.37 percent), and Uttar Pradesh (80 percent). In the case of other states the ratio was close to the national average. Thus, a substantial portion of land-owning households in the Scheduled Castes resorted to wage employment due to the small size of their land holdings. In fact in 1987–88, 75 percent of land-owning wage labour households owned less than 1.5 acres.

The year 1987–88 was a drought year and therefore the proportion of rural labour households with land holdings was relatively high in most of the states. The year 1983 presents a more normal situation. During that year about 38 percent of the labour households owned some land. In fact at the all-India level, 66.80 percent of lands owning households come from the less-than-one-acre category, and another 25.55 percent from the 1 to 2.50 acre ownership category. It is important to note that in a fairly large number of states, the proportion of rural labour households belong to the farm size category of less than one acre. In a few states like Jammu and Kashmir, Andhra Pradesh, Kerala, Madhya Pradesh, Rajasthan and Tamil Nadu the proportion of rural labour households was relatively high and it varied from 30 percent to 45 percent. In some states like Gujarat, Kerala, Madhya Pradesh, Maharashtra, Punjab, almost one-fifth of rural labour households owned 2.50 acres and above. A high incidence of rural labour households among the land owning households indicates both the small size of land they possessed and low land productivity despite IRDP and JEP land and irrigation improvement programs for Scheduled Caste marginal and small farmers.

Casual Wage Labour in Urban Areas

Turning to the urban areas, the proportion of casual labour among the Scheduled Caste households was again much higher than for other households (Table 3C). In 1993–94, the percentage of casual labour among the Scheduled Caste was 27 percent which was two and half times more than that of other households. The ratio was three times higher times in 8 states, four to five times in 2 states, one and half times higher in six states, and eight times in one state. About 62 percent of the total households in urban Kerala were casual labour, as against 26.6 percent for other households. The proportion of casual labour was comparatively higher among the Scheduled Caste households in Kerala (61.74 percent), Tamil Nadu (42.86 percent), Haryana (34:64 percent) and Karnataka (34.49 percent).

In the case of regular wage and salaried persons, the proportion of Scheduled Castes was less than that of other households; however, the differences were not as large as for casual labour. The reservation policy for government jobs seems to have helped the Scheduled Castes catch up with the other segments of the population. In about 12 states the share of Scheduled Caste regular wage and salaried households was less than that of others. In Andhra Pradesh, Gujarat, Himachal Pradesh, Punjab and West Bengal, however, their share was more than that of other households.

Disparities in Unemployment and Underemployment

Since more than 60 percent of Scheduled Caste workers in rural areas and more than 30 percent in urban areas depend mainly on wage employment, their earnings are obviously determined by level of employment and wage rates. It is possible that Scheduled Caste workers suffer discrimination in the employment market. Table 4 shows the unemployment rates of the Scheduled Caste vis-a-vis other workers for 1977–78, 1983, 1987–88 and 1993–94. Some important features about the unemployment situation of Scheduled Castes and other groups emerged quite clearly. In the case of "usual status" there are no significant differences in the unemployment rates of the Scheduled Caste and others, either in rural or urban areas. This is not surprising as a person is considered to be "usually employed" if he or she worked for more than 180 days in a year. Since Scheduled Caste workers have limited alternative sources of income other than wage employment their participation in such work on a yearly basis is likely to be higher than that of others. When we move to the unemployment rate based on current weekly status and current daily status the picture changes completely.

In the case of urban areas a nearly identical picture is observed (see Table 5). In all the four years, i.e., 1977–78, 1983 and 1987–88, and 1993–94 the unemployment rate based on usual status and current weekly status for males and females of Scheduled Caste households tends to be slightly higher than others. Thus the difference between the unemployment rate of Scheduled Caste households and other households based on current weekly status and on usual status is marginal. But as we move on to daily status the gap between Scheduled Castes and others is quite clear both for males and females. For example the unemployment rates based on daily status for Scheduled Caste males were 4.90 percent, 7.3 percent, and 7.20 percent in 1993–94, 1987–98 and 1983–84 respectively. For others the rates were 3.3 percent, 5.35 percent and 5.28 percent respectively during these years.

At the state level, to varying degrees across years, unemployment rates for Scheduled Caste males were higher than for other males. This was true in 11 of 17 states in 1993–94, 14 of 17 states in 1977–78, and 12 of 17 states in 1983–84. In the case of females the unemployment rates based on daily status were higher for all states in 1977–78, 1983–84 and in 12 states in 1993–94. It may be mentioned that even in the case of principal and subsidiary status in 9 of 17 states unemployment rates for Scheduled Caste males were higher than those of other households.

High Incidence of Poverty

With a higher incidence of wage labour associated with high unemployment/ Underemployment rates, the Scheduled Castes are more likely to suffer from low income and low consumption and hence from a higher incidence of poverty. Table 6A and 6B presents the poverty ratio for Scheduled Castes and others for 1987–88 and 1993–94 at the all-India level, combined and separately for self-employed and wage labour households both in rural and urban areas. The poor households among these two occupational groups have been the target of self-employment and wage-employment programs for quite some time. In 1993–94 about 48 percent of Scheduled Caste households were below the poverty line in rural areas, compared to 31.29 percent for the general population. The poverty level for Scheduled Castes was thus 17 percentage points higher than for others (Table 6A).

What is striking is the magnitude of poverty among the various household types. In 1993–94 the incidence of poverty was about 60 percent among agricultural labour, followed by 41.44 percent among non-agricultural labour. Even among households engaged in self-employed activities in agriculture and households in the (rural) non-agricultural sector 38 percent and 38.19 percent, respectively, were below the poverty line. In each of these household categories the proportion of Scheduled Caste households below the poverty line was much higher than that of their counterparts among the other groups.

In urban areas about 50 percent of the Scheduled Castes were below the poverty line in 1993-94, as compared to 29.66 percent among the others. (Table 6B) Further, the incidence was astonishingly high among the casual labourers (69.48 percent). Even among the self-employed the level of poverty was about 52 percent for Scheduled Caste households, compared to 34 percent for other groups. The incidence of poverty was also 35.28 percent among regular wage/salaried persons, which was much higher than that of other groups (19 percent). The disparities in the level of urban poverty between the

Table 3C: Magnitude of Casual Labour among Scheduled Castes - Urban (% to Total Urban Household)

	Casual Labour				Regular Wage Earner/Salaried			
	1987–88		1993–94		1987–88		1993–94	
	SC	OT	SC	OT	SC	OT	SC	OT
Andhra Pradesh	33.6	15.6	29.55	15.12	32.5	3.81	43.75	38.37
Assam	10.1	7.3	24.01	6.32	52.8	47.7	35.85	46.15
Bihar	29.8	10.2	23.82	9.63	39.5	39.5	33.82	36.30
Gujarat	32.6	11.9	15.64	10.25	51.3	45.2	48.14	38.73
Haryana	22.1	10.3	34.65	6.88	44.1	39.2	35.39	44.62
Himachal Pracesh	16.4	6.1	16.74	3.98	37.4	47.4	47.78	43.44
Jammu and Kashmir	25.0	4.5	13.04	1.51	35.5	41.7	42.75	53.34
Karnataka	26.9	16.4	34.49	12.66	24.8	38.2	40.00	44.76
Kerala	59.6	18.6	61.74	26.65	24.8	35.1	23.06	30.18
Madhya Pradesh	23.1	7.6	27.17	9.76	41.8	48.9	43.49	47.13
Maharashtra	24.7	9.1	23.18	6.80	50.2	55.1	48.96	52.62
Orissa	27.3	6.4	17.84	6.65	19.8	48.6	38.25	50.55
Punjab	27.4	5.9	22.43	7.23	32.7	39.8	42.77	41.26
Rajasthan	23.8	6.9	17.92	5.29	42.7	46.6	33.39	43.43
Tamilnadu	37.4	13.7	42.86	11.33	39.4	47.7	26.83	41.06
Uttar Pradesh	20.7	7.4	28.95	7.69	29.3	35.7	30.72	34.04
West Bengal	15.0	8.3	16.08	10.32	46.7	54.3	52.01	49.79

Note: SC = Scheduled Caste, OT= NON SC/ST

Source: National Sample Survey Employment and Unemployment, 1987–88 and 1993–94 Delhi.

Table 4: Unemployment Rate (Age 5 Years and Above) in Rural Areas

	Male				Female			
Category/ Year	Usual Principal Status	Usual Status	Current Weekly Status	Current Daily Status	Usual Principal Status	Usual Status	Current Weekly Status	Current Daily Status
Scheduled Caste								
1993–94	0.90	0.60	1.90	4.30	0.30	-	1.10	2.00
1987–88	1.30	0.90			1.40	1.10		
1983	1.10	0.76	3.22	7.16	0.40	0.23	2.16	2.23
1977–78	1.10	0.00	2.93	6.73	2.20	0.00	1.90	4.00
Others								
1993–94	1.20	0.90	1.60	2.70	0.44		0.80	1.11
1987–88	1.70	1.10	-	-	0.48	0.70	-	-
1983	1.30	1.90	2.15	4.03	0.43	0.29	0.91	1.72
1977–78	1.57	0.00	2.15	3.90	1.53	0.00	0.97	0.97

Source: National Sample Survey Employment and Unemployment, 1987–88 and 1993–94 Delhi.

Table 5: Unemployment Rate in Urban Areas

Category		Usual Status			Current Weekly Status			Current Daily Status		
		1977 –78	1983 –84	1993 –94	1977 –78	1983 –84	1993 –94	1977 –78	1983 –84	1993 –94
S.C.	Male	3.4	3.20	2.6	4.50	4.4	3.30	7.37	7.20	4.90
	Female	3.40	0.80	0.00	1.1	1.20	0.00	4.20	1.7	1.7
O.T.	Male	3.33	3.1	2.40	4.24	4.0	2.70	5.35	5.35	5.28
	Female	2.60	0.90	1.10	0.00	1.0	1.30	0.000	1.42	1.4

Note: SC = Scheduled Caste; OT = non SC/ST

Source: NSS Employment/Unemployment Reports 32nd, 38th and 43rd, and 50th Round.

two social groups were relatively high in the case of self-employed and regular wage earner/salaried workers but lower in the case of casual labour.

Table 7 presents the poverty ratios by state for Scheduled Castes and all groups, including Special Castes for the years 1983, 1987–88 and 1993–94. Significant inter-state and inter-social group disparities in the level of rural and urban poverty are evident. The poverty ratio in rural areas for the Scheduled Castes varied between 18 percent in Himachal Pradesh to 70.56 percent in Bihar. The incidence was particularly high in Bihar (70.56 percent), Uttar Pradesh (59 percent) and low in Punjab and Andhra Pradesh.

In urban areas the poverty ratio varied between 14.34 in Assam to 62 percent in Tamil Nadu, the level being higher than the national average in Uttar Pradesh (50 percent), Karnataka (61 percent) and Bihar. The ratio was relatively low in Himachal Pradesh, Haryana, Kerala and Punjab. It is important to recognise that in all the states the incidence of poverty was higher for Scheduled Castes as compared to others both in rural and urban areas.

This comparative account of the economic position of Scheduled Castes and others does provide convincing evidence of the continuing economic inequalities associated with caste. The proportion of self-employed persons among the Scheduled Castes is extremely low and as a result the level of manual wage labour is astonishingly high. The high incidence of wage labour among the Scheduled Castes, however, is not matched by a favourable employment rate or wages. The unemployment rate for Scheduled Castes is more than double that of other groups. Given the higher level of wage labour and higher unemployment rates, the poverty level is high as compared to the rest of India's population. This is particularly the case of wage labour that constitutes bulk of the workers among the Scheduled Castes. It is thus beyond doubt that the historical impact of traditional caste based restrictions on the ownership of property, employment and occupation are still visible to significant extent.

Table 6A: Percentage of Persons below Poverty Line by Household Type for Each Social Group

	Rural											
Category	Self-employed in agriculture		Self-employment in non-agriculture		Agriculture labour		Non-agriculture labour		Others		All	
Year	1987-88	1993-94	1987-88	1993-94	1987-88	1993-94	1987-88	1993-94	1987-88	1993-94	1987-88	1993-94
Scheduled Caste	41.21	37.70	41.6	38.19	59.77	60.00	46.49	41.44	29.98	29.00	50.07	48.14
Others	25.57	25.57	31.42	29.49	53.30	52.34	34.45	35.59	19.26	20.19	34.37	31.29

Table 6B: Percentage of Persons below Poverty Line by Household Type for Each Social Group

Categories	Self-employed		Regular Service/ Wage Earner		Casual Labour		Other		All	
Year	1987-88	1993-94	1987-88	1993-94	1987–88	1993–94	1987–88	1993–94	1987–88	1993–94
Scheduled Caste	61.48	54.60	43.69	35.28	73.45	69.48	56.84	45.00	56.84	49.90
Others	33.60	33.64	25.26	19.04	70.1	60.60	32.21	26.06	37.21	29.66

Source: Based on Consumption Expenditure Survey, NSSO, 1987–88 and 1993–94.

Table 7: Percentage of Poor: Head Count Ratio

	Rural						Urban					
	1983		1987–88		1993–94		1983		1987–88		1993–94	
State	SC	All	SC	All	SC	All	SC	All	SC	All	SC	All
Andhra Pradesh	37.41	26.50	51.36	40.13	29.58	29.92	54.70	44.63	26.00	15.92	43.82	41.51
Assam	43.05	42.60	48.74	26.38	36.76	39.35	30.09	17.39	45.39	45.01	14.34	13.15
Bihar	80.89	64.30	52.82	50.42	65.90	52.63	69.14	57.71	70.66	58.21	55.16	45.34
Gujarat	39.21	29.80	47.61	40.63	39.63	28.67	52.43	39.63	32.26	22.18	44.99	27.07
Haryana	36.44	20.56	44.45	23.48	27.88	16.22	33.88	17.79	46.56	28.03	23.58	13.09
Himachal Pracesh.	27.35	17.00	14.11	9.23	20.13	16.28	15.40	6.18	38.39	30.34	18.52	8.58
Jammu and Kash-mir	41045	26.04	0.00	17.14	37.70	25.70	36.60	14.82	NA	NA	NA	NA
Karnataka	52.68	36.33	54.38	43.37	52.30	32.87	64.93	49.06	46.36	29.88	61.59	40.21
Kerala	62.24	39.03	62.06	48.65	38.28	29.10	62.00	43.63	36.43s	25.76	31.59	29.57
Madhya Pradesh	58.42	48.90	70.24	54.69	51.72	41.52	68.85	48.17	45.83	40.64	65.00	49.70
Maharashtra	59.32	45.23	64.96	40.57	53.80	40.78	69.00	38.99	51.64	37.93	52.56	34.03
Orissa	75.84	67.58	65.95	50.61	67.60	57.64	62.68	44.11	48.95	49.72	47.45	40.59
Punjab	25.30	13.20	36.59	23.86	27.93	12.60	26.60	12.91	22.08	14.95	27.96	9.08
Rajasthan	40.47	33.50	51.79	40.37	37.87	33.22	55.36	38.99	38.38	26.26	48.63	31.63
Tamilnadu	67.46	53.99	72.28	49.22	64.05	45.80	63.37	43.88	44.05	32.48	61.00	44.34
Uttar Pradesh	57.20	46.45	56.63	50.27	56.49	41.10	57.28	45.22	58.99	42.28	58.02	36.06
West Bengal	72.53	63.05	47.77	32.21	53.59	48.30	45.60	32.84	45.29	40.28	37.73	22.51
All India	57.77	45.61	56.41	42.15	50.58	39.06	36.48	40.12	48.11	37.27	49.48	33.66

Source: NSS Consumption Expenditure Surveys, 1983, 1987–88 and 1993–94.

Economic Discrimination and Private Sector

To what extent these economic inequalities between Scheduled Castes and others are historical, and to what extent they are due to continuing economic discrimination in the market and outside the market are the big questions. While we do know in some measure about the first question, little is known about the second, i.e., market discrimination.

Economists in India have given less attention to the analysis of economic discrimination relating to caste and untouchability than to the question of economic discrimination arising out of race, ethnicity and other social institutions. Consequently, although we recognise inequality associated with caste we know much less about the forms, mechanisms and magnitudes of caste-based discrimination in factor and product markets.

The issue of market and pre-market discrimination acquired urgency in the context of the mega move towards privatising and channeling of jobs, capital, inputs and social services through the market. At present the Scheduled Castes are protected against economic discrimination, particularly in the job market, by the reservation policy in government and public sector jobs and services and preferential treatment in various state run programs (described in the preceding section). But with the declining role of the government and the public sector, the Scheduled Castes now increasingly depend on the market, which suffers from various kinds of imperfections including caste-based market discrimination. This has policy implications for the private organized and unorganised sectors.

Very few studies have tried to understand the phenomenon of caste-based market discrimination. The macro and some micro level evidence, however, indicate the presence of discrimination against the Scheduled Castes in rural and urban markets. The macro level evidence presented in the preceding section reveals a very high incidence of landlessness and near landlessness among the Scheduled Castes. The lack of access to agricultural land could be due to the weak resource position of Scheduled Castes. But a few studies also point toward discriminatory processes in the land markets where Scheduled Caste is limited (Nanchariah 1988; Mandavdhare 1996, Thorat and Deshpande 1998). Similarly, the National Sample Survey data shows that the unemployment rate (based on current, weekly and daily status) is much higher for the Scheduled Castes. The Rural Labour Enquiries also show that the wage rate received by Scheduled Caste rural labour in rural farm and non-farm activities tends to be lower, particularly in rural non-farm activities.

To what extent the differences in unemployment rate and wage rate of manual and semi manual labour are due to differences in productivity, and to what extent they are due to job and wage discrimination is an issue which needs detailed examination.

Some micro-level studies reveal the presence of discrimination in markets against the Untouchable. Banerjee and Knight (1995), and Deshi and Singh (1995) have brought out the significant presence of caste and untouchability-based economic discrimination. In the study of the urban labour market in Delhi during 1975–76 they observed that: "Use of the standard methodology showed that there is indeed discrimination by caste, particularly job discrimination through the estimation of occupational higher attainment function and it is quantitatively more important." They further observed that the "discrimination appears to operate at least in part through traditional mechanism, with untouchables disproportionately represented in poorly-paid dead-end jobs. The discriminators are likely to be other workers and employers." Even if discrimination is no longer practiced, the effects of past discrimination could carry over to the present—for instance in the choice of occupation. This may help explain why discrimination is greatest in operative jobs, in which contacts are more important for recruitment, and not in white-collar jobs in which recruitment involves formal methods. The economic system's advantage to favoured castes suggests that taste for discrimination is based, consciously, or unconsciously, on economic interest, thus making prejudice more difficult to eradicate."

The study by Dhesi and Singh (1995) conducted in Delhi in 1971 also observed "differences in jobs associated with education and labour market distortion arising out of caste and religious background of persons." Among the micro-level studies, the studies on Andhra Pradesh (Venketeswarlu 1990) and Karnataka (Khan 1995) also provided evidence of economic discrimination in occupation, employment, wages and loans and in other economic spheres. The Andhra Pradesh study indicated that "when untouchables want to switch over from their traditional occupation in the rural areas to some other occupation, they were abused or beaten." The Karnataka study revealed that nearly 85 percent of the respondents continued with their traditional occupation and only 15 percent could make a switch. In the urban areas, however, 56 percent had expressed a shift in the traditional occupation. The Orissa study of 1987–88 (Tripathy 1994) observed discrimination in land lease, credit and labour markets in rural areas. Nearly 96 percent of untouchable respondents in one village, and all untouchable respondents in the second village were discriminated against in wage payment; 28 percent in one village and 20 percent in the other faced discrimination in the share of rent. Discrimination in interest rates charged by the moneylender was found in both villages.

Conclusion

It has been observed that a very large section of the Scheduled Caste population is engaged in rural and urban informal or unorganised sectors.

About three-fourths of them live in rural areas. Among the total rural households an astonishingly high proportion of them—i.e., nearly 63 percent—earned their living as wage labour and the remainder are engaged in self-employed economic activities of various kinds. The remedial measures developed for wage labour households are mainly supplementary employment programs to maintain minimum income levels, particularly of those below the poverty line. Despite the wage employment programs targeted at poor and vulnerable sections, for the last four decades they have not been able to provide a minimum living to a large number of the Scheduled Caste population. Nearly 60 percent of agricultural labour households and a little more than 40 percent of wage labour in the rural non-farm sector are below the poverty line and have failed to achieve a minimum level of income and consumption. Thus, the remedial programs have not helped the vast majority of Scheduled Caste wage labour households in rural and urban areas secure a minimum income and living standard.

In the case of self-employed persons, the remedial measures have likewise helped only to a limited degree. At all-India level, 70 percent of the Scheduled Caste households were landless and near landless (i.e., owning less than one acre of land). The distribution of surplus land through land reform measures has failed to improve the access to land in substantial measures. Therefore, although 87 percent own some land, only 19 percent could achieve the status of self-employed cultivator. The land and irrigation improvement measures under IRDP and JEP and other programs could not make more than 19 percent viable producers. Even among self-employed households, about 38 percent of those in agriculture were below the poverty line, and another 38 percent in rural non-farm activities were also below the poverty line. It is quite clear that the Scheduled Castes are engaged in petty and low productivity self-employed activities. The IRDP and wage employment programs have helped some to improve income levels but they are inadequate in magnitude and coverage. The vast majority of Scheduled Castes—particularly wage labourers who constitute more than 60 percent of Scheduled Castes workers—lack adequate income.

In urban areas the situation is equally alarming. The remedial programs of a promotional nature, such as credit and training support for self-employment, and wage employment for wage labour, started much later than in rural areas and the marginal impact of these measures is quite clear. The level of poverty among casual labour is nearly 70 percent, followed by 55 percent among the self-employed and 35.25 percent among regular wage earner/salaried persons. This high level of deprivation and poverty exposes the inadequacy of these programs in urban areas.

There is a need to improve the efficiency and coverage of self-employment and wage-employment programs. Moreover, in the case of

Scheduled Castes the issue of economic discrimination in factor and product markets—particularly in employment, wage and capital markets—also needs to be addressed. The protections against economic discrimination against the Scheduled Castes in government and public sector establishments are nearly absent in the private organised and unorganised sectors. In view of the growing privatisation and increased dependence on the markets for jobs, capital and social services, it will be necessary to extend job reservation protection in the agriculture and the urban industrial sectors.

References

Akerolof, George. 1976. The economics of caste and of rat race and other woeful tales. *Quarterly Journal of Economics* 90(4) (November):599–617.

Banerjee, Biswajit and J. B. Knight. 1995. Caste discrimination in Indian urban labour market, pp. 158–88. In *Economics and discrimination, Volume 2,* edited by William A. Darity, Jr. Elgar Reference Collection (USA).

Birdsall Nancy and Richard Sabot, (Eds.). 1991. *Unfair advantage in developing countries.* The World Bank.

Darity, Jr., William A., (Ed.). 1995. *Economics and discrimination, Volume I.* Elgar Reference Collection (USA).

Das, Meenakshi. 1996. *Employment, wages and earnings of rural labour: A comparative study of Scheduled Caste, Scheduled Tribes and others.* M Phil Dissertation, Centre for the Study of Regional Development, Jawaharlal Nehru University, New Delhi.

Deshi A. K. and H. Singh. 1995. Education, labour market distortions and relative earning of different religious caste categories in India. *Canadian Journal of Development of Studies* (December 21).

Dreze, Jean and A. K. Sen. 1991. Public action for Social Security foundation and strategy. In *Social Security in developing countries,* edited by Ahmed et. al. Oxford: Clarendon Press.

Hauff, Von Michael. 1995. *Social Security in India some interpersonal and inter-regional features.* Institute of Economic Policy, University of Kaiserslautern (Germany).

Khan, Mumtaz Ali. 1995. *Human Rights and the Dalits.* Delhi: Uppal Publishers.

Lal, Deepak. 1988. *Hindu equilibrium, Volume I: Cultural stability and economic stagnation.* Oxford: Clarendon Press.

Nancharaiah, G. 1988. *Land and caste.* Himalaya, Delhi.

National Commission for Scheduled Castes and Scheduled Tribes. 1998. *Fourth report, 1996–7 and 1997–98,* Vols. I and II. Delhi.

Parvathamma. C. 1984. *Scheduled Castes and tribes: A Socio-economic survey.* New Delhi: Ashish.

Renteln, Alison Dunds. 1988. Relativism and the search for Human Rights. *American Anthropology* 90(1): 50–56.

Sasikumar, S. K. and R. K. A. Subrahmanya. 1996. Social Security for the unorganised sector in India. *The Indian Journal of Labour Economics* 39(4).

Shah, Ghanshyam. 1998. Caste and untouchability: Theory and practice. Paper presented at the Seminar on *Ambedkar in retrospect,* Jawaharlal Nehru University, Delhi.

Thorat, S. K. 1996. Ambedkar on economics of Hindu social order: Understanding its orthodoxy and legacy. In *The emerging Dalit identity,* edited by Walter Fernandes. New Delhi: Indian Social Institute.

———. 1999. Poverty, caste and child labour: Plight of Dalits and Adivasi children in India. In *Child labour in India, Vol. I,* edited by Klus. Delhi.

——— and Ram Deshpande. 1998. Caste system and economic inequality: Economic theory and evidence. In G. Saha (Ed.), *Dalit identity and politics.* Delhi: Sage.

Tripathy, R. B. 1994. *Dalits: A sub-human society.* Delhi: Ashish Publishing.

Venkateswarlu, D. 1990. *Harijan-upper class conflict.* Delhi: Discovery Publishers.

• CHAPTER TWELVE •

Racial and Ethnic Inequality—Is Political Moblilization the Remedy? The Case of Dalits and Tribals in Kerala, India

BRUCE P. CORRIE
Associate Dean
Undergraduate Studies, College of Business and Organizational Leadership
Professor of Economics
Concordia University—St. Paul
Editor, www.policybriefs.org

There is extensive literature on the important role of conscientization in strategies for human liberation. The failure of trickle-down economics to benefit the poorest of the poor in a significant way has been linked to fatalistic and passive attitudes of the poor—the so-called "culture of poverty." If conscientization is an important element of strategies for human liberation it would be helpful to have some quantitative evidence of both the level of conscientization as well as the link between conscientization and improvements in the living standards of the oppressed. Fortunately in the case of Kerala in India there is quantitative evidence on both the level of conscientization as well as possible links between conscientization and improvements in the living standards of some traditionally oppressed groups—Dalits (untouchables, Scheduled Castes, harijans) and Tribals (adivasis, scheduled tribes).

There is a very rich literature on the "Kerala Model of Development"—namely how a state in India with one of the lowest levels of economic development has high levels of social development (high literacy rates and low infant mortality rates). Among the reasons offered for this paradox has been the role of political mobilization by caste, class and religious group. This political mobilization has, in turn, resulted in the Keralite being highly conscious of rights and public resources.

First, some evidence of the level of conscientization of Dalits and Tribals in Kerala: the majority of Dalits work as agricultural laborers. Alexander (1989) illustrates how agricultural laborers in Kerala have much more progressive attitudes than their counterparts in the nearby states of Karnataka, and Tamil Nadu. Agricultural workers in Kerala scored the highest on the Ideological Orientation Scale constructed by him to measure traditional and egalitarian attitudes. Mahadevan and Sumangla (1987) constructed an index of modernization for married couples in Kerala and Andhra Pradesh and found the level of modernization to be higher in Kerala.

Next is the evidence of the link between the level of conscientization and political mobilization. Alexander (1989) illustrates in his comparative study of attitudes of agricultural laborers in the three states mentioned above, the strong positive association between the respondents' ideological orientation and their participation in political parties and class organization. This was especially true for agricultural laborers in Kerala.

The evidence of the link between the level of conscientization and positive improvements in the lives of the oppressed is given directly by Alexander (1989) and Mahadevan and Sumangla (1987), and indirectly by Panikkar and Soman (1984). Alexander (1989) provides evidence to show how agricultural laborers in Kerala gained greater benefits from land reform movements than their counterparts in the nearby state of Tamil Nadu. Mahadevan and Sumangala (1987) provide evidence about the positive links between progressive attitudes of Keralites and the low levels of fertility observed in Kerala. Panikkar and Soman (1984) in attempting to explain the paradox observed in Kerala—namely lower nutritional intake levels of Keralites as compared to people in other states in India but a relatively better nutritional status than the people in other states—posit this thesis: People in Kerala, being aware of their rights and claims against the state, make prompt use of health facilities thereby reducing the duration and intensity of illness and resulting in positive impacts on their nutritional status.

Specifically in the case of Dalits and Tribals in Kerala, Corrie (1994; 1995) illustrates how the status of the Dalit child in Kerala is much better than that of their counterparts in the rest of the country. An important question is whether Dalit living standards have improved in the course of Indian development. Fortunately the Kerala Statistical Institute has some micro surveys documenting their status during the period 1986–87 to 1990–91. The significance of this longitudinal data becomes all the more relevant because of the many unique factors in the lives of Dalits and Tribals in Kerala, one of which is the role of political mobilization around caste and class.

Micro level data based on village surveys over the period 1986–87 to 1990–91 provide an insight into the social dynamics of Kerala. For instance, in terms of rural households with good housing facilities (tile or concrete roof houses, electricity, and modern sanitation facilities), Dalits and Tribals had the highest gains relative to the upper caste groups. Dalits and Tribals had a 58 percent increase in households with tiled roofs compared to an 11 percent increase for the upper castes. Similarly they had a 48 percent increase in households with electricity compared to an 11 percent increase for the upper castes. There was a 98 percent increase in Dalit and Tribal households with adequate sanitation facilities compared to a 46 percent increase for the upper castes.

The average household size fell for all groups but declined the most for Dalits and Tribals. The age of marriage, another indicator of social development, also reflected an upward trend, with fewer Dalit and Tribal females getting married in their late teens. Finally, in terms of educational levels Dalits and Tribals show significant gains in narrowing the gap between them and the upper castes. The ratio of Dalit and Tribal literacy rates to that of the higher castes showed a significant narrowing of the educational gap. For Dalit and Tribal males the ratio was 0.65 for the age group 35+, 0.85 for the age group 20–24 and 0.97 for the age group 10–19 years. The corresponding ratios for females were 0.42, 0.72 and 0.92, respectively.

The above analysis leads us to the next question—can the Kerala model be replicated in other part of India and the world? The answer is both yes and no! Certain factors unique to Kerala such as ecological conditions, historical emphasis on education and caste and class dynamics make this model difficult to replicate. However some broad insights of the Kerala model can help other parts in India achieve their goals for human liberation.

Alexander (1989) points to some important preconditions for success in both conscientization and political mobilization: first, a critical mass of people having the same identity is important for successful political mobilization; second, there has to be a transformation in the consciousness of the people such that they develop new values which in turn motivates them to change the unjust conditions of their existence; third, the presence of alternative economic opportunities is important, as it will help reduce opposition to reform movements; finally, there is the need for sustained activities by agents of change in order for societal transformation to occur.

Last, we turn to the central question of this paper—is political mobilization the remedy to racial and ethnic inequalities? Political mobilization is a remedy that has to be complemented with other strategies aimed at improving economic opportunities for all people in the area. Kerala illustrates this situation very vividly. Economic development has not kept pace with progressive politics and as a result there is lot of frustration and unemployment present.

This contradiction exposes the limitations of the Kerala model of development. Further, we need true social transformation—a rejection of the old patterns of oppression. In Kerala, caste still remains a potent barrier for societal transformation. An effective remedy for racial and ethnic inequality calls for conscientization, economic development, and ultimately, human liberation.

References

Alexander, K. C. 1989. Caste mobilization and class consciousness. In *Dominance and state power in India,* edited by Francine Frankel and M. S. A. Rao. New York: Oxford University Press.

Corrie, Bruce. 1994. The Kerala Model of Development from the perspective of the Dalit child in India. Paper presented at the International Conference of Kerala Studies, Thiruvanthapuram, August 27–29, 1994.

———. 1994. The case for integrated child focused development strategies. *Community Development Journal* 29(3): 251–256.

———. 1995. A human development index for the Dalit child in India. *Social Indicators Research* 34: 395–409.

Kerala Statistical Institute. 1992. *Socio-economic changes in Kerala.* Thiruvanthapuram: KSI.

Mahadevan K., and M. Sumangla. 1987. *Social development, cultural change and fertility decline.* New Delhi: Sage Publications.

Panikkar, P. G. K., and C. R. Soman. 1984. *Health status of Kerala.* Thiruvanthapuram: Center For Development Studies.

• CHAPTER THIRTEEN •

Remedying Racial and Ethnic Inequality in New Zealand: Reparative and Distributive Policies of Social Justice

MARILYN E. LASHLEY
Associate Professor
Department of Political Science
Howard University

The social, economic and political position of New Zealand Maori—the *tangata whenua* (literally, the people of the land)—is similar to that of Native Americans and African Americans in the United States in several respects. Foremost, Maori are indigenous Polynesians whom western legend says traveled to New Zealand by canoe using celestial navigation around 900 AD. Since signing the Treaty of Waitangi with the British in 1840, Maori people have experienced on-going dispossession and marginalization. Similar to Native Americans, Maori people were dispossessed of their lands, fisheries and forests and reduced to near extinction by colonization and abrogated treaty rights. European officials and citizens progressively refused to honor and enforce the Treaty's guarantees for Maori people by confiscating Maori lands under government sanction. Similar to Native American and White settler relations, Maori-*Pakeha* (European) relations are marred by land wars and subordination that combined to jeopardized the very viability and survival of Maori people well into the 1930s.[1]

Today, like African Americans, Maori people are approximately fourteen percent of the population; have the highest and most disproportionate rates of unemployment, poverty, crime and incarceration; and are identified as the "problem" minority. Maori people experience greater social and economic inequality than all other population subgroups in New Zealand and hold the lowest social and economic position.

The Treaty of Waitangi, Founding Document of the New Zealand State

New Zealand was established as a British Commonwealth nation by treaty cession achieved by means of the unilateral actions and declarations of William Hobson, Lieutenant-Governor of the British Settlements. The treaty was written in English and Maori. On February 6, 1840, forty-six Maori chiefs signed a Maori language translation of The Treaty at Waitangi, which subsequently was taken around New Zealand and signed by approximately 500 additional Maori representatives. The core provisions of the Treaty are embodied in three articles:

> Article I
>
> The Chiefs of the Confederation of the United Tribes of New Zealand, and the separate and independent Chiefs who have not become members of the Confederation, cede to Her Majesty the Queen of England, absolutely and without reservation, all rights and powers of sovereignty which the said Confederation or individual Chiefs respectively exercise or possess, or may be supposed to exercise or possess, over their respective Territories as the sole sovereigns thereof (English text).
>
> The Chiefs of the Confederation and all the Chiefs who have not joined that Confederation give absolutely to the Queen of England forever the complete government over their land (English translation of Maori text, Kawharu 1989).
>
> Article II
>
> Her Majesty the Queen of England confirms and guarantees to the Chiefs and Tribes of New Zealand and to the respective families and individuals thereof the full and exclusive and undisturbed possession of their Lands and Estates, Forests Fisheries and other properties which they may collectively or individually possess so long as it is their wish and desire to retain the same in their possession; but the Chiefs of the United Tribes and the individual Chiefs yield to Her Majesty the exclusive right of Preemption over such lands as the proprietors thereof may be disposed to alienate at such prices as may be agreed upon between the respective Proprietors and persons appointed by Her Majesty to treat with them in that behalf (English text).
>
> The Queen of England agrees to protect the chiefs, the subtribes and all the people of New Zealand in the unqualified exercise of their chieftainship over all their lands over their villages and over all their treasures. But on the other hand the Chiefs of the Confederation and all the Chiefs will sell land to the Queen at a price agreed to

> by the person owning it and by the person buying it (the later being) appointed by the Queen as her purchase agent (English translation of Maori text).

> Article III

> In consideration thereof Her Majesty the Queen of England extends to the Natives of New Zealand Her royal protection and imparts to them all the Rights and Privileges of British Subjects (English text and English translation of Maori text).

As the founding document of the New Zealand State, Maori claims for redress and social justice necessarily are grounded in the Treaty of Waitangi. Maori people understood the Treaty of Waitangi as a power sharing and governance contract between two parties, Maori people and the Crown, whereby Maori people were equal parties with the British in the cultural, social, economic and political life of New Zealand (Interviews: Kingi and Henare). However, the English and Maori texts of the Treaty differ profoundly. According to the English text, indigenous Maori ceded all the rights and powers of sovereignty over their respective territories to Queen Victoria. Maori people retained full exclusive and undisturbed possession of their lands and estates, forests, fisheries and other properties (Article II) in return for royal protection and all the rights and privileges of British subjects (Articles III). According to the Maori text, Maori ceded *kawanatanga* (governance *not* sovereignty and retained *rangatiratanga* (chieftainship). For Maori, this distinction is paramount. The fundamental difference between the two texts, from the Maori perspective, is that confirmation of chieftainship also confirms sovereignty, in return for a *limited* concession of power.

Context of Contemporary Race Relations in New Zealand

The dominant ethos, "the dream of one people," that led many to describe New Zealand as free of discrimination and different from other industrialized nations, was never realized. Maori historically have held a subordinate and marginal position to Europeans that policy makers neglected to address. In the watershed 1961 Report by the Department of Maori Affairs on August 24, 1960, then Acting Secretary for Maori Affairs, J.K. Hunn, identified significant disparities between Maori and Europeans in income, housing and education. Despite many New Zealanders' characterization of the post-war period as one of racial assimilation and tranquillity, the Hunn Report found that racial problems festered during this period and culminated in the exclusion of the Maori from meaningful economic participation. More important, the Report showed that Maori land holdings actually diminished under the 1953 Maori Affairs Act and the 1953 Town and Country Planning Act.[2] In 1960 there were 3,168 leases involving 466,194 acres. By 1965 there were 3,481 leases involving 618,580 acres, and sales escalated from 5,245 to 51,824 acres for this period (Schwimmer 1968, 24). By 1990 government sanctioned land alienation, including confiscation and compulsory sale, had reduced Maori land holdings to only 5 percent of 60 million acres.

In response to mounting land loss and the highly contested 1967 Maori Affairs Bill that merely modified the language of compulsory sale of Maori lands but not the means and ends, a Maori protest movement developed.[3] In 1968, young, urban-based and largely university educated Maori formed the pantribal organization, *Nga Tamatoa* (the Young Warriors) to draw attention to the Treaty of Waitangi and demand both restoration of tribal lands and redress of grievances common to all tribes (Interviews: Kingi and Te Hemara). *Nga Tamatoa* took a militant stance in advocating for the use of Maori language as an official language, return of illegally confiscated lands, restoration of abrogated treaty rights and recognition of Maori culture and people as one of the two signatory parties to the Treaty of Waitangi. *Nga Tamatoa* redefined Maori identity and constructed a framework of "ethnic nationalism" by drawing upon the U.S. Civil Rights, American Indian and women's movements and from the "black identity and black consciousness" writings of Franz Fannon, Charles Hamilton and Stokeley Carmichael. This new identity proclaimed the unique political capacity of Maori culture as the basis for self-determination. Ethnicity emerged as the key weapon to counter the prevailing ideologies and resolve grievances over the loss of language, land and power (Greenland 1991, 91).

By the 1970s the older generation of Maori leaders also became more active in advocating return of Maori land and Maori rights as indigenous people and treaty party. Most prominently, Dame Whina Cooper (1895–1994), one of Maoridom's most distinguished and respected elders and former President of the Maori Women's Welfare League, at eighty years old led the historic 1975 Maori Land March from Auckland to Wellington. Both the Land March and the 1977 Bastion Point Protest and subsequent occupation were pan tribal protests organized by *Nga Tamatoa* in conjunction with established Maori organizations representing a wide spectrum of opinions on Maori issues. The resurgence of Maori culture and demands for equality, equity and social justice also led some Maori leaders to espouse separatism and absolute Maori sovereignty.[4] Although most New Zealanders dismiss Maori demands for sovereignty, restoration of *te tino rangatiratanga*, as absurdly radical or merely rhetoric (McHugh 1991, 49), some Maori remain quite serious in the demand for Maori self-government. Several Maori activists maintain there is a legal basis for Maori self-government and some still work toward this end (Interviews: S. Jackson and M. Jackson). However, consensus on an operative definition of sovereignty has not been reached and Maori demands range from

Maori self-government, to separate Maori development, to a separate system of justice for Maori (parallel legal system).

Government's Response: Reparative and Distributive Policies of Social Justice

In all nations both the role of the State and policy mechanisms for providing social justice remain highly contested, if not contentious, questions among policy makers, voting majorities and marginalized groups. Generally policy makers pursue social justice as reparative or distributive policies that seek to ameliorate the grievances of harmed groups yet insure minimal economic, political and social costs to voting majorities. Reparative justice (also called restorative justice) seeks to restore harmed parties to the position they would have held in the absence of the wrongful act(s), whereby the notion of unjust enrichment governs the nature and amount of reparations or compensatory damages (Miller 1991). Reparative justice is most often (and most narrowly) applied to breached rights to property caused by dispossession. On the other hand, distributive justice seeks to allocate public honors, wealth or other rewards and penalties of society either on the basis of merit and dessert or need and equality. Distributive justice presumes the equality of opportunity and that each person's social position and material rewards correspond as far as possible to merit (talents and efforts). Distributive justice is applied to problems of economic need or equality of opportunity and often employs instruments of positive discrimination as targeted policies to improve the relative economic and social position of a specific group or groups within a society. Targeted policies provide material uplift and increased opportunity to offset the harm of previous discrimination and, thereby, move society toward equality.

Responding to heighten Maori activism, New Zealand policymakers sought to provide social justice by enacting both reparative and distributive policies targeted to Maori people and by placing the Treaty of Waitangi at the center of New Zealand governance and policymaking. Policymakers primarily pursued two strategies of social justice: restorative (reparative) strategies of biculturalism and treaty settlement, and distributive strategies of positive discrimination as affirmative action and targeted social policy. Over the last two decades, government's pursuit of distributive strategies has waxed and waned while its pursuit of tribally grounded restorative strategies continues to course through the judicial apparatus. The settlement of claims of breached rights under the Treaty of Waitangi remain a salient policy priority for both Labour Party and National Party governments and, thus far, have been the most sustained group mechanism for providing social justice to Maori people.

Social Justice as Treaty Settlement

Foremost, policy makers provided social justice to Maori people by placing the Treaty of Waitangi at the center of New Zealand governance and policymaking. Invoking the rule of *contra preferentum*, which holds that where a divergence or ambiguity in a treaty document between two parties results, a provision should be construed against that party which drafted the document, in 1975 Parliament enacted the Treaty of Waitangi Act (Kingi 1984).[5] The 1975 Treaty of Waitangi Act reasserted the importance of the Treaty of Waitangi as the founding document of New Zealand and created a standing Tribunal to hear claims of breached treaty rights and investigate all new legislation from 1976 onward for possible treaty breaches. The Treaty of Waitangi Tribunal was charged with investigating treaty breaches by determining the meaning and effect of the Treaty of Waitangi as embodied in the two texts [English and Maori], and deciding issues raised by the differences between them (Treaty of Waitangi Act 1975 s. 5(2)). The 1975 Act also established the Waitangi Tribunal as a Division under the Department of Justice, comprised by a chairperson (chief judge of the Maori Land Court) and up to sixteen appointed members and staffed by civil servants.

In 1985, the Labour Government of Prime Minister David Lange (1984–1989) amended the 1975 Treaty of Waitangi Act and greatly enlarged its scope. The 1985 Treaty of Waitangi Amendment Act increased the Waitangi Tribunal from three to seven members, with four seats reserved for Maori, and made its jurisdiction retroactive to February 6, 1840, the date of treaty cession. In 1988, Tribunal membership was further increased to seventeen, including chief judge of the Maori Land Court, and the majority Maori membership requirement was removed. The Tribunal's main function has evolved to making inquires into claims submitted by Maori and making recommendations upon its findings to the Crown. The Tribunal makes findings that are not legally binding (with four exclusions) and may make proposals for long term restoration of land, but cannot recommend the return of land (Durie 1996). In short, the Treaty of Waitangi Tribunal functions as a commission of inquiry; it is not a court and is not bound by rules of evidence.

Claims of breached treaty rights were filed almost before the ink was dry on the Treaty of Waitangi. Although treaty-based appeals were made to the Crown by Maori Chiefs as early as 1847, the landmark settlements are due to the Treaty of Waitangi Act of 1975 and Treaty of Waitangi Amendment Act of 1985. The Treaty of Waitangi is a legal obligation between individual *iwi* and *hapu* (tribes and subtribes) and the Crown. Claims are filed under Article II for wrongful alienation of tribally-owned private assets. In general, claimants seek public acknowledgment by the Crown for wrongdoing, restoration of sovereignty over sacred sites, and redress (compensation or restoration) for the illegal confiscation of private assets. Treaty settlement is a restorative process that seeks to provide fair compensation for lands, fisheries, forests and other tribally-owned tangible assets unjustly confiscated by the Crown. Any or all Maori can bring a claim against the Treaty of Waitangi but they must demonstrate prior ownership of tangible assets (Interview: Graham).

Types of Claims

Claims of breached rights under the Treaty of Waitangi are filed either on behalf of a specific tribe or group of tribes as *iwi*-based claims or on behalf of all Maori people as pantribal claims. In the main, land was alienated under state sanction by means of purchase, gifting and confiscation. Consequently, it is possible to file four general types of claims of breached treaty rights; as old, gifted, crown purchase (pre and post 1865) or confiscation (*raupatu*) claims (Office of Treaty Settlement 1996). Old claims are filed for land alienated prior to British sovereignty. *Raupatu* claims are filed for land wrongfully confiscated as punishment of Maori tribes who rebelled. Gifted claims are filed for land made available for temporary purchase that was to be returned when the original purchasers left, died or no longer used it for the purposes of the original gift. Government has pursued settlement of both *iwi*-based (tribal) claims and complex claims on behalf of and affecting all Maori (pantribal claims).

Iwi-Based Claims. The Treaty of Waitangi stipulates obligations between Maori people, as a collective and as individual iwi and hapu (tribes and subtribes), and the Crown. Treaty settlements are provided via tribal mechanisms—Maori culture. Settlements of iwi-based claims are negotiated, implemented and administered by individual iwi as assets collectively held in tribal Trusts. In addition to administering tribal business, Tribal Trust Boards maintain official registers of iwi ancestry, kinship networks and membership. The benefits from treaty settlement are accessed by individual Maori through iwi membership or affiliation as Maori culture through the Marae. The Marae is the cornerstone of Maori culture and provides spiritual, economic, social and political organization as well as, literally, [venerated] tribal meeting house. When and where treaty settlements (and other targeted policies, e.g., affirmative action, biculturalism, language preschools and economic and social programs) have been most effective and successful, they have been implemented and accessed by means of the Marae structure as iwi-sponsored activities. For example, the Tainui Trust and the Ngai Tahu Trust utilize the Marae to provide community-based educational, social and health services and economic development to tribe members.

Pan Tribal Claims. In addition to claims filed on behalf of specific tribes and sub tribes, several "pan tribal" claims have been filed on behalf of "all

Maori." For example, the Te Reo Maori Claim (Maori language claim) is a pan tribal claim filed with the Tribunal May 3, 1984. In its April 29, 1986, Report, the Tribunal recommended enactment of legislation obligating Government to use Maori language in all official business and to promote and enable use of Maori language nation-wide. Another active claim filed October 9, 1991, on behalf of te iwi Maori (the Maori people) still before the Tribunal seeks to protect the use of indigenous flora and fauna, cultural and intellectual property, and base resources from exploitation (e.g., bioprospecting and bio-engineering genetic materials). Claims of these types account for nearly one-third of all claims brought before the Treaty of Waitangi Tribunal. However, the most prominent and perhaps most important treaty claim heard by the Tribunal is also a pan tribal claim: the commercial fisheries claim that was settled in 1992.

Adjudicated Claims

As of October 1998, 745 claims were filed under the 1985 Treaty of Waitangi Amendment Act. More than 254 claims have been adjudicated (settled, dismissed or withdrawn). Of the adjudicated claims, settlements of the most significant and most substantial economic development benefit are the pan tribal commercial fisheries claim (a.k.a. the Sealords Deal) and separate sets of claims by the Tainui tribes and by the Ngai Tahu tribes. The commercial fisheries claim was settled in September 1992 and established the Treaty of Waitangi Fisheries Commission. The initial fisheries settlement provided a fishing quota of 30 percent and NZ$ 150 million to promote Maori commercial fishing and to establish ten tribally-owned companies, including Sealord Products Limited and Moana Pacific Fisheries. These commercial fisheries have generated millions of dollars in assets, however, the schedule for asset allocation and the process for distribution among tribal groups is besieged by legal challenges and, to date, no assets have been disbursed. A Deed of Settlement also was reached with the Tainui tribes in May 1995. This agreement provided compensation of NZ$ 170 million, a public apology to Tainui-Waikato Maori from the Queen (Crown), the return of 14,164 hectares of land valued at NZ$ 100 million and a trust fund valued at NZ$ 65 million.

The other major and significant claim is actually a set of claims filed by the Ngai Tahu in 1986. This set of claims is perhaps the most complex claim because it involves almost the entire South Island and sweeps nine major and diverse claims under one umbrella.[6] Although the Waitangi Tribunal ruled Ngai Tahu claims valid and recommended settlement in 1991, a Heads of Agreement was reached only on October 5, 1996 and a Deed of Settlement was signed on November 21, 1997. Although the current value of assets appropriated from the Ngai Tahu are estimated at more than $20 billion, the terms of settlement provide, foremost, a formal public apology by the Crown and a redress package. Redress includes but is not limited to payment of $170 million plus interest that can be used to purchase Crown-owned assets, transfer of ownership of Crown-owned *pounamu* land (greenstone), restoration of ownership and title to Mt. Aoraki (Mt. Cook which Ngai Tahu will gift back to the nation), provision of up to $2.5 million to settle more than 30 small ancillary land claims and restoration of other assets including reserves, *mahinga kai* (food resources) and forests (Ngai Tahu Negotiating Group 1997).

Social Justice as Biculturalism

In 1984, the Labour Government of Prime Minister David Lange introduced the policy of biculturalism to provide Maori greater inclusion within New Zealand society and to recognize and restore the special status of Maori culture and Maori people as the other signatory party to the Treaty of Waitangi. The concept of biculturalism ensues from the "partnership" notion inherent in the Treaty of Waitangi and seeks to maintain Maori language, artifacts, customs and institutions intact. Biculturalism acknowledges the existence of only two ethnic groups as founders of the New Zealand State with particular and distinctive claims as New Zealander citizens: Maori *tangata whenua* and *Pakeha.*

Biculturalism buttresses on-going policymaking in New Zealand. Policymakers enacted the 1985 Law Commission Act that proclaimed a new national ethos for New Zealand as a bicultural nation and a multicultural society. Later that year, the Ministerial Advisory Committee for a Maori Perspective was established by the Department of Social Welfare. The Committee was charged with investigating and identifying the most effective approach to meet the needs of Maori people in policy, planning and social service delivery. In a landmark document, *Puao-Te-Ata-tu* (Day Break), the Committee identified biculturalism as the most appropriate policy direction for race relations in New Zealand and the essential prerequisite to development of a multicultural society (Department of Social Welfare 1986). The Committee defined biculturalism as "understanding and sharing the values of another culture, as well as understanding or preserving another language and allowing people the choice of the language in which they communicate officially" (Ibid., 19–20). The Maori Language Act is the capstone of biculturalism. Enacted in 1987, the Maori Language Act recognized Maori as an official language of New Zealand and established the Maori Language Commission to foster the use and development of Maori language. Today government documents, official signage and public announcements are rendered in Maori as well as English while fluency in Maori language is increasing among Maori and *Pakeha.*

Social Justice as Affirmative Action

New Zealand policy makers introduced policies of affirmative action much earlier than other western nations. Positive discrimination was first implemented in New Zealand in 1867 to provide direct political representation by reserving four parliamentary seats for Maori. Parliament established the Department of Maori Affairs in 1953 and the Maori Education Foundation in 1961 to address the unique social and educational needs of the Maori.[7] Special Polynesian preferences were given as early as 1951 when two places were set aside for Maori World War II veterans to attend the University of Otago Medical School. In 1975, the number was increased to six places out of 200. From 1951 to 1974, 32 applicants were admitted to the 48 places that were made available. (Out of 48 places set aside, 30 Polynesians qualified, one resigned and one died.) A system of preferences targeting Polynesians was implemented at the University of Auckland Medical School in 1972; 18 Polynesian applicants were selected out of a total of 81 applicants between 1972 and 1978. However, Polynesians admitted to the University of Auckland Medical School under the special preference scheme had higher bursary marks than the lowest marks for non-Polynesian admissions (Spoonley 1990, 91).

Affirmative action was extended to employment and economic development as well as other areas of education (tertiary, university and other training institutions). In 1980, the Government introduced the Maori and Pacific Island Recruitment Scheme to increase the participation of Maori and Pacific Islanders in the public service and move them through the senior levels. In 1987, the Race Relations Conciliator proposed that government implement a comprehensive system of affirmative actions "to improve the collective welfare of the community by the just distribution of success and status according to the situation faced by different groups" (Race Relations Conciliator 1987, 90). Similar to its American prototype, New Zealand's policy of affirmative action was formulated to address the unique circumstances and needs of Maori people as marginalized citizens in order to attain equality of results. In 1988, the State Sector Act mandated government departments to establish equal employment opportunity programs, and required that departments publish these program plans annually. Although this Act sought equality of outcomes, quotas and other numerical requirements were excluded.

Despite the absence of numerical requirements, affirmative action both created and expanded the Maori middle class and inducted significantly greater numbers of Maori into the ranks of mid and senior level management in the public and private sectors. Until the mid 1980s, Maori society was predominantly working class and dominated by unskilled blue-collar laborers in the primary sector. Census data shows that less than four percent of all Maori workers held professional, technical, administrative or managerial employment in 1981 while nearly 20 percent of *Pakeha* held employment in these occupations (Lashley 2000, 23). Although Maori held employment in diverse high skilled occupations requiring higher education (e.g., from medicine, science and opera to religion, law and politics) such employment accounted for less than one percent of the Maori labor force. By 1996—and despite increasing income inequality, with Maori median family income (NZ$ 28,695) only 58 percent of *Pakeha* median family income (NZ$ 49,424)—approximately 22 percent of all Maori workers were employed in professional, technical, administrative and managerial occupations (Ibid, 21 and Martin 1995).

Social Justice as Targeted Economic and Social Programs

Simultaneous to introducing biculturalism, government decision-makers also introduced distributive policies of positive discrimination targeted to Maori development and material uplift. Although Parliament earlier established the Department of Maori Affairs (DMA) in 1953 and the Maori Education Foundation in 1961 to address the unique social and educational needs of all Maori, in the 1980s Government expanded Maori affairs programming to include economic, education, health and social service initiatives. For example, in 1981 the Department introduced the first of several education programs to revitalize Maori language, *Kohanga Reo* (language nests) and in FY1989/90, funding for Maori language education in primary schools reached NZ$ 2.1 million (Ministerial Planning Group 1991, 17). In October 1984, the Minister of Maori Affairs, Koro Wetere (1984–1990) convened the Maori Economic Development Summit Conference in Wellington that brought Maori leaders and activists together with government officials to identify Maori social and economic needs and to consider proposals for improving Maori well-being. The three-volume proceedings document formed the basis for developing targeted programs subsequently adopted by the Department of Maori Affairs and launched the Development Decade (1984–1994). Equally important, the budget authority for Maori affairs was increased substantially, from NZ$ 67 million to NZ$ 250 million in 1985 in order to carry out these policies (Gardiner 1994).

In follow-up to Maori Summit recommendations, the Department of Maori Affairs increased funding and initiated several economic development programs directed to all Maori. DMA contracted with *iwi*-based and pan tribal organizations and private enterprises to deliver a wide range of pantribal health and social services as well as employment training and economic development programs to Maori people. Under the Crown Health Enterprises Act, the Ministry of Health implemented a major health initiative within several government departments in coordination with DMA to improve Maori physical well-being and life expectancy by lowering rates of mortality associated with poverty and limited information and access to services and treatment. Economic development programs included the Mana Enterprises and the less successful Mana ACCESS schemes. Mana ACCESS was established in 1987 to provide employment training to disadvantaged and unemployed Maori and required that training services be purchased from Maori providers. In FY 1989/90, more than NZ$ 66 million was allocated to Mana ACCESS training but only 24 percent of trainees secured employment, and 25 percent enrolled in further training at the completion of the initial course (Ministerial Planning Group 1991, 52). Similar to job training and employment programs in the U.S., job creation lagged behind job creation, and retraining older workers for new jobs requiring highly technical skills proved more difficult than expected.

The Mana Enterprises program was initiated in 1985 within the Department of Labour as a pan tribal scheme to promote job creation. In 1987, administration of Mana Enterprises was shifted to Maori Affairs and its goals were redirected to increasing Maori employment opportunities by promoting *iwi*-based business formation and expansion. In 1989, the goals of the Mana Enterprises scheme were redirected yet again, to develop and expand the commercial viability of new and existing Maori businesses by providing equity capital, loans and financial marketing advice. Thus the scheme's emphasis also was shifted from increasing employment opportunities for individual Maori to increasing the profitability of tribally-owned commercial ventures (Ibid. 43). By 1990, more than NZ$ 49.5 million was allocated to the Mana Enterprises scheme.

In this final form, Mana Enterprises was highly effective at assisting Maori in securing the necessary venture capital for creation and expansion of Maori-owned businesses. The scheme produced several highly successful commercial ventures, and undoubtedly the two most outstanding successes are the Maaori Development Corporation and the Ngai Tahu Holdings Corporation, whose combined lifetime earnings and assets exceed NZ$ 20 billion. In 1987, the Tainui Maaori Trust in the North Island formed the Maaori Development Corporation (MDC) with NZ$ 26 million in venture capital from government (NZ$ 13 mil), the Maori Trustee (NZ$ 7 mil) and two private companies, Fletcher Challenge Group (NZ$ 2 mil) and Brierley Investment Ltd. (NZ$ 2 mil). By 1993, MDC holdings included national chains of 81 Deka and 47 Farmers Trading Ltd. department stores, 11 Toy Warehouse stores, 52 Venture discount department stores and four James Smiths department stores based in Wellington with combined total annual sales exceeding NZ$ 1 billion. Today, MDC is wholly owned by the Tainui Maaori Trust, and is primarily engaged in financial investment and lending (principally minority technology start-ups), and asset management. In addition to financial investment and lending, the Tainui Maaori Trust owns and operates commercial fisheries and retail, mining, sports teams, casinos, substantial hotel and tourism ventures, as well as provides a range of health and social services. The Tainui Maaori Trust's portfolio includes Tainui Group Holdings Ltd, MDC Investments Holdings Ltd and other holding companies.

Similarly, the Ngai Tahu of the South Island also utilized the Mana Enterprises scheme to provide investment capital for new and existing *iwi*-based commercial ventures. Ngai Tahu Holdings Corporation (NTHC) was established by the Ngai Tahu Trust in 1987 to manage and operate the tribe's wholly owned commercial fisheries and property investments. In 1996, NTHC's investments included Ngai Tahu Fisheries Ltd., Property Group Ltd., Finance Co. Ltd., Ryman Healthcare Ltd., Whale Watch Kaikoura Ltd., and other holdings with a combined asset base valued at NZ$ 207 million. Since settlement of the Ngai Tahu treaty claim in 1998, the Ngai Tahu Holdings Corporation has broadened its investment base, which now includes management of post settlement purchase of Crown owned assets valued at NZ$ 250 million.

The Mana Enterprises scheme was a primary catalyst of economic growth and development for some Maori *iwi* (tribes). In particular, commercial ventures of the Tainui Maaori Trust and Ngai Tahu Trust were capitalized, which substantially and significantly increased *iwi* earnings and investments and, thereby, the collectively-held wealth of each tribe. However, to date, few of the economic benefits accruing from these ventures have trickled down to individual Maori households (Lashley, 35 and 40). By 1997, only a small percentage of investment earnings were disbursed directly to individual Maori, largely as tertiary and university scholarships. Although both Trusts provide some social services directly to tribe members (e.g., employment training, housing assistance and advocacy and educational activities) and treaty litigation on behalf of the tribe, the Trusts' Board members maintain that the provision of social welfare is the province of government. However, recent treaty settlement packages have provoked much debate and fueled criticism of both the Tainui and Ngai Tahu Trusts' opposition to direct disbursements of commercial and treaty assets to tribal members and use of these assets to provide social welfare assistance to Maori.[8]

Collision of Social Justice with Economic Restructuring and Public Sector Reforms

During the 1980s, New Zealand policymakers also enacted macroeconomic policies to restructure an ailing economy and to reform the public sector that collided with social justice policies enacted to address Maori grievances. Prime Minister David Lange's Labour Government not only implemented sweeping macroeconomic and public sector reforms aimed at stabilizing the economy and reducing government expenditures but also simultaneously amended the Treaty of Waitangi Act and greatly enlarged its scope. The 1985 Treaty of Waitangi Amendment Act produced a profusion of claims of breached Treaty rights while the hundred-year old Department of Maori Affairs was eliminated. From 1984 to 1994 successive Labour Party and National Party Governments—the new Right—enacted radical economic and social policy reforms that departed sharply from the long-established tradition of democratic socialism in order to reverse the economy's downward spiral. Upon assuming office in 1984, Prime Minister David Lange confronted a monetary crisis compounded by enormous budget deficits and massive deindustrialization. Conservative fiscal and monetary policies initiated in 1984 by the Labour Government's Minister of Finance, Roger Douglas, were continued and extended by the National Party from 1990. By July 1994 Prime Minister Jim Bolger (1990–1997) announced that National Government had achieved a fiscal surplus, increased economic growth three years running (by 4.6 percent), lowered inflation to under two percent, and was expected to reduce net public debt by nearly half of GDP in 1997 (from 60 percent to 30 percent).

Highly acclaimed by the International Monetary Fund, government's economic restructuring and public sector reforms—the New Zealand Experiment—accomplished a budgetary and social policy revolution. Foremost, import controls and tariffs were removed to stimulate and stabilize economic growth and private and public sector employment was deregulated. The 1987 Labour Relations and State Sector Acts overhauled employee-employer relations by limiting union organizing, and the 1991 Employment Contracts Act abolished compulsory union participation, effectively re-organizing work—primarily into sets of part time jobs at lower pay with greatly abridged employee rights and without health or other fringe benefits. On the fiscal side, Government introduced a 10 percent goods and services tax in October 1986 that was raised to 12.5 percent in June 1989, increased indirect taxes and substantially reduced personal tax rates for medium to high wage earners. Government also authorized the sale of state-owned enterprises and other government assets, instituted user fees for government services previously provided free of charge and assessed market rates for estate (public) housing, which further reduced the disposable incomes of lower income persons. Universal medical coverage was eliminated and medical care to the uninsured and low-income groups was rationed while hospitals were consolidated or closed. In short, government departments, programs and activities were devolved—eliminated, downsized or reorganized.

Impact of the New Zealand Experiment on Social Justice

Shifting Maori from Targeted into Universal Programs: Devolution and Mainstreaming

Devolution. Prime Minister Lange's program of devolution extended to phased-out elimination of both the Department of Maori Affairs in 1985 (effective October 1, 1989) and the centralized administration of targeted pan tribal economic and social programs. The language of devolution was not only used to transfer power, resources and responsibility to sub national or local level government, foremost, devolution restructured the partnership between Maori people and the State. In 1989, DMA was replaced by the Ministry of Maori Affairs and the Iwi Transition Agency (Ministry of Maori Affairs Restructuring Act 1989). The Ministry of Maori Affairs was charged to provide policy planning advice to the Iwi Transition Agency. Responsibility for administering Maori affairs was devolved to the Iwi Transition Agency. The Iwi Transition Agency was established to: a) acknowledge the enduring traditional significance of iwi; b) identify the characteristics by which iwi are to be recognized; c) provide for the incorporation of runanga (Maori councils, literally tribal collectives) to represent iwi; d) provide a process for the resolution of conflicts between iwi; and e) provide registration of iwi by any iwi of a body corporate as the authorized voice of the iwi (Runanga Iwi Act 1990, 2). The Runanga Iwi Act created a sub national governance structure headed by a chief executive (general manager) that linked the State to tribal entities and utilized Maori input and expertise to provide community-based programs and social services. The Iwi Transition Agency contracted directly with iwi and other Maori tribal organizations to deliver economic development programs and social services to Maori locally. Both elimination of the Department of Maori Affairs and establishment of the Iwi Transition Agency met with strident opposition from many Maori and further divided Maori leadership on the basis of tribal (iwi-based) and pan tribal approaches to Maori development and social justice.

Mainstreaming. In 1991, Prime Minister Bolger's (1990–1997) National Government disestablished the Ministry of Maori Affairs and the Iwi Transition Agency. Programs previously delivered by these units were transferred to mainstream host agencies and a new ministry, the Ministry of Maori Development, Te Puni Kokiri (TPK), was established in 1992. This new Ministry's function was primarily passive, to provide policy advice and to promote increases in the levels of achievement attained by Maori with respect to education, training and employment, health and economic and resource development; [and] monitor and liaise with each department and agency that provides services to Maori…(Ministry of Maori Development Act 1991 (s5)). Under mainstreaming, Maori policy was shifted from a two-pronged strategy of social justice requiring both pantribal distributive and tribally based reparative mechanisms to a strategy primarily focused on providing reparative justice via iwi-based mechanisms. According to Minister of Justice Doug Graham, the objective was to mainstream Maori into universal programs with the aim of providing social policy to Maori consistent with Article III of the Treaty: citizenship benefits and privileges. Maori were to be treated like every body else (Interview: Graham). Therefore, targeted social and economic programs previously administered by Maori Affairs, as related sets of bureaucratically coordinated initiatives, were transferred to government departments (including social welfare, education and health) and contracted out to non profit and private providers of social welfare services.

For example, under mainstreaming, New Zealand's Social Welfare Agency contracted the delivery of social services to external providers via its sub-unit, the Community Funding Agency (CFA). CFA was established to contract with private and nonprofit providers to deliver health, employment training, and other social services directly to New Zealand citizens in their communities. One such provider is the urban Maori authority, Waipareira Trust. In 1984, leaders of 40 Maori organizations, representing a *whanau* (family) of Maori organizations in West Auckland, established the pantribal organization—Te Whanau O Waipareira Trust (Waipareira Trust)—to assist impoverished Maori concentrated in West Auckland by providing community-based social welfare services and economic development. Waipareira Trust, like many other non-profit organizations throughout New Zealand, secures grants from CFA to deliver social services locally. Largely by contracting with an array of government departments with earnings from modest commercial ventures (including a Maori-owned and operated security firm), Waipareira Trust established a remarkable track record of providing urban Maori, who reside in economically distressed Auckland communities, much needed health and social services. These include employment training, residential mental health and juvenile habilitation centers, health care services, vocational and technical education, and small-scale economic development schemes. Nevertheless, under mainstreaming, in 1993 CFA funding to Waipareira was cut. However, in 1998, using venture capital from government and private sources, Waipareira Trust opened a mega shopping mall at the north-western end of the Auckland motorway, the Westgate Shopping Centre, in which it owns 48 percent of all shares—an asset valued at NZ$ 47 million. The Trust's success in attracting substantial government and private investment is due as much to its advocacy on behalf of detribalised urban Maori and pursuit of pan tribal remedies of social justice in the face of strident opposition as to its successful track record of delivering social service programs.

In an effort to have CFA funding restored, in 1994 the Trust filed a claim under both Article II (as treaty partner) and Article III (rights of equal access to social services) with the Treaty of Waitangi Tribunal that attracted considerable attention. The submission held that the Trust is a treaty partner representing the West Auckland community and further argued that the Crown, by reducing funding to the Trust, had failed to recognize both the representative and the trust status of Waipareira Trust as a treaty partner. Waipareira Trust's treaty claim also argued that welfare funding is not only for *iwi*. The Trust also attracted formidable criticism and opposition from prominent Maori *iwi* leaders when it joined with the Manukau Urban Maori Authority and other tribal entities in July 1995 and initiated litigation in the New Zealand High Court—and subsequently appealed the High Court's ruling to the Court of Appeals and the British Privy Council—challenging proposals by the Treaty of Waitangi Fisheries Commission to utilize *iwi*-based mechanisms for allocation and distribution of fisheries assets (Lashley 2000, 40–45). In early rulings, both the Tribunal and the Court of Appeals upheld that *iwi* is defined as "nation people," not tribe, and that settlement of all commercial fishing rights and interests of Maori is ultimately for the benefit of all Maori (New Zealand Court of Appeals 1996, 27).

Under mainstreaming, the Government shifted social policy implementation and administration to host agencies and utilized *iwi*-based mechanisms to deliver programming to Maori. Equally important, budget authority for targeted policy initiatives and programs previously administered by the Department/Ministry of Maori Affairs was transferred to mainstream host agencies, and staff levels were cut from approximately 1500 to 304 persons. For example, TPK records show that NZ$ 53.9 million allocated to DMA for Maori job training under the Maori ACCESS program was shifted to the Ministry of Education in 1992 (Ministry of Maori Development 1994). Budget authority for administering DMA, which peaked at NZ$ 270 million in FY1989/90, was reduced to NZ$ 36 million in FY1993/94 for the Ministry of Maori Development (Gardiner 1994). The 1994 TPK Summary of Mainstreaming shows that more than NZ$ 121.1 was transferred from eleven TPK programs to other government departments in FY 1992–93. Although this study does not permit analysis of total budget authority shifted from Maori programs to mainstream government departments and host agencies, it appears that total funding for Maori programs transferred to the relevant government units exceeded the DMA high mark of NZ$ 270 million.

The Fiscal Envelope

In 1994, wearied of the political and economic costs of the tribunal process and treaty settlements, government proffered a plan to settle all pending and future treaty claims in perpetuity. The National Government of Prime Minister Jim Bolger proposed a time-delimited full, final and permanent settlement in the amount of NZ$ 1 billion as total compensation for all outstanding claims and any future claims. The Crown Proposals for the Settlement of Treaty of Waitangi Claims, commonly called "the fiscal envelope" were presented in a set of three bilingual briefing booklets that specified treaty settlement processes, structures, submission guidelines and schedules, and venues for public hearings on the proposals. Beginning on February 2, 1995, a series of thirteen regional hearings, *hui*, were convened by the Minister in Charge of Treaty of Waitangi Negotiations and Minister of Justice, Doug Graham, and other government officials, to present the Crown Settlement Proposals, describe the process of implementation and address questions. In *hui* after *hui*, Maori people resoundingly and with mounting outrage rejected the fiscal envelope wholesale. After the conclusion of the March 25, 1995, *hui* at Christchurch, Minister Graham canceled the remaining *hui* scheduled for Porirua, Wellington. Discussions on the "fiscal envelope" continued amidst protest for several months after the canceled *hui*, and during that period Prime Minister Jim Bolger, Justice Minister Doug Graham and officers and staff of the Ministry of Maori Development lost considerable face. The Crown proposals were quietly shelved while Government publicly refused to amend the proposals and signaled its intentions to salvage the plan at a later date.

Conclusion: Increasing Racial and Ethnic Income Inequality

During the past two decades—and despite reparative and distributive policies of social justice aimed at compensating Maori with tangible assets for breaches of the Treaty of Waitangi and providing material uplift—the gap between Maori and *Pakeha* economic and social well-being is growing. Increasing racial and ethnic income inequality has resulted from the devolution of distributive programs targeted to all Maori in the wake of economic restructuring and public sector reforms. Census data show more than 40 percent of all Maori are reliant on government benefits, the "dole," as the sole source of income and are a disproportionate share of New Zealand's expanding underclass (SNZ 1991 and 1996). New Zealand's new urban underclass exhibits the same characteristics and pathologies as the American urban underclass. Many urban Maori are concentrated in neighbourhoods that have high rates of poverty, joblessness, teenage pregnancy and out-of-wedlock births, school drop-out without certification, crime and incarceration. Although targeted economic and social programs were effective, the programs were short-lived. The collective effect of former Prime Ministers David Lange's devolution and Jim Bolger's mainstreaming was, *de facto*, a retreat from the nascent centralized coordination and administration of social policy targeted to all Maori people initiated under Labour. Even former National Government's Minister of Finance, Ruth Richardson (1990–1994) later charged that the dismantling of the Ministry of Maori Affairs effectively substituted the vote for Maori social policy to treaty settlement.

Despite sustained reparative policies of treaty settlement, the collectively held *iwi*-owned treaty settlement assets by-pass most Maori people. Seventy percent of all Maori people are urban, do not actively affiliate with their tribes and cannot prove prior ownership of tangible assets. Article II, the tangible assets requirement, is a constraint to many Maori who are entitled to compensation due to the pervasive legacy of dispossession and marginalization. Although all Maori and their progeny remain victims of illegal land confiscation and unfairness, only a small proportion actively affiliate with *iwi* and *Marae* or have access to the substantial monetary and legal resources required for claims litigation. The economic benefits of treaty settlements and other earnings from successful *iwi*-based commercial ventures do not trickle down to most Maori households but are used to add asset value to the investment portfolios of the tribe. Moreover, most treaty settlements have not reached the asset distribution stage.

Increasingly many New Zealand policy analysts, community leaders and some politicians acknowledge that, in spite of their universality, economic restructuring and nearly two decades of public sector and social policy reforms not only have exacerbated poverty among the least advantaged, but also have rendered New Zealand a far less egalitarian society than it was (Easton 1994; Mowbray and Dayal 1994). For example, opposition leader Helen Clark characterized balanced budget and social policy reforms as "the Americanization of New Zealand" because they demonstrated the National Government's "preference for a booming economy at the expense of social justice with the attendant creation of a permanent underclass without any hope of getting out" (Clark 1995). Unlike the U.S., problems of poverty in New Zealand never were deemed intractable, racial or ethnic.

In conclusion, those Maori who are better off during this period are better off because of government's pursuit of both reparative and distributive policies of social justice. Nevertheless, neither reparative treaty settlement nor redistributive economic and social programs alone are sufficient instruments for providing the requisite material uplift to achieve equality and undo the harm done to all Maori people. In addition to restorative treaty settlements, biculturalism and *iwi*-based mechanisms, sustained distributive targeted economic and social programs that utilize pan tribal mechanisms are required in order to reduce racial and ethnic inequality and effectively blunt the disparate costs of economic restructuring and public sector reforms on Maori people.

References

Clark, Helen. 1995. Radio interview. Wellington: Radio New Zealand, March 26.

Department of Social Welfare. 1994. Statistical information report. Wellington.

———. 1986. Puao-te-Ata-tu/day break: The report of the Ministerial Advisory Committee for a Maori Perspective for the Department of Social Welfare. Wellington.

Durie, Edward. 1996. A judge's eye view of the Treaty of Waitangi Tribunal. Paper presented at the Indigenous Peoples Conference, Vancouver, British Columbia, Canada. March 20–22.

Easton, Brian. 1994. *The Maori in the labour force.* Wellington: Ministry of Maori Development.

———. 1986. *Wages and the poor.* Auckland: Unwin Paperbacks.

Gardiner, Wira. 1994. Setting the Scene, pp. 54–62. In the *Proceedings of the Maori health decade hui.* Wellington: Ministry of Maori Development.

Gardner, James. 1995. Ministers to get guards for huis. *Dominion.* Wellington. February 13: 1–2.

Graham, Douglas. Interview. Minister of Justice and Minister in Charge of Treaty of Waitangi Negotiations. Wellington, November 23, 1994.

Greenland, Hauraki. 1991. In *Naga Take: Ethnic relations and racism in Aotearoa/New Zealand,* edited by Spoonley, Pearson and Macpherson. Auckland: Dunmore Press.

Hazelhurst, Kayleen. 1993. *Political expression and ethnicity.* Westport CT: Praeger.

Hardy, Jean. 1961. Interpretation of plurilingual treaties by international courts and tribunals. *British Yearbook of International Law* 37: 72–98.

Henare, Manuka. Interview. Head, Maori Studies, Victoria University at Wellington, September 9, 1994.

High Court of New Zealand. *Judgement.* April 30, 1996.

Hunn, J. K. 1961. *Report on the Department of Maori Affairs.* Wellington: Government Printer.

Iwi Transition Agency. *Report of the Iwi Transition Agency Working Group on the Runanga Iwi Bill.* Local Government Amendment Bill (No. 8) and the Resource Management Bill. January 30, 1990.

Jackson, Te Moana Nui A Kiwa. Interview. Maori Legal Services. Wellington, November 24, 1994.

Jackson, Syd. Interview. Activist. Auckland, November 4, 1994.

Kawharu, I. H. 1989. *Waitangi: Maori and Pakeha perspectives on the Treaty of Waitangi.* Auckland: Oxford University Press.

Kingi, Pauline. Interview. Regional Director, TPK. Auckland, March 11, 1994.

———. 1984. The Treaty of Waitangi. Harvard University: Unpublished Master of Laws Thesis.

MacDonald, Robert. 1990. *The Maori of Aotearoa-New Zealand.* London: The Minority Rights Group.

Martin, Barry. 1995. *The New Zealand family and economic restructuring in the 1980s.* Hamilton: Population Studies Centre Discussion Papers, University of Waikato, May, 1998. Personal communication.

Miller, David. 1991. Justice in *Blackwell Encyclopedia of Political Thought,* edited by David Miller, J. Coleman, W. Connolly and A. Ryan. Oxford: Blackwell Publishers.

Ministry of Maori Affairs. 1984. Maori Economic Development Summit Conference. Wellington: TPK.

Ministry of Maori Development. 1997. *Review of the Ministry of Education Service Delivery to*

Maori. Wellington: Government Printer.

———. 1994. *Summary of mainstreaming*. Wellington: Government Printer.

———. 1986. *Te Urupare Rangapu (Partnership Agreement)*. Wellington: Government Printer.

Mowbray, Mary. 1993. *Incomes monitoring report*. Wellington: Social Policy Agency.

——— and Neela Dayal. 1994. The Fall and Rise of Household Incomes. *Social Policy Journal of New Zealand* 2(July): 114–122.

New Zealand Race Relations Conciliator. 1982. *Race against time*. Wellington: Human Rights Commission.

Ngai Tahu Negotiating Group. 1997. *Crown Settlement offer*. Christchurch: Ngai Tahu Publications.

Office of Treaty Settlement. 1996. *Briefing to incoming government*. Wellington: OTS.

———. 1995. *Crown proposals for the settlement of Treaty of Waitangi claims*. Wellington: DJ.

Race Relations Conciliator. 1987. *Towards an equitable society, Affirmative action*. Auckland: Race Relations Office.

Report of the Royal Commission of Inquiry. 1972. *Social security in New Zealand*. Wellington.

Schwimmer, Erik G. 1968. *The Maori people in the Nineteen Sixties*. Auckland: Blackwood and Janet Paul.

———. 1960. Government and Changing Maori. *New Zealand Journal of Public Administration* 22(2): 13–37.

Spoonley, Paul, David Pearson, and Ian Shirley, (Eds.) 1994. *New Zealand society*. Palmerston North, New Zealand: Dunmore Press.

Social Policy Agency. 1993. *Social environment scan, Brief for the Minister of Social Welfare*. Wellington: Department of Social Welfare.

Statistics New Zealand. 1996. *Census of population and dwellings: 1991 and 1996*. Wellington: SNZ.

• CHAPTER FOURTEEN •

A Call for Public Policy Review: The Indian Gaming Regulatory Act and Native American Development

GARY C. ANDERS
Professor of Economics, School of Global Management and Leadership
Arizona State University, West Campus

Since the passage of the Indian Gaming Regulatory Act (IGRA) in 1988, casino gaming has quickly become the single most important economic activity on many reservations. In 1995 there were 120 casinos operating in 26 states. Net revenues were estimated to be about $4 billion. By 2004 tribal casinos generated over $18.5 billion in annual revenue. Compared to the $10.6 billion earned by Nevada gambling establishments, it is easy to appreciate the scale to which this enterprise has grown in just a few years (Stearns, 2005).

The character of Indian gaming depends on the proximity to highly populated areas or major highways. Reservation casinos range from the Foxwoods Casino in Connecticut which is one of the largest in the world to trailers that offer a few slot machines in remote locations. Although it is difficult to generalize, given these differences, this chapter attempts to objectively discuss both the positive and negative aspects of Indian gaming. The discussion focuses on those issues that are relevant to the development of healthy Native American communities. First, I will briefly discuss the problems of poverty and underdevelopment that have long plagued Native Americans. Next, I will provide an overview of the positive aspects of Indian gaming and the ways that tribes have benefited from casinos. Following this, I consider some of the more controversial aspects of gambling, including the current conflicts between tribes and state governments, over such issues as, regulatory supervision, sovereignty and the displacement of expenditures from taxable to nontaxable sectors of state economies. The conclusion, suggests four changes in the current law, which if enacted may improve the IGRA as a public policy.

Any serious discussion of contemporary Native Americans must consider the long-standing economic and social problems of Indian reservations. It is only in this context that we can more fully appreciate how gaming has affected tribes. Specifically, it is important to keep in mind, the high rates of poverty and unemployment that have persisted on Indian reservations. According to the 2000 census, the number of Native Americans living in poverty is more than twice the percent of all other races in the United States (U.S. Department of Commerce, Bureau of the Census, 2001). In 1999 only 62% of the total Native American work force was employed full-time year-round. Unemployment rates on reservations can be as high as 80% of the total labor force. Substandard housing and physical isolation further compounds other social problems that include chronic diseases such as diabetes, as well as drug and alcohol abuse. Under the "new federalism" programs of previous Republican administrations there were significant cuts in government spending for Native Americans programs. Because few reservations had marketable resources or business opportunities most families relied upon seasonal agricultural work and transfer payments. Long mired in poverty and underdevelopment, the introduction of legalized gambling, provided Native Americas with the first major non-governmental stimulus for economic development.

Positive Impacts of Indian Casinos

In addition to reducing the number of families living in poverty, Indian leaders such as Rick Hill, Chairman of the National Indian Gaming Association, point out that casinos reduce dependence upon the state and federal government (Hill, 1995). Gambling can be very profitable—generating millions of dollars for some tribes—and there are numerous ways that individuals tribal members can benefit from gaming. First, some tribal compacts provide for a per capita distribution of revenues. This means that enrolled tribal members receive a yearly payment from their gaming profits. The creation of new job opportunities is a second way that tribal members can directly benefit through gaming. For example, the two Gila River casinos located near Chandler, Arizona have a work force of about 1,300 employees. According to tribal officials, more than 90% of the casino workers are Indians. Many of those who find employment have been able to move out of welfare and for the first time are able to provide for their families without governmental assistance. Third, tribes have used gaming revenues to build hospitals and clinics, construct new housing, provide much needed police and fire protection, establish college scholarships, as well as provide many other social services.

For the past thirty years tribal leaders have been searching for an economic development approach that would improve the living conditions of their members. From the revenues derived from gaming, tribes have expanded community social services, upgraded the quality of education, increased availability of health services, and provided better for tribal elders and other needy members of their community. Successful casinos have empowered the tribes with funds to undertake infrastructure improvements and investments in related non-gaming businesses. In many instances, the thrust of these economic development efforts is toward establishing competitive down-stream linkages with gaming. Examples of this diversification effort include: hotels, conference centers, restaurants, RV parks, and golf courses. The principal objective is to encourage new business ventures and create more jobs by expanding the tribal economic base beyond gambling.

Through casino gaming, Indian tribes that were once poor and entirely dependent upon transfer payments, are developing managerial and professional competencies that strengthen their ability to assert tribal concerns and effectively negotiate with outside entities including state and local governments. One can therefore argue that a long-term benefit from gaming is that it enhances community development through increased employment in tribal enterprises, the construction of much needed infrastructure, expanded social services, as well as through increased participation in tribal business operations, and more effective representation of Native American business interests.

Furthermore, the money that the casinos earn elevates the standing of tribes with respect to white communities and makes them an effective political force. Today, casinos and bingo halls represent economic clout that brings tribal members together and connects their individual interest to larger national issues. Such political mobilization can provide a useful training ground for younger leaders, and a mechanism whereby Native Americans cultivate their leadership skills to effectively interact with non-Indians.

While there are strong critics of casinos let us not forget that gambling is a *voluntary* transfer that people participate in by choice. Retirees and the elderly are one of the largest segment of the casino market. During visits to casinos, I asked older people about their decision to gamble at tribal casinos. They told me that they like to go to casinos for entertainment because it provides a safe, comfortable environment. Many of them do not have the physical stamina to engage in other activities, and find visits to casinos, particularly ones that offer free shuttle service and inexpensive buffets, to be a fun, relatively inexpensive group activity. From an economic point of view,

Indian gaming has increased the range of consumer entertainment choices, despite what some economists perceive as a regressive unproductive transfer.

Negative Impacts of Indian Casinos

Until fairly recently, there were not that many college educated tribal leaders. Given the relatively low levels of community capital, the unprecedented success of gambling can rapidly outstrip a tribe's ability to manage the huge inflows of cash. Although the situation is changing, Indian casinos are often managed by non-Indian companies and receive up to 40% of the total profits. Any time there is a cash-based business of this magnitude there are opportunities for criminal infiltration. Such concerns have been a source of conflict between states and tribes over the adequacy of employee background checks, and the supervision of tribal gambling operations.

Another concern is that gaming may undermine traditional Native American culture and values. There are several dimensions of this problem. The first, deals with the integrity of the tribe and tribal governments that represent the legitimate interests of Native Americans. Because of the profits associated with casinos, groups with a minimum, if any Indian blood, are motivated to seek recognition from the Department of Interior. These groups want to get federal recognition so that they can establish a reservation, and then build a casino. Currently, there over 109 groups seeking such recognition. A proliferation of Indian casinos will increase competition between tribes for a given segment of gaming market. Over time profits will diminish as a result of market saturation. Tribes, in general, have done a good job discouraging their own members from gambling in the casinos, but this could change with increased competition.

Another negative feature deals with the infiltration of existing tribes by non-Natives who seek to claim membership in order to receive gaming payouts. A number of tribal casinos generate hundreds millions, and in some cases even billion of dollars a year, and the political competition for control of the tribal government can further politically fragment tribes. Questionable individuals seeking tribal membership to realize personal gain have lead to legal battles that undermine communities. The Shakopee Mdewakanton Dakota Community is a high profile example. The Mystic Lake Casino, located on the Prior Lake reservation of the Mdewakanton, has been embroiled in a legal battle for control of the tribe's gaming operations. Louis B. Smith, the oldest member of the tribe, filed a legal challenge to tribal elections. She contested the election of Stanley Crooks as Tribal Chairman on the grounds that 43 people added to the tribal enrollment were not eligible to participate in the tribe's elections. "Ms. Smith contends an enrollment ordinance used to adopt new members is illegal and does not meet the criteria of the tribal constitution. She says that people who are not qualified under the tribal constitution are being adopted into the community for the sake of financial benefit and to bolster Mr. Crooks' political power base" (Melmer, 1995). There are numerous other cases where co-optation and infiltration of a small tribe can threaten the very institutions created to preserve their identity.

Casino gaming exacerbates inequalities between tribes in terms of market access to heavily trafficked locations (close to urban areas or interstate highways versus sparsely populated rural areas). There are cases where small tribes with less than a few hundred members operate highly profitable casinos and are thereby able to make lavish per capita payments (i.e., Foxwoods' revenues are over $1 billion annually, and Mystic Lake has paid $40,000 to $50,000 per month to enrolled tribal members). On the other hand, there are tribes like the Hopi and, until just recently, the Navajo who have chosen not to participate in gaming, but suffer extremely limited economic and employment opportunities.

There is also the danger that gaming can subvert traditional culture and values. Most of us realize the importance of education and saving in order to build-up human and financial capital. But providing large per capita payments, some tribes distort incentives and weaken the motivation to get an education, take a job, or invest. In this way, gaming payouts are analogous to welfare, except that the check is bigger. Large per capita payments also provide an incentive to increase family size. Thus, birth rates have increased because females can collect more money for each additional child.

With regard to the argument that gambling provides economically disadvantaged Native Americans with jobs, critics point out that the majority of the jobs in casinos are low hourly wage positions requiring at least a high school education (i.e., money changing, servicing slot machines, and janitorial). The higher paying jobs are professional and technical in nature, typically require a college degree (i.e., auditing, payroll, accounting, marketing and human resources management). Unless the tribe has a strong program that provides training and scholarships for college, these jobs will continue go to outsiders.

The new wealth brought in by casinos can change the way that non-Indians people think about Native Americas. When literally vast amounts are being spent to build Las Vegas type casino, the general public is exposed to a false illusion that all reservations are becoming rich. This is clearly not the case. As the 2000 census data point out there are many reservations where the economic conditions have been relatively unchanged by gaming.

No discussion of casino gaming is complete without mentioning gaming's attendant social costs. These externalities include: compulsive gaming, increased drug and alcohol abuse, crime, neglect and abuse of children and spouses, and missed work days. Various researchers have estimated these social costs at between $12,000 and $50,000 for each problem gambler. The number of compulsive gamblers can range as high as 4–5% of the general adult population (Thompson, Gazel, and Rickman, 1995).

The only survey of Indian gaming patrons, conducted with tribal support, indicates that the poor (incomes under $15,000 per year) and elderly (over 65-years old) participate in casino gambling much more than the general population (Thompson, Gazel, and Rickman, 1995). Gambling much more than other any other legal activity is regressive, in other words, it is supported predominantly by people from lower income levels.

While being generally in favor of Native American gaming, I am concerned about the economic impacts of casinos on local economies. One aspect of these impacts is the displacement of state tax revenues and increasing costs exacerbated by problem gaming. My research on the impact of reservation casinos in or near Maricopa County, Arizona indicates that significant displacement in sales tax revenues occurred with the opening of the casinos. These findings suggest that increases in gaming profits come at the expense of other taxable sectors of the economy, and since Indian casinos do not pay state taxes, sales tax revenues can be significantly reduced (Anders, Siegel, and Yacoub, 1998). More research needs to take place before we can generalize this finding. Currently, I am looking other dimensions, such as changes in employment and taxes in states where gambling has been legalized, to better understand how casinos affect local economies.

Suggested Changes in the IGRA

For the first decade, the main problem with Indian gaming was its uncertainty. In light of the often combative political climate, tribal leaders adopted a short-run time horizon. They feared that they might have only a few years to make as much money as possible, before the federal government reversed its position and repealed the IGRA. In light of this uncertainty, tribes tended to be very closed about their gaming operation. Almost all information on tribal profits is kept confidential. Given the lack of hard data, it is easy to see why there have been very few studies to confirm or deny assertions about the benefits and costs of gaming. It is hoped that the IGRA will be comprehensively reviewed in the near future, and with this, there should be a rigorous study of gaming to assess the policy approach. With this in mind, I would like to offer the following suggestions:

First, Congress should provide public disclosure by requiring that tribes report relevant financial information. This means that all tribal casinos provide information on the size of their casinos, the square footage of gaming area, the total number of gaming devices and tables, and report the revenues the same way that publicly-owned casinos do in states where gambling has been legalized. This availability would provide the necessary information to more accurately gauge the economic contribution of gaming, and facilitate better coordination between states and tribes.

Second, there is a serious need to create more oversight capability at the national level by strengthening the National Indian Gaming Commission (NIGC). The scope of the NIGC is quite broad, but the staff is small and there is not enough regulatory oversight to provide adequate protection and enforcement.

Third, an amendment to the IGRA is needed to reduce the built in inequality by providing a mechanism for the redistribution of gaming revenues to rural tribes. This could take the form of the 7i provision in the Alaska Native Claims Settlement Act (P.L. 92–203). This aspect of the law requires a distribution of Alaska Native Regional Corporation revenues from subsurface projects, such as mines and oil fields, to all the Alaska Native Regional Corporations. While potentially unpopular, this is one way that the benefits of gaming can be spread more equitably to tribes, that do not by virtue of their location, have any hope of developing profitable gaming operations.

Fourth, IGRA should be revised to provide a uniform revenue sharing arrangement between gaming tribes and their respective state governments. My research indicates that states lose a significant amount of sales taxes, as the result of the shift from taxable purchases to non-taxed gaming. In addition, states must cover the rising cost of traffic, crime and social problems resulting from gaming. As it currently stands, revenue sharing between tribes and states ranges from 25% in Connecticut to 0% in several states. Such variance, not only minimizes the need for states to be adequately compensated, but it creates discrepancies that further exacerbate inequalities between tribes.

Conclusion

Economic development of Native American communities has long been a goal of the federal government. From allotment programs to industrial parks, almost all the federal policies and projects, failed to provide a sustainable basis for reservation economies. Although forced by the realization, the Supreme Court would likely support the sovereignty of Indian tribes to engage in gaming. Congress passed IGRA in an attempt to reconcile Native American rights with interests of the established gambling industry (Eadington, 1990). No one at that time could have anticipated that Native American gaming would grow so large.

The purpose of this discussion has been to demonstrate that tribes can effectively use gaming to become more self-reliant, but that there are also problems with the current law. In order to improve IGRA as public policy, Indian gaming operations must become good corporate citizens. There is a serious need to widen the distribution of benefits and minimize the negative aspects of gaming. Changes to the IGRA, along the lines suggested here, will be difficult to pass because of tribalism and vested interests. A strong gambling lobby can thwart the policy review process and stalemate modifications that would be in the greater public interest. Nevertheless, it is hoped that Congress can approach the revision of IGRA with a clear intent to strengthen the law and improve the distributional effects while safeguarding the long-term interests of Native American communities.

Gary Anders is a Professor of Economics, School of Global Management and Leadership, Arizona State University at the west campus. He wishes to express his appreciation to Samuel L. Myers, Jr. and Bruce P. Corrie for their comments on an earlier draft of this chapter.

References

Anders, G., D. Siegel, and M. Yacoub. 1998. Does Indian casino gambling reduce state revenues? *Contemporary Economic Policy* 16(3): 347–355.

Eadington, W. R. 1990. *Native American gaming and the law*. Reno, NV: Institute for the Study of Gaming.

Hill, Rick. 1995. Indian gaming and tourism. *Indian Gaming Magazine*, February, p. 4.

Melmer, David. 1996. Shakopee election challenged. *Indian Country Today*, February 8, A1.

Thompson, W., R. Gazel, and D. Rickman. 1995. The economic impact of Native American gaming in Wisconsin. *Wisconsin Policy Research Institute Report* 8(3) (April).

Stearns, John. 2005. U.S. tribal casinos won $18.5 billion in 2004. *Arizona Republic*, February 16, D–1.

U.S. Department of Commerce, Bureau of the Census. 2001. *2000 Census of population and housing*. Washington, D.C.: U.S. Government Printing Office.

• CHAPTER FIFTEEN •

Economic Security for All: A Necessary Condition for Eliminating Racial Economic Inequality

SHEILA D. COLLINS
Professor of Political Science
Director, M.A. in Public Policy and International Affairs
William Paterson University

There is abundant historical evidence to demonstrate that in climates of economic scarcity, racism, misogyny, and various kinds of scapegoating are fueled. One has only to recall the experience of post-World War I Germany or, more recently, the racial rioting that accompanied the Indonesian financial collapse. In times of scarcity, politicians and employers also rediscover convenient excuses for reneging on social and economic commitments, and the always fragile political identities that weave different ethnic groups into a single national polity break down. General economic insecurity, then, is a triggering mechanism for racial and ethnic injustice, and general economic security is a necessary, precondition—although not a guarantor—for achieving the elimination of racial and ethnic inequality.

In an age of globalization, economic scarcity within a particular nation is no longer the only harbinger of racial economic discrimination. With the ability to move anywhere in the world in search of cheaper labor or a more favorable "business climate," transnational corporations have created a climate of general economic insecurity even among relatively affluent workers in the advanced industrial countries. By the same token, uneven development among nations fosters waves of impoverished migrants seeking work in the more affluent sectors of the world economy, thus providing employers with a convenient pool of cheap labor. The creation of racially and ethnically segmented low-wage immigrant labor markets may threaten the jobs and wages of low-skilled native workers[1] and may even pose a psychological threat to more affluent native workers, generating anti-immigrant bashing and xenophobic nationalisms. How else to explain the rise of Joerg Haider's Freedom Party in Austria or the resurgence of neo-Nazi groups and far-right parties even in the traditionally tolerant Scandinavian countries.[2]

Economic Security: The Essentials

Three conditions are essential to general economic security: full employment; adequate income support for those who cannot work either because of family care responsibilities, handicapping conditions, or old age; and environmental sustainability. In the absence of these conditions, no attempts to eliminate racial and ethnic injustice can ultimately be successful.

To provide real economic security, the concept of full employment must include the ready availability of employment opportunities for all who need them. This means that people must not be made to endure long spells of unemployment before reentering the labor market. It also means that jobs should be available where the unemployed could be expected to take them and that they provide incomes and benefits that enable people "to establish a command over a range of goods and services needed to insure a decent standard of living" (United Nations Development Programme 1996, 87).

Full employment also means that jobs must be equitably distributed across various groups in terms of both quantity and quality. A few groups must not bear the burden of most of the "bad" jobs. Training and supportive services for those who want to work but have often been excluded from the workforce (women with children, those with disabilities who could work with the proper support, those who have turned to crime because of despair over finding a decent job) must also be readily available.[3]

Even with full employment, however, there will be people who will need state support: people between jobs, those with severe disabilities, people (usually women) with very young children or elder care responsibilities, and the elderly. Real economic security means recognizing that family care responsibilities are social obligations of the entire society that ought to be compensated, and that no one should fear poverty because of conditions over which they have no control.

And finally, economic security requires environmental sustainability. Real economic security means that people must have access to the resources that are needed to freely develop and exercise their basic capabilities without jeopardizing the ability of future generations to meet their needs. Amartya Sen (1999, 74, 87), the Nobel economist, argues that the capability of "choosing a life one has reason to value" is an essential form of human freedom and that income security is one of the major means of achieving that capacity.

Diminishing Global Employment Security

How do we stand at the beginning of the twenty-first century in regard to these necessary preconditions for eliminating racial economic inequality? World economic growth, which should contribute to these preconditions, has resulted in a tripling of average per capita income over the past half century, providing more opportunities for people than ever before (United Nations Development Programme 1999, 25). Yet that growth has been highly uneven. While 33 countries achieved an annual average per capita growth rate above 3 percent between 1980 and 1997, 59 countries had negative growth rates (27) and 16 countries experienced reversals in human development since 1990 (129). Income gaps within and between countries have been widening over the past four decades. In 1960, those in the top fifth of the richest countries had 30 times the income of the poorest 20 percent. By 1997, the richest fifth had 74 times the income of the lowest fifth. In East Asia, per capita incomes today are more than seven times what they were in 1960, but in Sub-Saharan Africa, and other regions, they are lower than they were thirty years ago (36).

Rapid globalization, though requiring countries to increase their investments in skills development and training may, ironically, be leading to just the opposite for the most vulnerable workers, reducing their opportunities and incentives for training (International Labour Office 1999b, 1–7). Across the world, economic dislocations caused by globalization and structural adjustment programs imposed by the International Monetary Fund and World Bank have resulted in heavy job losses and worsening employment conditions. The International Labour Organization (ILO) has estimated that about a billion people—a third of the world's work force—are either unemployed or underemployed.[4] This is especially true for young people. About 60 million young people between the ages of 15 and 24 are in search of work according to the ILO. "Unemployment early in life," it points out, "has been shown to increase the probability of future joblessness and lower future wages" (Lisk 1999, 1). Contingent work and work in the informal sector—that is, work not tied to long-term labor contracts, government protections or employer-provided benefits—appears to be on the rise, within both the developed and developing world.[5] The ILO contends that the task of creating sufficient new jobs to overcome unemployment, underemployment and problems of low pay ranks as the primary challenge for economic and social policy in countries at all levels of development across the globe" (International Labour Organization 1995).

Nowhere is the prospect for real economic security as far off as it is in Africa, with more than 30 countries that are classified as least-developed (International Labour Organization 1999a, 11). Sub-Saharan Africa is particularly hurting. Although its growth rate has improved since 1995, for the previous two decades it had experienced economic retrogression. Declining prices for its commodity exports, environmental disasters and high rural to urban migration caused by the collapsing agricultural sector has led to a strong decline in employment since the mid-1980s. On average, low-productivity work in the informal sector—the kind of employment that Eatwell (1995) calls "disguised unemployment" was believed to employ over 60 percent of the urban labor force in 1995, while unemployment ranged between 15 and 20 percent, compared to around 10 percent in the mid–1970s (International Labour Organization 1995, 65). That leaves about 20–25 percent of the labor force who might be said to be "gainfully employed." Moreover, the cost reduction measures associated with structural adjustment plans have reduced living standards. It is estimated that more than half the people live in absolute poverty (International Labour Organization 1999a, 9, 12).

Despite improved macroeconomic indicators, much of Latin America and the Caribbean have also seen a steady fall in modern sector employment, reversing the trend of the previous three decades. Unemployment has remained high in several countries for the last decade and increased between 1990 and 1997 in Argentina, Brazil, Colombia, Costa Rica, Ecuador, Jamaica, Mexico, Peru, Uruguay and Venezuela (International Labour Organization 1999b, Table 1.8 "Labour market indicators for selected Latin American and Caribbean countries," 21). Not surprisingly, employment in the informal sector has risen. Between 39 and 68 percent of all workers in 13 Latin American countries were employed in the informal sector where wages are half of what they are in the formal sector and where workers usually lack benefits and even written contracts (Table 1.10, 22–23). In most countries, the average real wage fell during the 1980s, but began to recover during the 1990s. However, in 5 out of 11 countries analyzed, real wages in 1997 were still lower than in 1980 (23).

Growing populations and shrinking jobs have plagued Middle Eastern and North African countries for the past decade. Across the region both unemployment and underemployment rose by up to one percent a year between 1990 and 1995. Especially severe is youth unemployment—in countries like Algeria and Palestine rising to 50 percent or more (Cordahi and Horan 1995).

In several of the industrialized countries of northern Europe where, following World War II, the unemployment rates were once the envy of the world, unemployment rates have been in the double digits for the past decade, though between 1998 and 1999 there was some recovery. In Germany, the official unemployment rate had risen to 12 percent by the beginning of 1997—the highest since the 1930s—though by the end of 1999 it had fallen to 9 percent.[6] Still, one researcher has suggested that the jobless rate could be almost double the official rate if one counted the so-called "silent reserve" of unemployed who don't show up in the unemployment statistics—the discouraged and contingent workers (Huffschmid 1996). In France unemployment at the end of 1999 was 10.4 percent, while in Spain it was 15 percent.

In most of the countries of the former Soviet Union which once experienced virtual full employment, the situation is even worse. With the exception of Poland, the Czech Republic and Hungary, the much touted "transition to democracy" has resulted, not in greater economic prosperity, but in a free-fall into unemployment, soaring inequality, corruption and political instability. Poverty has escalated sharply and wage levels generally remain far lower than they were in 1989 (International Labour Organization 1999b, 18–19).

With an official unemployment rate of 4 percent as of January 2000, the United States appears to be in an enviable position vis-à-vis its European and developing-world counterparts. And indeed, the U.S. approach to employment—flexible labor markets, a weak welfare state, and maximum freedom for capital—is increasingly seen as the model for employment growth for the rest of the world.

Yet the official picture is misleading. In spite of continuous, albeit unspectacular, growth and low inflation, a majority of Americans feel less economically secure than they did twenty years ago.[7] The United States has traded fuller rates of official employment for greater job insecurity and workplace stress for those with jobs, as well as greater income inequality. While the income of the richest fifth of the population increased from 48.9 to 49.2 percent of total household income between 1993 and 1998 and the share going to the richest 5 percent increased from 21 to 21.4 percent, the income of the poorest fifth of the population registered no increase at all. Their share remained at only 3.6 percent between 1993 and 1998.[8] In fact, 80 percent of the U.S. population have seen their share of total household income decrease since 1967 (U.S. Census Bureau 1999, xiv).

For increasing numbers, full-time jobs and lifetime security have been replaced by rising rates of part-time and contingent work. Real wages, which had fallen over two decades have begun to rise again, but in the "booming" economy of 1998, with the lowest unemployment rate in nearly 30 years, *one quarter* of all full-time workers 16 years and older still had weekly earnings below the poverty line for a family of four (U.S. Bureau of Labor Statistics 1999); in 1997, nearly 35 million people (12 percent of all U.S. households) lived in food insecure or hungry households.[9] Increases in overtime, multiple job-holding, and more family members sent into the labor market enable many families to cling to middle class lifestyles at the cost of increasing levels of individual and family stress.

While segmented labor markets—for women, racial/ethnic minorities and the disabled—have long represented the principal basis of economic inequality, employment trends in the United States are increasingly showing patterns throughout the labor market of inequality among equally credentialed workers even in the same workplace. Many employers are now offering two-tiered wage structures, one for a small core of permanent, highly paid workers and the other for a larger group of part-time and contingent workers, each doing the same work. The growing use of outsourcing has also led to increased workplace inequality.

Beyond increasing job insecurity, inequality and workplace stress, U.S. unemployment rates mask other discouraging labor market realities. Official statistics on unemployment leave out those who have become so discouraged that they have given up looking for work. Looking through want ads but not finding anything doesn't qualify one to be counted as "unemployed." The person must be immediately available for a job and have actually contacted employers in the four weeks prior to the survey. Moreover, the unemployment statistics count as "employed" involuntary part-time and temporary workers, and those who have dropped from family supporting jobs into the informal, underproductive low-wage category of the "disguised unemployed." And unemployment statistics fail to count the close to two million people who are now incarcerated—the majority of whom are people of color. Many of them are very likely behind bars because they despaired of ever finding a niche in the legitimate economy. The growth of the prison population and the increasing use of prison labor should be seen as a kind of reinstitution of the system of slavery—this time under coloration of constitutional authority, since it is only in prison that slavery is still countenanced by the 13th Amendment.

Adding up all these uncounted and undercounted types puts the real U.S. jobless rate at something over twice the official rate. In January 2000, when the official unemployment rate registered 4 percent (or 5.7 million workers officially "unemployed"), a total of 13.3 million people or 9 percent of the labor force were either officially unemployed, working part-time because they couldn't find full-time work or were so discouraged that they had given up looking for work and thus were uncounted in the official unemployment rate.[10] In comparison to our European counterparts, the supposed advantage of the flexible American labor market entirely disappears.

What is there left for models? The S.E. Asian "Tigers" that just a few years ago were being hailed as the new models of development saw their economies plummet almost overnight and their triumph new middle classes suddenly disappear. Although they are now recovering, according to the World Bank, "the incomes to the low and middle classes have yet to be restored and the 15 million or so people that the crisis pushed below the poverty line can as yet take little solace from these improvements."[11] Even in Japan, with its lifetime guarantee of job security and low official unemployment rates the figures are deceiving. Only about one-in-five male workers has been offered lifetime security. The number of discouraged workers (not counted in

Japan's official unemployment rate) rose from 870,000 in 1992 to 1.2 million in 1995, making the total jobless rate comparable to that of the United States (Takahashi 1996). Japan also has a larger proportion of people who are either self-employed or who work in family businesses. These people don't show up in the unemployment statistics even when business turns bad and they can't make a living. According to Eatwell (1995, 34), Japan's rate of disguised unemployment "is truly extraordinary and totally transforms the traditional employment picture of the economy." In 1990, when Japan's official unemployment rate was 2.1 percent, its "true unemployment rate"—that is, the officially unemployed plus the disguised unemployed, was 18.7 percent (35).

The lifetime security model for core workers is on its way out. In 1995, the Japanese Federation of Employers' Associations, under pressure from international markets, suggested that Japan's lifetime security be changed to a more flexible two-or three-tiered approach, such as that emerging in the United States. Though the changes are as yet modest and evolutionary, as the *New York Times* reported, "together, they may add up to a revolution that would have far-reaching reverberations for Japan and for competing economies in the United States and elsewhere" (WuDunn 1996). Workers over the age of fifty and young workers are the first to feel the pinch. In September 1995, the *New York Times* reported that recent Japanese college graduates—once the envy of the world—"faced the most forbidding season in years, and many have settled for jobs [as receptionists, retail clerks, etc.] they would have once dismissed" (Andrews 1995).

The Attack on the Welfare State

Added to the specter of global unemployment and underemployment is the almost universal contemporary attack on the welfare state that, along with active labor market policies, had brought an earlier generation out of a period of extended economic crisis, racial violence and war. In the developing world the destruction of state welfare institutions has been underway for some years as these countries, financially strapped by external debt, have been forced by international lending agencies to restructure their economies. More recently, the industrialized countries as well—led by the United States and Britain—faced with their own "structural adjustment" pressures from international financial institutions and global corporations have been engaged in a massive downsizing of their state structures.

In August 1996, the United States Congress took the potentially explosive step of ending one of the pillars of its 1935 Social Security Act: the entitlement of the poor to government support. While the poor will continue to get some government help, it is now time-limited and no longer guaranteed as a kind of tacit "right." The so-called "welfare" programs—once mandated and largely administered by the federal government—have been renamed "personal responsibility and work opportunity" programs and turned over to state governments to design and administer. A series of punitive conditions and eligibility restrictions have been attached to such monies, eliminating some groups like undocumented workers and many legal immigrants from these benefits and making the stigma attached to being poor even more onerous. The results of the first four years of welfare repeal have been drastically reduced welfare rolls but a greater disproportion of people of color left on the rolls, deepening poverty among the poor, and an increase in the ranks of the working poor.[12] For example, the average amount by which the incomes of poor families fell below the poverty line was $245 greater per family member in 1998 than in 1995 (before the repeal of "welfare") (Dalaker 1999, v; Center on Budget and Policy Priorities 1999). Poverty rates among children in single-mother families were particularly striking: 55 percent of such children under six lived in poverty in 1998. The figures were even higher for black children—60 percent; and Hispanic children—67 percent (Dalaker 1999).

Europe, too, has been engaged in public downsizing under pressure from the structural adjustment requirements of the Maastricht Treaty. Here, the story is more mixed than it is in the United States and Britain. Most Western European governments start from a much higher base of public support, so that the erosion of public services has not yet created the level of inequality one sees in the U.S. and U.K. The pace of change is also tempered by the level of public resistance to these policies. In both France and Germany massive demonstrations and strikes of public workers and students initially slowed the downsizing process and caused political alarm bells to ring among the ruling parties. In Norway, the voters opted to stay out of the European Union with its stringent entrance requirements and have continued to have both a buoyant economy and near full employment with equity (Ibrahim 1996). In Sweden, however, which was, as late as 1990, the world's most advanced welfare state, and the cuts have been draconian, with growing but not yet massive public resistance (Ginsburg 1996).

For eastern and central Europe, the Baltic countries and the Russian federation, with a few exceptions the transition to capitalism has not resulted in greater economic security but in "a deterioration of unparalleled proportions," according to a 1994 UNICEF report. The privatization or bankrupting of state social services has resulted in soaring inequality and in a health crisis "unprecedented in the peacetime history of Europe in this century" (Crossett 1994). Malnutrition, mass epidemics, increases in suicides, alcoholism, drug addiction and crime are rampant.

Environmental Sustainability in Trouble

While there is some good news in selected areas of the world on the environmental front, the overall picture is not a sanguine one. According to the Worldwatch Institute, annual emissions of greenhouse gases have climbed to a new high, and there is now a consensus among scientists that the erratic climate changes we are experiencing are signals of increased global warming. Since the Rio Earth Summit in 1992, the planet's biodiversity has been irreversibly diminished. The growth in food production is slowing while the growth in demand—driven by both population growth and rising, if uneven, affluence—continues. The desertification of sub-Saharan Africa continues at an alarming pace, and in many parts of the world, water is an increasingly scarce commodity. More and more, environmentalists point out, ethnic and racial animosities are being fed by fights over scarce resources. Though governments have given lip service to the need to maintain environmental sustainability, in reality their actions are lagging far behind the degradation of the earth's physical resource base (Worldwatch Institute 2000).

Economic Insecurity and Racial Discrimination

It is not hard to make the connection between economic insecurity and racial/ethnic discrimination and conflict, yet it is surprising how few of the world's policymakers acknowledge the linkage. Diminishing economic returns for some groups—especially in a climate of rising expectations—and increasing wealth for others generates anger and social hostility that has historically been played out either in revolutions or racial/ethnic conflicts and civil war.

With soaring poverty and unemployment brought on by the disruption of traditional agriculture and degradation of the environment, sub-Saharan Africa has been embroiled in a series of inter-ethnic conflicts which Western policy makers attribute to some kind of suigeneris "tribalism." While the sources of these conflicts are complex, they are in large part conflicts over who will control the dwindling employment opportunities and natural resources of the region. A similar "tribalism" has engulfed many of the successor states to the Soviet Union. As unemployment rates have risen, state services have been slashed as the region faces profound environmental crisis. Across the Islamic world, a fanatical brand of Islam is bred among enclaves of the unemployed and impoverished young.

In the United States, as unemployment climbed and wages fell among the majority white population from about 1973 to the mid-1990s, we saw a concomitant increase in immigrant bashing, attacks on affirmative action, and the growth of white supremacy groups. In Western Europe, too, it is not surprising that double digit unemployment rates and the erosion of public benefits have led to increased rates of anti-immigrant sentiment, anti-Semitism, and neo-fascist violence. In such a climate some opportunistic politicians find it all too easy to get votes by appealing to racism. Europe has seen the growth of xenophobic far-right political parties.[13]

While the connection between general economic insecurity and racial/ethnic conflict may be salient, what about the connection between general economic insecurity and racial discrimination in the workplace? William Julius Wilson and others have pointed out that racial discrimination varies depending on the tightness of the labor market. In a slack market, employers can afford to be more selective in hiring and promotion. They will create new job prerequisites and exaggerate the amount of experience that is needed. Those with the fewest credentials (disproportionately racial/ethnic minorities and women) will be screened out. Such groups then get discouraged and drop out of the labor market. In tight markets, however, they are drawn in (Wilson date unknown, 19).[14]

The history of young black male employment in the United States bears this out. Employment for young African American men was greatest in the near full employment climates of the 1940s and 1960s and declined in the 1950s and 1980s (Carnoy 1994, 24–25). Studies by Osterman (1991) and Freeman (1991) of local labor markets demonstrate that in climates of near full employment, even those considered most "unemployable" (young African American men without high school diplomas) are drawn into the labor market, reducing their poverty dramatically. Tight labor markets also provide both the political and psychic space for racial minorities to challenge labor market segmentation. In the tighter labor markets of both World War II and the 1960s, African Americans and women were able to challenge racial and gender segmentation and to enter some previously closed occupations.

The erosion of the welfare state, while creating more general economic insecurity, is also particularly devastating for racial/ethnic minorities in two ways. First, because of their historic exclusion from private labor markets, they have been disproportionately dependent on social services. Cutbacks in these services therefore mean increasing economic vulnerability for these groups. Second, racial minorities particularly in the United States have been disproportionately employed by state welfare institutions. Indeed, over the past three decades, employment in this sector has been the ticket for large numbers of African Americans into the middle class.

When the five-year time limit for receipt of welfare in the United States kicks in, there will be more people competing for scarce minimum wage jobs in the private market than ever before. Although the U.S. government does not keep job vacancy surveys like many European governments do, what research has been done indicates that there are always twice as many job seekers—even for low-wage jobs in good economic times—and incrementally more people needing jobs than jobs available when overall unemployment goes up (Abraham 1983; Newman 1995; Jeter 1995; Goldberg, Collins, Gingsberg and Harvey 1996; Harvey 2000). The U.S. may be creating a vicious game of musical chairs in which former welfare recipients will be competing with the working poor, the newly arrived immigrant, the laid-off civil service worker and, in some cases, the recent college graduate. The potential for racial/ethnic conflict in such a situation is all too ripe.

Learning from History

Policy makers today appear to have learned nothing from the experience of earlier generations. In 1944, emerging from a more than two-decade long period of economic scarcity marked by explosive racism and two terrible world wars, the leaders of the so-called "free world," in a moment of unusual clarity, realized—as President Franklin Roosevelt (1966, 1288) stated it—that "true individual freedom cannot exist without economic security and independence. Necessitous men are not freemen. People who are hungry and out of a job are the stuff of which dictatorships are made."

In a generation that remembered the hard times after World War I and was haunted by memories of the depression, there was "near hysteria over the specter of unemployment," a former White House reporter wrote (Donovan 1977, 107). And so in 1944, both the Democratic and Republican platforms endorsed the idea of government guaranteed full employment, and their presidential candidates gave it unqualified support. Public opinion was also on the side of full employment, and nearly every major religious and civic organization endorsed the idea. In his State of the Union address in 1944, President Roosevelt (1966, 1288) enunciated a new Economic Bill of Rights, "economic truths [that] have become accepted as self-evident." Among these were: "the right to a useful and remunerative job in the industries, or shops, or farms of the Nation; the right to earn enough to provide adequate food and clothing and recreation; the right of every family to a decent home; the right to adequate medical care and the opportunity to achieve and enjoy good health; the right to adequate protection from the economic fears of old age, sickness, accident and unemployment; the right to a good education." Roosevelt's Economic Bill of Rights was modeled on a New Bill of Rights that had been set out by his National Resources Planning Board, a document which "encompassed human rights in general, without rigidly separating the economic from the civil-political" (Gross 1988).

While Roosevelt's Economic Bill of Rights did not include civil and political rights, the rest of the world saw that the three kinds of rights could not be so separated. They enshrined these rights in several documents, including the

U.N. Charter, the Universal Declaration of Human Rights, and the International Covenant on Economic, Social and Cultural Rights, among others. The world, it seemed, had learned the lessons of the 30s. But while Europe and Japan moved to institutionalize economic security through the provision of generous social welfare, state-corporate planning, and active labor market policies, United States business interests, in collusion with a coalition of Republicans and conservative Democrats (from the still racially segregated South) in Congress moved quickly to nip this broadening rights movement in the bud. They defunded the National Resources Planning Board and forbade the President from transferring its functions to any other agency, effectively killing a source for progressive economic analysis and innovative policy planning. They defeated the 1945 Full Employment Bill which, if passed, would have committed the federal government to guaranteeing every American the right to useful and remunerative employment, and in its place, passed the Employment Act of 1946, an emasculated version of the original bill which called only for *maximum* instead of *full* employment and required the government to use only *practical* means of attaining its goals. Thereafter, even this diluted bill was more often honored in the breach.

In spite of the major flaw at the heart of our domestic policy—the continued exclusion of people of color from the full rights and responsibilities of citizenship—the U.S.'s position of economic superiority in the post war world enabled an expanding American pie to promise a period of relative hope for economic security and upward mobility to most in the white working class. As a result, in this more secure climate, the African American community was encouraged to fight for its own inclusion. Economic security for the white working class enabled blacks to break the hegemony of white dominance and to expose the virulence and absurdity of white supremacy to the world.

It is thus not surprising that the return of economic insecurity for the white working class during the late 1970s—the result of a restructuring of the international economy which put the dictates of capital, rather than concern for human rights and social peace, back in charge of the agenda—coincided with a reversal in the hope for racial economic inequality that the Civil Rights era had begun to produce. Black men in *every educational category* earned a lower real hourly wage in 1993 than in 1979, but the only group of white men to see their earnings rise since the late 1970s have been men with post-graduate education (Henwood 1995, 5).

With few exceptions the policy elite around the world—but especially in the United States—remain oblivious to the danger signs, although a few are now beginning to raise alarms. One of them, Ethan Kapstein, Director of Studies at the Council on Foreign Relations, warns that today "the world may be moving inexorably toward one of those tragic moments [which in the past led to either war or revolution] that will lead historians to ask, why was nothing done in time?" (Kapstein 1996) What we need says Kapstein is a return to the kind of leadership that led America and the world in the immediate post-war decades, in which "statesmen...designed a liberal world economy that maintained an active domestic role for the state in order to ensure that equity and growth went hand in hand." Billionaire investment philanthropist George Soros (1997) has issued a similar warning and prescribed a similar solution, as has former World Bank Vice President and Chief Economist, Joseph Stiglitz (February 1999; April 1999; 2000). Though there is some recognition of the problem among the international policy elite, as of this writing there are no aggressive national levels or international programs to turn the situation around. As a follow-up to the 1995 UN Social Summit, the International Monetary Fund and the International Labour Organization have agreed to strengthen cooperation to boost global employment, but so far this amounts to dialogue and information sharing (Washington Branch of International Labour Organization 1995). An OECD paper released in late 1996 called for more empirical study of specific policy options (*OECD Economic Outlook* 1996). Perhaps this is progress, but the more common approach being adopted among the world's policy makers is to boost overall economic growth rates through supply-side monetary policies. Though they admit that this "creative destruction" will create some losers, they assume that the benefits will eventually trickle down to the unfortunate. We should be mindful that it took the near collapse of the world's economy, the impoverishment of millions, and a terrible world war before the policy elites of an earlier era adopted policies to ensure that growth would be accompanied by some kind of equity.

The Solution Lies in Politics

Contrary to mainstream economic propaganda there is no technical barrier to creating economic/job security for everyone. As the Commission on Employment Issues in Europe, headed by former Austrian chancellor Bruno Kreisky, pointed out to the European Community some years ago, the problems of unemployment and increasing income polarization are not economic but political. They are the result of specific restrictive economic policies that have kept aggregate demand too low. The recommendation of the Kreisky Commission was *not* to adopt the flexible labor market policies of the United States, but to institute active labor market policies, job creation with *real* wage growth, and international cooperation to stabilize prices (Commission on the Employment Issues in Europe 1989). Unfortunately, the Kreisky Commission's proposals went unheeded.

If we are not to embody Santayana's dictum that those who ignore history are condemned to repeat it, we cannot wait for the policy elites to come to their senses. Jobs and economic security for *all* must be seen as the condition sine qua non for racial economic equality. Full employment is a necessary, though partial condition for racial and ethnic peace. Overcoming the political inertia to enact full employment policies will require building a new mass political movement that seeks to operationalize—in this and every other country—the economic rights which the world community has so eloquently articulated and which were recently reiterated by U.N. Secretary General Kofi Anan in his call for a "Citizens" Compact on the United Nations and Corporations."[15]

The building of such a movement requires three strategic steps. First, it requires the capacity to dispel the economic myths and distortions that policy makers, in thrall to market economics, use to justify the return to laissez faire capitalism with its savage inequalities. Academics committed to racial and economic justice have a crucial role to play in articulating an alternative set of economic premises. They must undertake the research necessary to demonstrate that jobs for all at decent wages is economically feasible as well as socially desirable in the late twentieth century. Much of this research exists but needs to be made available to the lay public.

Barring peaceful electoral change, people increasingly beleaguered by economic insecurity will engage in extra-electoral challenges to power. This can take the form of either progressive equity-generating movements or reactionary ones. In the United States and across Europe we have witnessed the growth of neo-fascist and paramilitary movements. But we have also witnessed major strikes of workers during 1995 and 1996 in France and Germany protesting the loss of economic security, calling for a different relationship between economic and political power, and demanding a social policy that provides equity and security.

Second, the constituencies that have a stake in full employment (the vast majority of the world's people) need to begin working together instead of in separate racial/ethnic, issue-oriented or national enclaves. This has already begun to happen through the growth of the NGO community and their impact on the various U.N.-sponsored global summits (on the environment, women, urbanization, etc.). The international protests against the World Trade Organization in Seattle, Washington, in November 1999, in Davos, Switzerland, in December 1999 and in Washington, D.C., in April 2000 are further evidence that such a global civil society is coming together. Such work at the international level must be augmented by international networks of social scientists, such as the Workshop on Alternative Economic Policy in Europe, which brought economists from eight EU member countries together in October 1995 and by religious institutions and trade unions that have the capacity for broad national and international networking. Third, the enormous dominance of private economic power over the institutions of democracy must be challenged by counter-power, through the development of parties and candidates committed to economic equity and security. Some indications of movement in this direction are the development of new political parties in the United States (particularly the Labor Party, the Green Party and the New Party), the movements to reform campaign spending and to hold corporations accountable, and efforts to rebuild communities shattered by corporate flight from the bottom up through democratically designed development strategies.[16] The resurgence of the Labour Party in Britain, the renewed concern among French Socialists for job creation, the election of the Social Democratic Party in Germany and of a center-left coalition in Italy may be further indications of a shift, however limited.

The policy agenda that is beginning to emerge from such activities (with the exception of the neo-fascist movements) is remarkably similar across the globe. It consists of at least eleven broad policy goals.[17]

Full Employment

The private market never has and never will provide for true full employment. Governments must do this through a variety of direct and indirect market place carrots and sticks as well as by serving as a direct employer of last resort.

Affirmative Action to Redress Discrimination

Full employment would do much to reduce social tensions caused by racial and other forms of discrimination, but it would not automatically eliminate the disparities that exist in the labor force due to entrenched, institutionalized racism and sexism. If we are to reduce group-related inequality there must be—for the foreseeable future—some form of active commitment to redressing systemic barriers.

Affirmative action is infinitely easier to enforce in a climate that promises economic security for *all*, and affirmative action must apply not only to inequalities within nations but to inequalities between nations. The rich countries of the North must contribute funds to an international development bank for the poorer countries of the South, as well as engage in debt relief and other measures. The Jubilee 2000 campaign of religious organizations' call for cancellation of the debts of impoverished countries in Africa, Asia and Latin America and President Clinton's gesture in promising a cancellation of debt owed to the U.S. are major signs of movement in this direction.[18]

Income Support

Full employment would significantly reduce the need for unemployment insurance and welfare. However, some kinds of government-provided income support will be necessary for those who cannot work in the paid labor force. This includes the temporary or permanently disabled, the caretakers of infants and very young children, the elderly and their caretakers, those left bereft of the primary breadwinner, and workers who are between jobs.

Protection of Workers' Rights

The erosion of labor's power relative to that of capital has contributed to increased race-based poverty and inequality in the United States and in developing countries. Governments must ensure that workers and their organizations' rights are protected in law and strictly enforced. At a minimum, the International Labour Organization's core labor standards must be adopted and enforced by every country. Workers themselves, however, must work to democratize their own highly bureaucratic and sclerotic trade unions.

Holding Corporations Responsible and Accountable

Corporations have been recognized by the courts as "persons" with the same Constitutional rights as human beings. Yet too often they have not acted as responsible public citizens and the mechanisms for holding them publicly accountable are weak. A just society that seeks to eradicate racial economic inequality must correct this deficiency. Attaching strings to state and federal taxes and subsidies can influence corporations and banks to be responsible citizens. Some have called for the inclusion of labor, community and environmental advocates on corporate boards. Others have advocated a "stay or pay" policy that requires companies to negotiate with the workers and communities in areas that they plan to leave and to compensate them for the losses that will be incurred. Reforming economic accounting systems to include in the costs of doing business the social and environmental costs that are now "externalized" has been recommended by a large number of groups, and guidelines for doing this have been published by the United Nations. Restoring the U.S. corporate income tax to the levels that prevailed in the 1950s would reduce nearly two-thirds of the current deficit and free up that money to meet human needs and create jobs (Barlett and Steele 1994, 24). Government policies that make it more possible for worker/community ownership of major enterprises have also been recommended.

Limitations on Capital

Speculation in international financial markets has reached new and dangerous proportions, jeopardizing the health and stability of the world's economic system. Outlawing or taxing such dangerous forms of speculation is extremely important. A tax on foreign exchange transactions of only one-tenth of one penny on the dollar would raise $1 billion each trading day—nearly $250 billion per year—an amount adequate to finance the U.N. and all of its development and relief programs, and would contribute to deficit reduction around the world (Canova, Collins, Ginsburg, Goldberg, Rosen, and Zaccone 1995, 23).

How much wealth is enough? Inequality, particularly in the United States, has grown out of all proportion to anything that makes sense. A bill that was introduced in the British parliament would have limited corporate executives from exceeding 20 times the average pay of their non-managerial employees. In the United States, the Share the Wealth Project is promoting the idea that all incomes for tax purposes should be pegged to the minimum wage. Maximum income should then be capped—some have said at ten times the minimum, others at 50 times the minimum—and the excess recovered through the income tax system (Pizzagati 1994; Snyder 1995). Pegging the maximum wage to the minimum wage would give all taxpayers an incentive to raise the minimum wage to a level that was decent and livable. Others have proposed direct taxes on wealth similar to what eleven other industrialized countries now have (Wolff 1995, 51–7).

Cutting Military Spending

With the world's most lethal arsenal and enough nuclear weapons to kill everyone in the world several times over, there is no reason for the bloated military budgets maintained by so many governments. Military spending produces fewer jobs than spending in the civilian sector and diverts a country's best minds to developing the means to kill rather than creating a viable human habitat. Blocked military budgets weaken civilian manufacturing capacity, and drain treasuries of the resources needed to stimulate growth and meet peoples' needs. To insure against poverty and inequality, however, a shift from military spending would have to be done in the context of a planned conversion process so that defense industry workers were not sacrificed in the transition.

Universal Health Insurance

Recent cross-national studies have demonstrated that mortality and disease rates are closely associated with a nation's overall rate of inequality (*British Medical Journal* 1996; Kaplan et al. 1996; Wilkinson 1992; Waldmann 1992). Universal health care, provided through the tax system but democratically managed, has been demonstrated to be not only more effective in preventing disease but more cost-effective as well as providing a source of new jobs.

Universally Available Lifelong Education

The fastest growing jobs—especially in the advanced industrialized countries—are those that require higher levels of education and training than ever before. We cannot hope to rid ourselves of racial economic inequality without providing everyone with the access to affordable, quality education and training, including higher education that can be accessed at any time in a person's life. This requires increased funding for general education, compensatory education for those currently left behind, for providing the kinds of equipment (computers, etc.) that lower income students need in order to be able to compete in the labor market, and for school-to-work programs like the German apprenticeship program for the non-college-bound.

Rebuilding Our Cities

There has been tremendous damage done to cities across the U.S. and in the third world by public policies that support short-term profit-taking by private corporations instead of addressing the long-term needs of the cities' economies and people. Today, large sectors of America's cities are festering wounds of crime, drug addiction, family dysfunction, and environmental degradation; home to most of the nation's poorest citizens. In the Third World, as capitalist aid and trade displace rural peasants from their land, megacities of tens of millions have grown up without any of the urban amenities we take for-granted: running water, electricity, sewage removal, garbage collection, parks, playgrounds, museums and so on.

Cities have always been the lifeblood of a nation. Europeans know this much better than Americans and have sought to preserve the infrastructure and cultural heritage of their cities even as they modernize. A program to reduce poverty must place special emphasis on rebuilding the cities as places of hope, culture, beauty, creativity, and neighborliness.

Environmental Conservation and Protection

The economic health of people, communities and nations is intimately tied to the health of their surrounding environment. Through a number of major summits and projects on environmental protection, development and peace sponsored by the United Nations over the last thirty years, the international community has belatedly come to understand the links between poverty, inequality and environmental degradation. Eradicating poverty must therefore go hand-in-hand with concerted efforts to strengthen and expand environmental protection, education, and global governance. While environmental preservation can be a source of new jobs and tax revenues.

To preserve the earth and feed the world's people there must also be support to help family farmers and rural peasants succeed with technologies that do not require enormous uses of fertilizers and pesticides.

References

Abraham, Katherine G. 1983. Structural/frictional vs. deficient demand unemployment. *American Economic Review* 73(September): 708–724.

Andrews, Edmund L. 1995. Japan's job market shocks collegians. *New York Times*, 5 September, D2.

Barlett, Donald L., and James B. Steele. 1994. *America: Who really pays the taxes?* New York: Touchstone/Simon & Schuster.

Bean Frank D., and Stephanie Bell-Rose, Eds. *1999. Immigration and opportunity: Race, ethnicity and employment in the United States*. New York: Russell Sage Foundation.

Beveridge, William H. 1944. *Full employment in a free society*. London: Allen & Unwin.

Briggs, Jr., Vernon M. December 1990. *The changing nature of the workforce: The influence of U.S. immigration policy*. Washington, DC: National Planning Association.

British Medical Journal. 1996. Editorial: The big idea. *British Medical Journal* 312(April 20): 985.

Canova, Timothy, Sheila D. Collins, Helen Lachs Ginsburg, Gertrude Schaffner Goldberg, Sumner Rosen, and June Zaccone. 1995. *A growth agenda that works*. New York: National Jobs for All Coalition.

Carnoy, Martin. 1994. *Faded dreams: The politics and economics of race in America*. New York: Cambridge University Press.

Center on Budget and Policy Priorities news release. 1999. Low unemployment, rising wages fuel poverty decline. Washington, DC: Center on Budget and Policy Priorities. 1 October 1999.

Cohen, Roger. 1997. For France, sagging self-image and esprit. *New York Times*, 11 February, A1.

Collins, Sheila D., Helen Lachs Ginsburg, and Gertrude Schaffner Goldberg. 1994. *Jobs for all: A plan for the revitalization of America*. New York: The Apex Press.

———, Helen Lachs Ginsburg, Gertrude Schaffner Goldberg, Sumner Rosen, and June Zaccone. 1997. The challenge of full employment in the global economy. *Economic and Industrial Democracy* 18(1)(February, Special Issue): 5–33.

Commission on Employment Issues in Europe. 1989. *Program for full employment in the 1990s: Report of the Kreisky Commission on employment issues in Europe*. London: Oxford Pergamon Press.

Cordahi, Cherif, and Deborah Horan. Middle East labour: Political troubles burden job markets. InterPress Service, 27 April, 1995.

CorpWatch. 1998. Citizen's compact on the United Nations and corporations [online]. Available from World Wide Web: http://www.corpwatch.org

Crossett, Barbara. 1994. U.N. study finds a free Eastern Europe poorer and less healthy. *New York Times*, 7 October, A13.

Dalaker, Joseph. 1999. U.S. Census Bureau current population reports, Series P60–207, *Poverty in the United States: 1998*. Washington, DC: U.S. Government Printing Office.

DeFreitas, Gregory. 1998. Globalization and progressive economic policy. In *Globalization and progressive economic policy*, edited by Dean Baker, Gerald Epstein, and Robert Pollin. Cambridge, England: Cambridge University Press.

Donovan, Robert J. 1977. *Conflict and crisis: The Presidency of Harry S. Truman, 1945–1948*. New York: W.W. Norton.

Eatwell, John. 1995. Disguised unemployment: The G7 experience. Unpublished paper based on a Report to UNCTAD, G7 Unemployment: Disguised and Revealed (Contract no. CNF4C/082) (March).

Europe's Far Right. BBC News online: http://news.bbc.co.uk

Flavin, Christopher. 1997. The legacy of Rio, pp. 3–22. In *State of the world 1997*. Washington, D.C.: Worldwatch Institute/W.W. Norton & Co.

Freeman, Richard B. 1991. Employment and earnings of disadvantaged young men. In *The urban underclass*, edited by Christopher Jencks and Paul E. Peterson. Washington, D.C.: The Brookings Institution.

Ginsburg, Helen Lachs. 1983. *Full employment and public policy: The United States and Sweden*. Lexington, MA: Lexington Books.

———. 1996. Sweden: Fall from grace: Entrance in the EU has increased pressure on Sweden to dismantle its welfare state. *In These Times*, 23 December, 21 ff.

Goldberg, Gertrude Schaffner and Sheila D. Collins. 2000. *Washington's new poor law: Welfare reform and the roads not taken, 1935 to the present*. New York: The Apex Press.

Goldberg, Gertrude Schaffner, Sheila D. Collins, Helen Lachs Ginsburg, and Philip Harvey. September 1996. Welfare "reform": Where are the jobs? *Uncommon Sense* 5.

Gross, Bertram. 1988. From rhetoric to reality: Economic rights. Unpublished paper.

Hamermesh, Daniel S., and Frank D. Bean, Eds. 1998. *Help or hindrance? The economic implications of immigration for African Americans*. New York: Russell Sage Foundation.

Harvey, Philip. 2000. How many jobs are there? The need for a national job vacancy survey. *Uncommon Sense 15* (March).

Henwood, Doug. September 9, 1995. Race and money. *Left Business Observer* 69.

Hitchens, Christopher. December 2, 1996. Blue on the Danube. *The Nation*, p. 8.

Howell, David R., and Elizabeth J. Mueller. March 1998. Immigration and native-born male earnings: A jobs-level analysis of the New York City metropolitan area labor market, 1980–90. Unpublished paper. New School for Social Research, New York, NY.

Huffschmid, Jorge. April 1996. Alternative economic policy for full employment: Proposals for Germany. Unpublished paper.

Ibrahim, Youssef M. December 13, 1996. Welfare's cozy coat eases Norwegian cold. *New York Times*, p. A1.

International Labour Organization. 1995. *World employment report 1995*. Geneva: International Labour Office.

International Labour Organization. 1999a. *ILO activities in Africa: 1994–99, Report of the Director-General to the Ninth African Regional Meeting, Abidjan*, December 1999. http://www.ilo.org

International Labour Organization. 1999b. *World employment report 1998–9*. Geneva: International Labour Organization.

Jeter, Jon. December 11, 1995. Lack of entry-level work trips Md. welfare reform. *Washington Post*.

Johnson, Dirk. November 15, 1999. Tight labor supply creates jobs for the mentally disabled. *New York Times*.

Kaplan, George A., Elsie R. Pamuk, John W. Lynch, Richard D. Cohen, and Jennifer L. Balfour. 1996. Inequality in income and mortality in the United States: Analysis of mortality and potential pathways. *British Medical Journal* 312 (20 April): 999–1003.

Kapstein, Ethan. 1996. Workers and the world economy. *Foreign policy* (May/June): 16–37.

Kawai, Masahiro (EAPVPC) and Richard Newfarmer (EASPR). 1999. East Asia regional overview [online]. http://www.worldbank.org

Mishel, Lawrence, Jared Bernstein, and John Schmitt. 1999. Executive summary, p. 21. In *The state of working America 1998–99*. Ithaca, NY: Cornell University Press.

Lisk, Franklyn. 1999. Generating employment, labour rights and development, p. 1. Paper presented at 21st Annual United Nations Parliamentary Forum, New York, September 29–30, 1999.

Lohr, Steve. December 29, 1996. Though upbeat on the economy, people still fear for their jobs. *New York Times*.

Nasar, Sylvia with Kirsten B. Mitchell. May 23, 1999. Booming job market draws young Black men into fold. *New York Times*.

Newman, Katherine S. May 20, 1995. What inner-city jobs for welfare Moms? *New York Times*, p. A23.

North, David S. 1994. Enforcing the minimum wage and employer sanctions. *Annals of the American Academy of Political and Social Science* 534(July): 58–68.

OECD Economic Outlook No. 60, press release 18 December, 1996, Paris.

Osterman, Paul. 1991. Gains from growth: The impact of full employment on poverty in Boston. In *The urban underclass*, edited by Christopher Jencks and Paul E. Peterson. Washington, D.C.: The Brookings Institution.

———. 1999. *Securing prosperity: The American labor market: How it has changed and what to do about it*. Princeton, NJ: Princeton University Press.

Pizzagati, Sam. 1994. *The maximum wage: A common sense prescription for revitalizing America by taxing the very rich*. New York: The Apex Press.

Roosevelt, Franklin Delano. 1966. State of the Union Address, January 11, 1944, pp. 1288. In *The State of the Union messages of the Presidents 1790–1966*, edited by Fred L. Israel. New York: Chelsea House/Robert Hector Publishers.

Sen, Amartya. 1999. *Development as freedom*. New York: Alfred A. Knopf.

Singer, Daniel. October 26, 1996. Liberte, egalite, racisme? *The Nation*, pp. 19–21.

Smith, James P., and Barry Edmonston, Eds. 1997. *The new Americans: Economic, demographic and fiscal effects of immigration*. Washington, DC: National Academy Press.

Snyder, Bryan. July/August 1995. A maximum wage: How much is enough? *Dollars & Sense*, p. 30 ff.

Social summit follow-up: ILO, IMF agree to boost global jobs. Fall 1995. *ILO Washington Focus*.

Soros, George. 1997. The capitalist threat. *Atlantic Monthly* (February): 45–58.

State-level study finds over 15 percent of households food insecure/hungry in seven states, Ten percent or more in two-thirds of states. Medford, MA: Tufts University Center on Hunger, Poverty and Nutrition Policy, 22 October, 1997.

Stiglitz, Joseph E. February 1999. Participation and development: Perspectives from the comprehensive development paradigm. Paper presented in Seoul, Korea, February 27, 1999.

———. April 1999. Whither reform? Ten years of the transition. Paper prepared for the World Bank Annual Bank Conference on Development Economics, Washington, DC, 28–30 April, 1999.

——. 2000. Democratic development as the fruits of labor. Keynote address to the Industrial Relations Research Association, Boston, MA, January 2000. Papers are available from the World Bank at: http://www.worldbank.org

Takahashi, Yukichi. March 1996. Changes in the Japanese labor market and a sketch of lifetime employment in contemporary Japan. Unpublished paper.

United Nations Development Programme. 1996. *Human development report 1996*. New York: Oxford University Press.

———. 1999. *Human development report 1999*. New York: Oxford University Press.

U.S. Bureau of Labor Statistics. June 6, 1999. Labor force statistics from the Current Population Survey, Table 4: Quartiles and selected deciles of usual weekly earnings of full-time wage and salary workers by selected characteristics, Fourth quarter 1998 averages, Not seasonally adjusted.

http://stats.bls.gov/news.release/wkyeng.t04.htm

U.S. Census Bureau. 1999. *Current population reports, P60–206, Money income in the United States: 1998*. Washington, DC: U. S. Government Printing Office.

Waldmann, Robert J. 1992. Income distribution and infant mortality. *The Quarterly Journal of Economics* 107(November, 1): 1283–1302.

Washington Branch of International Labour Organization. 1995. Social summit follow-up: ILO, IMF agree to boost global jobs. *ILO Washington Focus* (Fall).

Whitney, Craig R. January 7, 1996. Europeans redefine what makes a citizen. *New York Times*, Sec. 4, 6.

Wilkinson, Richard G. 1992. Income distribution and life expectancy. *British Medical Journal* 304(January 18): 165–168.

Wilson, William Julius. Date Unknown. Poverty, joblessness, and family structure in the inner city: A comparative perspective. Unpublished paper prepared for presentation at the Chicago Urban Poverty and Family Life Conference.

Wolff, Edward N. 1995. *Top heavy: A study of the increasing inequality of wealth in America*. New York: The Twentieth Century Fund Press.

Worldwatch Institute. 2000. *State of the world 2000*. Washington, DC: Worldwatch Institute.

WuDunn, Sheryl. June 12, 1996. When lifetime jobs die prematurely. *New York Times*, D1.

•CHAPTER SIXTEEN•

If Not Affirmative Action, Then What?

SAMUEL L. MYERS, JR.
Roy Wilkins Professor of Human Relations and Social Justice
Hubert H. Humphrey Institute of Public Affairs
University of Minnesota

Affirmative action is a remedy (Kumar 1992). It is a remedy that was applied by the British government during the late 19th century in India to help create a civil service that reflected the caste makeup of Indian society. It is a remedy that was encoded in the Indian constitution after World War II designed to overcome generations of discrimination against the lower castes in education and in public employment.

Affirmative action is a remedy in New Zealand and in Australia. It is designed to correct years of neglect against aboriginal and native islander populations by providing direct monetary compensation for stolen land and providing education and public sector employment opportunities (Lashley 1996; Spoonley, Pearson and Shirley 1994).

Affirmative action is a remedy in the United States. It is a remedy adopted by U.S. government agencies to enforce existing presidential executive orders and civil rights laws (Anderson 1997). Affirmative action in the U.S. is a remedy to the legacy of unequal opportunities produced by State sanctioned and government enforced segregation and discrimination in employment, public education, and government contracting and procurement that directly contributed to current inequalities in these market sectors (Massey and Denton 1993; Myrdal 1962; Higginbotham 1978).

Affirmative action, then, is a means to an end. It is a means for remedying discrimination and for enforcing equal opportunity and civil rights laws.[1]

Affirmative action can mean anything from aggressive recruitment targeting under represented groups, to direct set-asides and numerical goals. The first form of affirmative action is the kind Robert Dole and Jack Kemp support as they declared, in their presentations before the National Association of Black Journalists.[2] Set-asides, numerical goals and timetables are supported by groups like the Minority Business Enterprise Legal Defense and Education Fund, headed by former Congressional Black Caucus Chair, Parren Mitchell.[3] A useful convention articulated by Barbara Bergmann (1996; 1997) is to avoid making fine distinctions between affirmative action that includes numerical goals and affirmative action that does not. Instead, a good definition embraces the whole range of affirmative remedies that seek to correct or compensate for prior discrimination.

Affirmative action, as a remedy to prior discrimination—narrowly tailored to the groups that have been discriminated against, and narrowly tailored to address specific forms of discrimination, often is fair, effective, efficient and legally sound public policy.[4]

However, not everyone would agree that affirmative action efforts are fair.[5] And many people believe they are not efficient.[6]

This essay addresses itself to the issue of whether we should abandon affirmative action in its broad range of manifestations because some forms of affirmative action are unfair. The essay then asks whether we should abandon all affirmative action because many forms of affirmative action are ineffective or inefficient.

First of all, what is "fair?" Two notions of fairness have currency in intellectual circles. The first is commonly adopted by whites when there is a discussion of affirmative action. This notion of fairness is one where an innocent white loses a job promotion because a less qualified nonwhite has been promoted (Glazer 1975; Fiscus 1992).

Suppose there are 100 applicants for a job. Only one person can get the job. There are two criteria for selection: one is performance on the test and the expectation that the selected person be among the top ten performers on the test. The second is a qualitative assessment based on the objectives of the public or private employer.[7] Suppose that this objective is understood to require that the selected applicant have "managerial ability."[8] Initially, assume that everyone is white and male and that everyone takes the test. The tenth ranked person gets the job based on the qualitative assessment of managerial ability plus the test scores.[9]

How many white people will feel that this selection procedure is unfair? Ninety-nine white men were turned down for the job. But were there 99 white men who were unfairly treated? No more than 9 whites can contend that the selection process is unfair. However, if the subjective indicator "managerial ability" is deemed to be a legitimate criterion for selection, then the resulting selection must be considered fair.

Under affirmative action, however, we often see quite a different scenario. Suppose there are 99 white men and one white woman taking the test. Now the second criterion for selection relates to remedying prior discrimination against women. This is an objective just like the objective of requiring managerial ability of the person selected. However, experience suggests that if the woman is the 10th ranked performer on the test and is awarded the job, more than 9 white men will say that the results are unfair. Perhaps 99 white men would claim that the resulting selection is unfair. This may arise because many white men feel that the white woman has stolen a job from them.

That brings up a second notion of fairness, which is more appropriate for application to situations such as affirmative action. This is what William Baumol (1986) calls "superfairness." A superfair distribution is one that would not cause envy if persons' positions were switched (Rawls 1971).

In other words, the scenario above would be considered superfair if a white male, not selected, would prefer to be a white male and not selected than to be a female—with her entire history of prior discrimination—and to be selected. That is to say, in order for the 99 white men to say that they feel the affirmative action is unfair, they would have to agree to switch places with the white women—live her life of insults and sexism and discrimination—and then be the beneficiary of the initiative that permits the 9th ranked person to be selected.

Put another way, superfairness requires that the person who divides the cake cannot also choose the slice. The "I cut, you choose" notion of fairness, then, suggests a different way of viewing whether this affirmative action effort really is "unfair" to 99 white men. Perhaps, in our example, the selection process is unfair to at most 9 white men. However, those same 9 white men would have been denied the job without the affirmative action. Thus, affirmative action cannot be the cause of the feeling of unfairness.

Quite distinct from the fairness issue is the problem of effectiveness or efficiency. The research by University of California economist Jonathan S. Leonard and the essays in William Darity's collected volume on the economics of discrimination clearly reveals that at least in employment, affirmative action works.[10] In some areas, as William Spriggs points out that the most successful affirmative action initiatives have occurred in the military (Myers 1997; Butler 1992, 196; Moskos 1996).

However, not all affirmative action efforts have helped minorities in ways they were intended to. For example, in an examination of the minority business set-aside program in the State of New Jersey, large white firms are found to have benefited more than small minority firms. This research suggests that affirmative action efforts do not always work, that they are not always efficient, and they do not always benefit the intended beneficiaries.[11]

The reason for much of the confusion over whether affirmative action is efficient is that economists and others have different notions of what they mean by efficient and/or effective. In the specialized jargon of economists, a remedy is efficient if it improves the welfare of the intended beneficiary without reducing the welfare of anyone else.[12] And, this idea of an efficient remedy requires at its root that the remedy help the person it is supposed to help.

But things can get a little more complicated if you are a policy analyst and move beyond the narrow confines of microeconomics. The policy analyst would want to know three additional things about affirmative action as a remedy:

Does it compensate for the discriminatory disparity and/or the unequal results?

Does it accomplish its goals better than any other method, such as a group-neutral approach?

Does it remedy the underlying discrimination that caused the unequal results to begin with?

Or put differently: Does it fix it? Does it fix it better than any other method? Does it fix it forever?

Of these three types of efficiencies, we only have positive answers to the first two. Clearly direct quotas, set-asides, and every other kind of offensive form of affirmative action one can think of—busing students, payment of damages to victims of discrimination, payment of reparations or other forms of direct compensation—satisfy the first form of efficiency. The literature on race-neutral remedies to racial earnings inequality and racial differences in admissions in higher education suggests efficiencies on the second of these two measures.

However, one can be convinced by something that former American Experiment President Mitch Perlstein said at the Wilkins Center National Conference on Race Relations and Civil Rights in 1994. Mitch alluded to the fact that affirmative action might be bad for race relations. Restated in the context of the third form of efficiency—does affirmative action eliminate discrimination? The answer is yes, it possibly can, but it generally does not.

This is a troubling conclusion for anyone who supports affirmative action, narrowly tailored and justified by prior or continuing discrimination. There is mounting evidence that affirmative action cannot, does not, nor will not eliminate racial discrimination among populations that are infested with racial animosities, racial hatred or institutionalized forms of racism. If the criterion for the efficiency of an affirmative action plan is that it eliminate the underlying cause of the inequality that makes the remedy needed, then most affirmative actions—from the far extremes of Dole and Kemp's aggressive recruitment definitions to the Black Caucus' pro set-aside positions—do not do the job.

To eliminate discrimination, we will need something else. That something else has yet to be proposed by anyone. And there is not one shred of evidence that any public or private policy has convincingly lead to permanent elimination of racial discrimination or racism in American society.

Both extremes can be faulted for being inefficient. The Dole-Kemp form of affirmative action cannot eliminate racial discrimination. If we vigorously recruit women and minorities and then do not set a goal to hire them, then in the presence of sex or race discrimination after the vigorous recruitment, we will still hire the "best-qualified" white male. It fails to address the underlying cause of the unequal outcomes.

At the other extreme—where there is a direct attempt to alter the outcomes—the underlying cause of the inequality also remains unaddressed. As research on minority business set-asides reveals, set-asides do not always eliminate or even reduce discrimination against minority businesses.

However, affirmative action should be supported, not because all affirmative action initiatives meet all three efficiency criteria. Affirmative action should be supported because it meets some of the efficiency criteria and generally passes the superfairness test when applied to specific cases of discrimination.

To understand why we should settle for second best, consider this: If we eliminated affirmative action, would we eliminate prior discrimination and its legacy against historically oppressed peoples? In other words, would eliminating affirmative action make minorities better off? Would eliminating the Dole-Kemp form of affirmative action make minorities better off? Would eliminating minority scholarships make minority students better off? The answer is no. As long as discrimination remains, affirmative action is needed.

Before all affirmative action is dismantled—even the portion that can pass the first two parts of the efficiency test and which can pass the superfairness test, what is going to be done about illegal discrimination? We have a highly imperfect weapon for remedying discrimination in our hands. Eliminate that weapon, and replace it with nothing at all, then we will revert to a world of utter racial separateness and isolation with no reasonable hope of narrowing the persistent discriminatory gaps in American society. Until someone comes up with a viable alternative to affirmative action as a means of redressing discrimination, we have to settle for the best we've got.

References

Anderson, Bernard. 1997. Affirmative action policy under Executive Order 11246: A retrospective view. In *Civil Rights and race relations in the post Reagan-Bush era*, edited by Samuel L. Myers, Jr. Westport, CT: Praeger Publishers.

Baumol, William. 1986. *Superfairness*. Cambridge: MIT Press.

Bergmann, Barbara. 1996. *In defense of affirmative action*. New York: Basic Books.

———. 1997. Is affirmative action a quota system? In *Civil Rights and race relations in the post Reagan-Bush era*, edited by Samuel L. Myers, Jr. Westport, CT: Praeger Publishers.

Bolick, Clint. 1996. *The affirmative action fraud: Can we restore the American Civil Rights vision?* Washington DC: Cato Institute.

Butler, John Sibley. 1992. Affirmative action in the military. *The Annals of the American Academy of Political Science* 523(September): 196–206.

Darity, Jr., William A., Ed. 1995. *Economics and discrimination. Volume II*. Aldershot UK: Elgar.

Eastland, Terry. 1996. *Ending affirmative action: The case for colorblind justice*. New York: Basic Books.

Fiscus, Ron. 1992. *The constitutional logic of affirmative action*. Durham, NC: Duke University Press.

Fosu, Augustin Kwasi. 1992. Occupational mobility of Black women 1958–1981: The impact of post-1964 antidiscrimination measures. *Industrial and Labor Relations Review* 45(2) (January): 281–94.

Franklin, V. P. 1991. Black social scientists and the mental testing movement, 1920–1940. In *Black psychology*, edited by Reginald L. Jones. Berkeley, California: Cobb and Henry Publishers.

Friedman, Lee. 1984. *Microeconomic policy analysis*. New York: McGraw-Hill.

Glazer, Nathan. 1975. *Affirmative discrimination: Ethnic inequality and public policy*. New York: Basic Books.

Heckman, James J., and Brook S. Payner. 1989. Determining the impact of federal antidiscrimination policy on the economic status of Blacks: A study in South Carolina. *American Economic Review* 79(1) (March): 138–77.

Higginbotham, Leon A. 1978. In *The matter of color: Race and the American legal process*. New York: Oxford University Press.

Kumar, Dharma. 1992. The affirmative action debate in India. *Asian Survey* 32(3) (March): 290–302.

Lashley, Marilyn. 1996. Remedying racial and ethnic inequality in New Zealand: Treaty settlement, affirmative action, and biculturalism. *International Policy Review* 6(1): 51–60.

Leonard, Jonathan S. 1984a. Anti-discrimination or reverse discrimination: The impact of changing demographics, Title VII and affirmative action on productivity. *Journal of Human Resources* 19(2) (Spring): 145–154.

———. 1984b. Employment and occupational advance under affirmative action. *Review of Economics and Statistics* 66(3) (August): 377–85.

———. 1984c. The impact of affirmative action on employment. *Journal of Labor Economics* 2(4) (October): 439–63.

———. 1985. What promises are worth: The impact of affirmative action goals. *Journal of Human Resources* 20(1) (Winter): 20.

———. 1990. The impact of affirmative action regulation and equal employment law on Black employment. *Journal of Economic Perspectives* 4(4)(Fall): 47–63.

Loury, Glenn. 1995. *One by one, from the inside out: Essays and reviews on race and responsibility in America*. New York: Free Press.

Lynch, Frederick. 1989. *Invisible victims: White males and the crisis of affirmative action*. New York: Greenwood Press.

Massey, Douglas S., and Nancy A. Denton. 1993. *American apartheid: Segregation and the making of the underclass*. Cambridge, MA: Harvard University Press.

Mezey, Susan Gluck. 1992. *In pursuit of equality: Women, public policy, and the federal courts*. New York: St. Martin's Press.

Moskos, Charles. 1996. Affirmative action in the army: Why it works. In *The Affirmative Action Debate*, edited by George Curry. Reading MA: Addison Wesley.

Myers, Jr., Samuel L. 1996. Who benefits from minority set-asides? The case of New Jersey. *Journal of Policy Analysis and Management* 15(2): 202–226.

———. Ed. 1997. Remedies to racial inequality. In *Civil Rights and race relations in the post Reagan-Bush era*. Westport, CT: Praeger Publishers.

———. 1999. Minority business set-asides. In *The encyclopedia of African American business history*, edited by Juliet E. K. Walker. Westport, Conn.: Greenwood Press.

———. (2004). Equity and social insurance." In *Strengthening community: Social insurance in diverse America*, edited byKathleen Buto, Martha Priddy Patterson, William E. Spriggs, and Maya Rockeymoore. Washington, D.C: National Academy of Social Insurance.

Myrdal, Gunnar. 1962. American dilemma. In *The Negro in America*, edited by Maxwell Slutz Stewart. New York: Public Affairs Committee.

Nelson, H. Camilla. 1996. Affirmative action in higher education: *Hopwood* and Beyond. Civil Rights Policy Director's unpublished paper. Minnesota Attorney General's Office.

Pearlstein, Mitch. 1997. Remedies to racial inequality. In *Civil Rights and race relations in the post Reagan-Bush era*, edited by Samuel L. Myers, Jr. Westport, CT: Praeger Publishers.

Rawls, John. 1971. *A theory of justice*. Cambridge: Belknap Press.

Reuters. August 24, 1996. Politics; Excerpts from remarks by Dole and Kemp to Black journalists' convention. *The New York Times*, Section 1, p. 10, Column 1.

Shade, Barbara J. 1991. African American patterns of cognition. In *Black psychology*, edited by Reginald L. Jones. Berkeley, California: Cobb and Henry Publishers.

Smitherman, Geneva. 1991. Talkin and testifyin: Black English and the Black experience. In *Black Psychology*, edited by Reginald L. Jones. Berkeley, California: Cobb and Henry Publishers.

Sowell, Thomas. 1994. *Race and culture*. New York: Basic Books.

Spoonley, Paul, David Pearson, and Ian Shirley, Eds. 1994. *New Zealand society*. Palmerston North, New Zealand: Dunmore Press.

West, Cornel. 1996. Staying on the path to racial equality. In *The affirmative action debate*, edited by George Curry. Reading, MA: Addison Wesley.

Williams, Robert L., and Horace Mitchell. 1991. The testing game. In *Black Psychology*, edited by Reginald L. Jones. Berkeley, California: Cobb and Henry Publishers.

Notes

Chapter Three: Local Global Racism in Latin America

1. There are no official statistics of Ecuador's population by race. Estimates place the African population at ten percent.
2. My translation of "aspiracional," not a word in Spanish either.
3. Elsewhere, we have developed the notion of racism as massive societal waste. See Feagin and Vera 1995.

Chapter Four: A Case of Culturalization: Haitians in the Dominican Republic

1. Estimates differ. Other sources report as many as 25,000 victims. See, for example, Wucker 1996.
2. Price-Mars's statement continues to be accurate, as Haitians "still cut the cane Dominicans will not touch" (Wucker 1999, 244).
3. With the election of a new president in Haiti and the Dominican Republic, there have been new developments and promise of presidential cooperation. Yet, recent news articles suggest the problems of these two countries are not over.
4. The extent to which this prejudice is enhanced by nationalism is not clear.
5. See Wucker 1996.
6. Ibid.
7. As cited in Ridgeway 1994.

Chapter Seven: Affirmative Action and International Law: A Test Case

1. One of the earliest instances of affirmative action was the 1969 "Philadelphia Plan" instituted by the United States Government to provide employment to African Americans in the construction industry. See John David Skrentny, *The Ironies of Affirmative Action*, (Chicago and London: The University of Chicago Press, 1996) 177. Even earlier, in 1965,

Executive Order 11246 provided for affirmative action in Government contracts. See Executive Order 11246, 30 F.R. 12319, Sept. 28, 1965; 30 F.R. 12935, October 12, 1965. The Supreme Court first authorized voluntary (as opposed to court-ordered) affirmative action in the case of *United Steelworkers of America v. Weber*, 443 U.S. 193 (1979).

2. This shift in perspective is effectively captured in an essay by George M. Fredrickson. See Fredrickson, George M. 1995. Demonizing the American Dream. Review of *The Politics of Race: Principles for a Multiracial Society*, by Dinesh D'Souza. New York Review of Books XLIII (October, 1995): 10–16.
3. These shakeups, and the effects they have had on middle class Americans, are documented in a series of articles published in book form as *New York Times, The Downsizing of America*, (New York: Times Books, Random House. 1996). See also, Jeffrey Madrick, *The End of Affluence*, (New York: Random House. 1996); Jeremy Rifkin, *The End of Work: The Decline of the Global Labor Force and the Dawn of the Post-Market Era*, New York: Putnam. 1995); and Robert J. Samuelson, *The Good Life and Its Discontents: The American Dream in the Age of Entitlement 1945–1995*, (New York: *New York Times*. 1996). Even though the unemployment rate, hovering around 4.3% for early 1998, is the lowest it has been in the United States in approximately thirty years, the attacks on affirmative action continue unabated.
4. The literature attacking affirmative action is voluminous. One of the more interesting critiques can be found in Michael Lind, *The Next American Nation: The New Nationalism and the Fourth American Revolution* (New York: Free Press, 1995). For an interesting review, see, Ryan, Alan. 1995. It Takes All Kinds. Review of *The Next American Nation: The New Nationalism and the Fourth American Revolution*. New York Review of Books, XLII (October 5,): 30–34. See also, Hacker, Andrew. 1996. *Goodbye to Affirmative Action?* Reviewing a series of books on the issue in New York Review of Books, XLIII (July 11): 21–29.
5. Some of the earlier cases decided by the U.S. Supreme Court in the 1980's are explored in Frank E. Deale, Affirmative Action: Unresolved Questions Amidst A Changing Judiciary, 18 *New York University Review of Law and Social Change*, 81 (1990–1991).
6. *Podberesky v. Kirwan*, 38 F.3rd 147 (4th Cir. 1994).
7. *Hopwood v. State of Texas*, 78 F. 3rd 932 (5th Cir. 1996).
8. *Taxman v. Board of Education of Piscataway*, 91 F. 3rd 1547 (3rd Cir. 1996).
9. The provision amends Section 31 of Article I of the California Constitution to read: "The state shall not discriminate against, or grant preferential treatment to, any individual or group on the basis of race, sex, color, ethnicity, or national origin in the operation of public employment, public education, or public contracting."
10. The vote was 4,736,180 votes in favor (54%) and 3,986,196 votes against (46%). *Coalition for Economic Equity v. Pete Wilson*, 946 F. Supp. 1490, 1495 n. 12 (N.D.Cal.1996) The Court noted that "white voters were the only racial or ethnic group supporting 209." Id.
11. *Coalition For Economic Equity v. Wilson*, 122 F. 3rd 692 (9th Cir. 1997).
12. See 118 S. Ct. 397 (1997). The Court also refused to hear appeals in *Podberesky*, 115 S. Ct. 2001 (1995) and *Hopwood*, 518 U.S. 1033 (1996). The Court agreed to hear *Taxman*, see 118 S. Ct. 362 but the case was settled and therefore dismissed. See 118 S. Ct. 595. See also Eva M. Rodriguez, *Rights' Group Settlement Settles Little*, *Wall Street Journal*, Nov, 24, 1997 at A3.
13. See U.N. GAOR, Res. 2106 A (XX), adopted December 21, 1965), entered into force, January 4, 1969, 660 UNTS 195, reprinted in, 5 ILM 352 (1966).

14. See id. at Article 1(4).
15. Id. at 2.1.
16. The African-American state schools included: Bowie State, Coppin State, Morgan State, and the University of Maryland Eastern Shore. According to the District Court in *Podberesky*, these institutions were "segregated, vastly underfunded, and consistently neglected." *Podberesky*, 838 F. Supp. at 1077. The Court further noted that "even federal land grant funds which were specifically designated for Maryland's Black colleges were diverted to White schools." Id. The Office of Civil Rights concluded that the traditional African-American colleges offered specialization in areas that were "notably less attractive" than the programs at the state's White universities. Id. at 1080.
17. The student was admitted over the objection of then University President, Harry "Curley" Byrd, who argued that "admission of African-Americans to the Graduate school would mean admission to College Park [where our girls are] and would destroy the very segregation idea for the undergraduate school." Byrd was President of the University of Maryland from 1935–1953, Id. at 1077 n.6, 1078, and recommended privatization rather than desegregation. Id.
18. Id. at 1078.
19. Id. Moreover, the school was also unsympathetic to the concerns of those African-American students who were admitted. In 1963, the school prevented African-American students from forming a chapter of the Congress of Racial Equality, and discouraged Martin Luther King, Jr. from speaking on campus. The next year however, George Wallace was allowed to speak. Id. at 1078.
20. Id. at 1079.
21. 347 U.S. 483 (1954).
22. See, 42 U.S.C. § 2000d et. seq.
23. This conclusion was based on findings that the university was not increasing its financial aid expenditures to African-American students, was not increasing dormitory integration, and was not providing aid for African-American fraternity and sorority housing even though it spent over a million dollars to build such housing for ten white fraternities and sororities during the late fifties and early sixties. Facilities housing Black student programs were found to have inadequate heating and broken toilets. See *Podberesky*, 838 F. Supp. at 1079.
24. *Podberesky*, 956 F. 2d 52, 55 (4th Cir. 1992).
25. This amounted to approximately 1% of the university's financial aid budget. *Podberesky*, 838 F. Supp. 1075, 1077 (D.C. Maryland, 1993).
26. Id. at 1082.
27. Id. at 1082.
28. The Francis Scott Key Scholarship Program is another scholarship program offered by the University of Maryland for which all students at the University may compete. These scholarships, which provide benefits equivalent to the Banneker scholarship, are available to 53 students each year. To be eligible for this scholarship, the applicant must have a "predictive index" of 60, calculated by reference to the Scholastic Aptitude Test score and grade point average.

    Over the years, the Key scholarships were administered as follows: "In 1992, out of thirty six Key scholarships awarded, African Americans received two, Asians Americans received ten, Hispanics received one and Whites received twenty three. In 1991, twenty seven Key scholarships were awarded: two to African Americans, five to Asian Americans, one to Hispanics and the remainder to Whites. In 1990 fifty-two Key scholarships were awarded: African Americans received two, Asian American received seven, Hispanics received two and Whites received forty-one. In 1989, forty seven scholarships were awarded: one to an African American, three to Asian Americans, two to Hispanics and forty one to Whites." *Podberesky*, 838 F. Supp. 1075, 1095 (D. Md. 1993).

29. His high school calculated his grade point average as "over 4.0." *Podberesky*, 956 F. 2d at 53, while the university calculated it at 3.56. These figures gave him a predictive index of 59, one point short of what was needed to be eligible for the Key scholarship.
30. See *Podberesky v. Kirwan*, 764 F. Supp. 364 (D. Md. 1991) and 838 F. Supp. 1075 (D. Md. 1993).
31. *Podberesky v. Kirwan*, 956 F. 2d 53 (4th Cir. 1992); 38 F. 2d 147 (4th Cir. 1994).
32. The trial court relied upon studies by a sociologist and a race relations consultant prepared for the University, known as the Allen Report and the Feagin Report. Both of the reports provided "overwhelming" evidence that UMCP continued to have a poor reputation among African-Americans. *Podberesky*, 838 F. Supp. at 1087.
33. The trial court found that 27.1% of graduating high school seniors in Maryland were African-American; that 22% of the high school students taking the S.A.T. were African-American; that 17.9% of the high school students who graduated with a course curriculum meeting the University's general requirements were African-American; 18.1% of all Maryland S.A.T. takers who scored over 380 on the math S.A.T. were African-American; and 19% of all Maryland S.A.T. takers who scored above 270 on the verbal S.A.T. were African-Americans. In contrast, only 13% of the incoming freshmen at UMCP were African-American. Id. at 1088.
34. The trial court found that for the entering class of 1989, only 62.4% of African-American freshman at UMCP remained after three years in comparison with 74.5% of white freshman and 73.4% of the total 1989 freshman population. For graduation rates, of the 1986 entering class of freshman, only 42.5% of African-Americans graduated after six years compared to 66.5% of white freshman and 63.5% of the total 1986 freshman population. Id. at 1091. This rate exceeded that of all other identifiable groups at the University. Id.
35. The trial court cited complaints of racism made to the university's Office of Human Relations; overtly racist comments by faculty and teaching assistants; the lack of African-American leaders on campus; failure of campus media entities to cover accomplishments of African-American faculty, students and staff; and a continuing segregated atmosphere. Id. at 1093.
36. *Podberesky*, 38 F. 3rd 147, 155 (4th Cir. 1994).
37. Id. at 158.
38. Id. at 158–159.
39. For example, the Court of Appeals said that the trial Court did not account for African American high school graduates who 1) chose not to go to any college; 2) chose to apply to only out of state schools; 3) chose to postpone application to four year schools; and 4) chose to attend the predominantly African-American institutions. Id. at 159–160.
40. Id. at 161.
41. *Taxman v. Board of Education of Township of Piscataway*, 91 F. 3rd 1547, 1551, 1578 (3rd Cir. 1996).

42. Id.
43. 91 F. 3rd at 1550, citing to N.J. Administrative Code Tit. 6 §§ 6:4–1.5, 6:4–1.6(a).
44. Id.
45. Id.
46. In explaining this decision, the Board President stated: "I have a general feeling during my tenure on the board that it was valuable for the students to see in the various employment roles a wide range of background, and that it was also valuable to the work force and in particular to the teaching staff that they have—they see that in each other…In my own personal perspective I believe that by retaining Ms. Williams it was sending a very clear message that we feel that our staff should be culturally diverse, our student population is culturally diverse and there is a distinct advantage to students, to all students, to be made—come into contact with people of different cultures, different background, so that they are more aware, more tolerant, more accepting, more understanding of people of all background…" *Taxman*, 91 F. 3rd at 1551–1552.
47. George H. Bush was President when the United States filed suit. In January 1995, during the Clinton Administration, the United States withdrew from the case on the ground that it could not support the judgment and conclusion of the District Court that Taxman had been unlawfully terminated. See *Taxman*, 91 F. 3rd at 1552.
48. See *United States v. Board of Education of Township of Piscataway*, 832 F. Supp. 836, 851 (D.N.J. 1993).
49. See *Taxman v. Board of Education of the Township of Piscataway*, 91 F. 3rd. 1547 (3rd Cir. 1996). Judges Mansmann, Becker, Greenberg, Cowen, Nygaard, Alito, Ross and Stapleton voted for the plaintiff. Judges Sloviter, Sciricia, Lewis and McKee dissented.
50. *Taxman*, 91 F. 3rd at 1558.
51. Id.
52. The Appeals Court noted the parties' stipulation that "neither the Board's adoption of its affirmative action plan nor its subsequent decision to apply it in choosing between Taxman and Williams was intended to remedy the results of any prior discrimination or identified underrepresentation of Blacks within the Piscataway School District's teacher workforce as a whole. Nor does the Board contend that its action here was directed at remedying any *de jure* or *de facto* segregation." *Taxman*, at 91 F.3rd at 1563.

    This stipulation has proven to be a matter of controversy. After reviewing the record of the case while it was pending in the Supreme Court of the United States, Rutgers Law School Professor Alfred Blumrosen noted that the stipulation "was based on a comparison with the largely White labor market to the south that ignored an equally close but better integrated labor market to the north." Blumrosen concludes that "[w]hen that labor market is included; the Board's employment of minority teachers appears so small that it justifies affirmative action under existing law." See Alfred W. Blumrosen and Ruth G. Blumrosen, *The Flawed Foundation of Piscataway High—A Misleading Stipulation, an Absence of Representation, and Uncertainty About Informal Affirmative Action*, 1 RUTGERS RACE & THE LAW REVIEW 319, 321 (1999).
53. Id. at 1550.
54. 91 F. 3rd at 1565.
55. Relying on Justice O'Connor's opinion in *Wygant v. Jackson Board of Education*, 476 U.S. 267 (1986), Judge Sloviter argued that promoting diversity among the faculty was a sufficiently compelling reason for affirmative action programs as to pass constitutional

review. O'Connor's opinion in *Wygant* was joined by Justices Marshall, Brennan, Blackmun and Stevens, each of whom approved some form of multi-ethnic representation in the faculty as a sufficient justification for affirmative action. *Taxman*, 91 F. 3rd at 1573.

56. See Sloviter J., dissenting, at 91 F. 3rd 1576: arguing that there is "no language in Title VII to suggest that a lottery is required as the solution to a layoff decision in preference to a reasoned decision by members of the school board, some of whom are experienced educators, that race of a faculty member has a relevant educational significance if the department would otherwise be all White." See also, McKee J., dissenting at 1578, expressing disbelief that Title VII requires the striking down of an action which assured "that the business department would retain the only Black teacher tenured in that department in anyone's memory."
57. "Indeed the Court in *Weber* explicitly cautioned that its holding in that case should not be read to define the outer boundaries of the area of discretion left to employers by Title VII for the voluntary adoption of affirmative action measures." *Taxman*, 91 F. 3rd at 1570 (Sloviter, J. dissenting.)
58. See *Taxman*, 91 F. 3rd at 1569, Sloviter, J. dissenting: "Notwithstanding the majority's literal construction of the language of Title VII, no Supreme Court case has ever interpreted the statute to preclude consideration of race or sex for the purpose of insuring diversity in the classroom as *one of many factors* in an employment decision..." (emphasis in original).
59. See *Hopwood v. State of Texas*, 78 F.3rd 932 (5th Cir. 1996).
60. Id. at 962.
61. Id. at 964.
62. Id. at 937.
63. Id.
64. Id. at 938.
65. Id. at 936, n. 4.
66. Id. at 951.
67. Id. at 936, n. 4.
68. Id. at 936.
69. Id. at 937.
70. *Texas v. Hopwood*, 518 U.S. 1033 (1996). The Court also refused to hear the appeal of the African-American student organizations who sought to intervene in the case to argue that the school's affirmative action policy was constitutionally sound. *See Texas v. Thurgood Marshall Legal Society*, 21 F. 3rd 603 (5th Cir. 1996), *cert. denied*, 518 U.S. 1033 (1996).
71. The law school policy declared unconstitutional by the Court of Appeals was revamped by the law school in 1995 in response to a ruling by the U.S. District Court for the District of Texas. As a result of this voluntary change, the relief provided to the plaintiffs by the District Court in the law suit was limited to the right to re-apply for admission under the revamped process. See *Hopwood v. Texas*, 861 F. Supp. 551, 582–583 n. 87. The Court of Appeals decision authorized additional relief, including money damages and/or immediate admission to the law school, because it was of the view that "there is no indication that in employing the new plan, the law school will cease to consider race *per se* in making admissions decisions." *Hopwood v. Texas*, 78 F. 3rd at 958. To justify this conclusion, the Court of Appeals seized upon a law school declaration that, even under the new plan, race was "necessary to the attainment of its goals." Id.

72. The ruling does not apply to private institutions because the strictures of the Fourteenth Amendment do not apply to private entities. See, U.S. Const., Amendment XIV: "...nor shall any State...deny to any person within its jurisdiction the equal protection of the laws." See also, *The Civil Rights Cases*, 109 U.S. 3 (1883).
73. The Fifth Circuit consists of the states of Texas, Louisiana, and Mississippi.
74. Since the University of Texas plan arguably went beyond what the Supreme Court authorized in *Regents of the University of California v. Bakke*, 438 U.S. 265 (1978), a similar plan would be vulnerable to challenge independent of *Hopwood*'s authority before another court. See, e.g., *Wessmann v. Boston School Committee*, 160 F. 3rd 790, 795–796 (1st Cir. 1998), (reversing Boston district court order upholding affirmative action plan allowing use of race and ethnicity in the selection of students to Boston's three prestigious examination schools, but disclaiming reliance upon *Hopwood*).
75. See *Hunter v. Erickson*, 393 U.S. 385, 390 (1969).
76. See *Washington v. Seattle Independent School District*, 458 U.S. 457, 485 (1982).
77. 116 S.Ct. 1620 (1996).
78. However, after the decision in *Roemer*, the United States Court of Appeals for the Sixth Circuit upheld a Cincinnati City Charter amendment which barred the adoption of laws providing protected status for homosexuals against a challenge that the amendment was in violation of the Equal Protection Clause. See, *Equality Foundation of Greater Cincinnati, Inc. v. Cincinnati, Ohio*, 128 F. 3rd 289 (6th Cir. 1996).
79. In the words of its proponents, the measure would (a) "Eliminate those affirmative action programs for women and minorities run by the state or local government in the areas of public employment, contracting and education that give 'preferential treatment' on the basis of sex, race, color, ethnicity, or national origin...In addition the measure would eliminate programs that give preference to women-owned or minority-owned companies on public contracts. The measure would eliminate or cause fundamental changes to voluntary desegregation spending that could be affected by the measure including the special funding given to (1) magnet schools in those cases where race or ethnicity are preferential factors in admissions of students to the schools, and 2) designated racially minority schools that are located in areas with high proportions of racial or ethnic minorities. In addition the measure would affect a variety of public schools and community college programs such as counseling, tutoring, outreach, student financial aid, and financial aid to selected school districts in those cases where the programs provide preferences to individuals or schools based on race, sex, ethnicity, or national origin. The measure would affect admissions and other programs at the state's public universities..." See, California Ballot Pamphlet, prepared by California Legislative Analyst's Office, quoted in *Coalition for Economic Equity v. Wilson*, 946 F. Supp. 1480, 1493–1494 (N.D. Cal., 1996).
80. In addition to the named party plaintiffs, plaintiff organizations include: the California NAACP, the California Labor Federation, the Council of Asian American Business Associations, the California Chinese American Citizen's Alliance, the California Chapter of the Women Construction Business Owners and Executives, United Minority Business Entrepreneurs, Asian Pacific American Labor Alliance, La Voz Chicana, the Black Advocates in State Service and the Black Chamber of Commerce of California. See *Coalition for Economic Equity*, 946 F. Supp. at 1490 n.5.
81. See *Coalition for Economic Equity v. Pete Wilson*, 946 F. Supp. at 1520.
82. Id. at 1508.

83. Id. at 1409.
84. Id. at 1508.
85. Id. at 1499.
86. Id. at 1517.
87. See *Coalition of Economic Equity v. Wilson*, 122 F. 3rd 692 (9th Cir. 1997).
88. In the words of the Court: "The first step in determining whether a law violates the Equal Protection Clause is to identify the classification that it draws. Proposition 209 provides that the State of California shall not discriminate against, or grant preferential treatment to, any individual or group on the basis of race or gender. Rather than classifying individuals by race or gender, Proposition 209 *prohibits* the State from classifying individuals by race or gender. A law that prohibits the State from classifying individuals by race or gender *a fortiori* does not classify individuals by race or gender. Proposition 209's ban on race and gender preferences, as a matter of law and logic, does not violate the Equal Protection Clause in any conventional sense." *Coalition of Economic Equity v. Wilson*, 123 F. 3rd at 702.
89. 122 F. 3rd at 708. As the Court held: "It is one thing to say that individuals have equal protection rights against political obstructions to equal treatment; it is quite another to say that individuals have equal protection rights against political obstructions to preferential treatment. While the Constitution protects against obstructions to equal treatment, it erects obstructions to preferential treatment by its own terms." Id.
90. 122 F. 3rd at 110, citing, *Griggs v. Duke Power Co.*, 401 U.S. 424, 431 (1971).
91. While the defendants have been deprived of this important interest, there is no corresponding guarantee that the plaintiffs would obtain what they sued for. Neither Hopwood nor her co-plaintiffs were guaranteed admission to the Texas law school, even without the affirmative action plan. Nor was there an obligation for the University of Maryland to provide more scholarship assistance to Podberesky, had it decided to dismantle the Banneker Scholarship Program and channel all non-need based scholarships through the Key Program, which already rejected Podberesky for non-racial reasons. Had the school district of Piscataway decided to toss a coin to determine whether Williams or Taxman should be laid off, as suggested by the majority opinion, Taxman could have lost the toss. Although the Supreme Court of the United States granted the petition of the Piscataway School district to hear this case, the case was settled under by unusual arrangement under which the Black Leadership Forum, a coalition of civil rights organizations, put up approximately $433,000 to facilitate the settlement. See Eva Rodriguez, *Rights' Group Settlement Settles Little*, WALL STREET JOURNAL, Nov. 24, 1997 at A3.
92. In discussing the expansion of the African-American middle class, the primary result of affirmative action programs, Queens College sociologist Andrew Hacker has stated that "...from Colin Powell to construction workers, this group would be much smaller were it not for extra efforts to put Blacks in places where they have been underrepresented. Nor should it be said that such efforts are no longer needed because legal barriers to opportunity have been overturned. As we have seen with corporations, some kind of pressure is still needed—from conscience, government, or concerns about public relations—to achieve even one Black Vice President." Hacker goes on to note that "affirmative action has been our most successful policy for bringing citizens of slave descent into the main currents of national life. Since 1970, Black families who are upper

middle class (incomes at least $50,000 in constant dollars) have grown from 11.6 percent to 21.1 percent, a sharper rise than for whites." See, Hacker, *supra*, n. 4 at 27.

93. See, UN General Assembly, Third Session, *Universal Declaration of Human Rights*, G.A. Res. 217, U.N. GAOR 3rd Sess., pt. 1 at 71 U.N. Doc A/810 (1948), Article 6 ["all are equal before the law and are entitled without any discrimination to equal protection of the law. All are entitled to equal protection against any discrimination in violation of this Declaration and against any incitement to such discrimination"]; Article 8 ["Everyone has a right to an effective remedy by the competent national tribunals for acts violating the fundamental rights granted him by the constitution or by law."]; UN General Assembly, Twenty-First Session, *International Covenant on Civil and Political Rights*, March 23, 1976, 999 U.N.T.S. 171, G.A. Res. 2200, U.N. GAOR, 21st Sess. No. 16 at 52 U.N. Doc A/6316 (1966), Article 26 ["All persons are equal before the law and are entitled without discrimination to equal protection of the law. In this respect, the law shall prohibit any discrimination and guarantee to all persons equal and effective protection against discrimination on any ground such as race, color, sex, language, religion, political or other opinion, national or social origin, property, birth or other status."]; UN General Assembly, *International Convention on the Elimination of All Forms of Racial Discrimination*, U.N. GAOR, Res. 2106 A (XX), December 21, 1965, Article 2.1 ["States parties condemn racial discrimination and undertake to pursue by all appropriate means and without delay a policy of eliminating racial discrimination in all its forms and promoting understanding among all races..."]. Each of these international instruments can be found in Center for the Study of Human Rights, *Twenty-Five Human Rights Documents* (New York: Columbia University, 1994).

94. Id.

95. International Convention on the Elimination of All Forms of Racial Discrimination at Article 1 (4): ["Special measures taken for the sole purpose of securing adequate advancement of certain racial or ethnic groups or individuals requiring such protection as may be necessary in order to ensure such groups or individuals equal enjoyment or exercise of human rights and fundamental freedoms shall not be deemed racial discrimination, provided however, that such measures do not, as a consequence, lead to the maintenance of separate rights for different racial groups and that they shall not be continued after the objectives for which they have been taken have been achieved."]

    Although affirmative action was not explicitly approved in the Covenant on Civil and Political Rights, *supra*, n. 88, "it was accepted during the drafting...that a prohibition of discrimination or distinction does not preclude positive measures taken in favor of disadvantaged groups." See B.G. Ramcharan, "Equality and Nondiscrimination" *in The International Bill of Rights: The Covenant on Civil and Political Rights*, Louis Henkin, ed., (New York, New York: Columbia University Press, 1981) at 259.

96. Statement by the Committee on the Elimination of Racial Discrimination at the World Conference to Combat Racism and Racial Discrimination, quoted in Theodore Meron, *The Meaning and Reach of the International Convention on the Elimination of All Forms of Racial Discrimination*, 79 Am. J. Int'l Law 283 (1985).

    For a favorable comparison of ICERD with the International Convention on the Elimination of Gender Discrimination, see Laura Donner, *Gender Bias in Drafting International Discrimination Conventions: The 1979 Women's Convention Compared With the 1965 Racial Convention*, 24 Cal. W. Int'l L. J. 241 (1994).

97. Senate Advice and Consent, 140 Cong. Rec. S7, 634 (daily ed. June 24, 1994).

98. In addition to hearing complaints from states-parties, a state-party may also elect to hear complaints filed by "individuals or groups of individuals within its jurisdiction claiming to be victims of a violation by that state party of any of the rights set forth in this convention." After so electing, the state-party must establish a domestic committee to hear such complaints. International Convention on the Elimination of All forms of Racial Discrimination, Article 14 (1,2). If the complaining individuals or groups do not receive satisfaction from this domestic committee within six months, the individual or group may petition the Committee on the Elimination of Race Discrimination. Id at Article 14 (5).

    The United States has chosen not to hear complaints filed by individuals against U.S. government practices, and has consequently failed to establish a committee to hear such complaints. See, Marian Nash (Leich), *Contemporary Practices of the United States Relating to International Law*, 88 Am. J. Int'l L. 719, 723 (1994). In the circumstances described in the text, where state actors and federal instrumentalities have worked to eliminate affirmative action programs that are arguably justified by the Convention, there is a need for separate federal litigation against the United States and state officials expressly claiming that the state programs are inconsistent with the Convention and should be rejected as a matter of international and federal law. See Jordon Paust, *Race Based Affirmative Action and International Law*, 18 Mich. J. of Int'l L. 659, 674 (1997) [arguing that "the recent effort in California to outlaw affirmative action is both inconsistent with the provisions of the treaty and superior federal policy set forth in the treaties and cannot prevail."]

99. Id. at Articles 8 (1) and 11 (1).

100. Id. at Article 11 (3) and 12 (1.a).

101. Id. at Article 13 (1, 2).

102. Id. at Article 13 (2, 3).

103. International human rights instruments have not been enforced by courts of the United States unless they were either self-executing or carried into force by domestic legislation. See, Restatement (Third) Foreign Relations Law of the United States, sec. 111 (3)(4); *Frovola v. USSR*, 761 F. 2d 370, 374 n. 5 (7th Cir. 1985); *Fuji v. State*, 38 Cal. 2d 718, 242 P. 2d 617 (Cal. 1952); *Asakura v. Seattle*, 265 U.S. 332, 341 (1924); *Foster v. Neilson*, 27 U.S. (2 Pet.) 253 (1929); *Ware v. Hylton*, 3 U.S. (3 Dall.) 198, 236–237 (1796).

104. These include Section 2 of the Thirteenth Amendment to the U.S. Constitution, Section 5 of the Fourteenth Amendment to the U.S. Constitution, Section 2 of the 15th Amendment to the U.S. Constitution, various provisions of legislation pursuant to those authorizations, including Titles II and VII of the Civil Rights Act of 1964, 42 U.S.C. 1981 and 1982, and the Voting Rights Act of 1965 and subsequent Amendments. See also, the Federal Pubic Works Act of 1977, 42 U.S.C. Sec. 6705 [10% of any grant thereunder be set aside for Minority Business Enterprises] upheld in *Fullilove v. Klutznick*, 448 U.S. 448 (1980).

105. It should be noted, however, that the Clinton Administration, through the Department of Justice, has proposed changes in affirmative action policies in awarding federal contracts by tightening certification and eligibility requirements for companies claiming minority status. See 61 Federal Register 26042 (May 23, 1996). The Department filed a brief in support of affirmative action and the University of Texas Law School in *Hopwood*, as did the state Universities of Arizona, Iowa, Oklahoma, and West Virginia. See Andrew Hacker, *supra*, n. 4 at 21, 25, n.3.

106. ICERD at Article 1(4). As a preliminary matter, an additional question which would have to be answered is whether private parties may either bring litigation in the federal courts against the under ICERD, or exercise the complaint procedure against the United States as a state-party which has not established a committee for handling such complaints.

107. As a result of the *Hopwood* decision, the entering class at the University of Texas Law School, formerly one of the nation's major educators for minority lawyers, had only four African-Americans and 26 Hispanics in its first year class. Among the freshman class of 6,500 at the University of Texas, there were only 150 African American students. At the University of California Law School, which can no longer use affirmative action in admissions because of Proposition 209, the number of entering African-Americans has plummeted from 20 to 1. See Sue Anne Pressley, *Court Ruling Turns Law School Pale*, MANCHESTER GUARDIAN WEEKLY, September 7, 1997 at 16.

In part because of these immediate consequences of the anti-affirmative action movement, Nathan Glazer, who was one of the first to launch an assault on affirmative action remedies in his 1975 book, AFFIRMATIVE DISCRIMINATION: ETHNIC INEQUALITY AND PUBLIC POLICY (New York: Basic Books 1975), has come around to the view that without affirmative action, few African-Americans would gain admission to highly ranked colleges, "undermin[ing] the legitimacy of American democracy." See, Nathan Glazer, *Why I No Longer Think Affirmative Action Is Unjust*, SACRAMENTO BEE, FORUM SECTION, April 12, 1998 at FO1; Brent Staples, *The Quota Bashers Come in From the Cold*, N.Y. TIMES, April 12, 1998 at sec. 4 p. 12 col. 1.; James Traub, *Nathan Glazer Changes His Mind, Again*, N.Y. TIMES MAGAZINE, June 28, 1998 at 23.

Moreover, shortly after the California vote, the voters of Houston, Texas rejected a similar attempt to eliminate affirmative action through a voter referendum. See Susan Estrich, *Affirmative Follies*, DENVER POST, Nov. 30, 1997 at GO3.

Chapter Ten: Unequal Opportunities in Education and Labour Market in India

1. These figures relate to mid 1980's. Data for 1988–89 suggest that the completion rate for the general population has improved (Singh 1993).

Chapter Eleven: Programs for Empowerment and Reducing Equality: A Long Way to Go for Untouchables

1. In this paper the terms untouchable and scheduled caste are used interchangeably. The name scheduled castes is used (for untouchable) by the Government for official purposes.

Chapter Thirteen: Remedying Racial and Ethnic Inequality in New Zealand: Reparative and Distributive Policies of Social Justice

1. *Pakeha* is the Maori term for Whites/Europeans. Some Whites regard this term as pejorative while others use it as an acceptable synonym. In official statistics and reports "European" is used to describe White settlers and immigrants and their descendants. Consistent with New Zealand journalism conventions, the author uses *Pakeha* and European interchangeably throughout the text.
2. The 1863 New Zealand Settlement Act was the first major legislation that sanctioned compulsory land confiscation as punishment for the Maori wars against European settlement and colonization; hence approximately 3.5 million acres were taken from Maori as a prize of war. In 1905 Maori Land Boards were authorized to compulsorily acquire land declared "not required for actual occupation by Maori." Between 1865 and 1899, approximately 11 million acres of Maori land was transferred to European hands under the land laws, leaving approximately 8 million acres in Maori freehold ownership. Between 1900 and 1930 another 4.5 million acres of Maori land were alienated and a further 3 million acres were leased. A 1920 survey estimated that 400,000 acres were occupied by Maori and 800,000 acres were available for Maori use (Ward 1997). Although government decision-makers slowed the pace of land confiscations by enacting the 1929 Native Land Amendment Act and Native Land Claims Act, the acts were reversed by the 1953 Maori Affairs Act. Under the 1953 Maori Affairs Act, any interested person could submit information to the Maori Land Court claiming a particular parcel of land was unproductive or had noxious weeds or unpaid rates and empowered Maori Trustees, who could alienate Maori-held land by leasing or selling these lands as they saw fit. The 1953 Town and Country Planning Act further restricted use of Maori-held lands via zoning laws.
3. The 1967 Maori Affairs Bill amended the 1953 Maori Affairs Act to render it less harmful to Maori while maintaining compulsory sale to Europeans of land held by multiple Maori owners. This Bill gave Maori incorporations greater consultation and rights of appeal, the option to trade shares and to retain unclaimed dividend, but sustained compulsory sale of multiple-owned Maori land on the basis of having ceased to be Maori land instead of being declared European land.
4. The operative meaning of Maori sovereignty remains an unsettled question both within Maoridom and New Zealand society. For comprehensive discussion see Donna Awatere *Maori Sovereignty*, (Auckland: Broadstreet Publications 1984), Lindsay Cox *Kotahitanga* (Auckland: Oxford U. Press 1993), Paul McHugh *Maori Magna Carta* (Auckland: Oxford U. Press 1991), Andrew Sharp *Justice and the Maori* (Auckland: Oxford U. Press 1991) and Alan Ward A *Show of Justice*, (Auckland: Oxford U. Press 1991).
5. The New Zealand Government accepted tenets of international law requiring that each of the of the parties to a treaty drawn up in two languages has the right to rely on its own version for purposes of interpretation, unless there is an express stipulation that only one of the texts shall be authoritative (Hardy 1961).
6. Claims include Otakou, Banks Peninsula, Murihiku, North Canterbury, Rakiura and Arahura purchases; Princess Street reserve; perpetual leases of Ngai Tahu reserves and *mahinga kai* (food resources).

7. Many argue that these government institutions historically functioned to the disadvantage of Maori people. See Hazelhurst 1995 and Spoonley 1990.
8. It is important to note that both the Tainui Maaori Trust and Ngai Tahu Trust also contract with government to deliver social welfare and other services to Maori. Maintaining that provision of social welfare is the responsibility of government, the Trusts deliberately refrained from disbursing Trust assets for these purposes and focused instead on providing tertiary and university scholarships. Given substantial settlement packages, recent court rulings on the definition of *iwi*, proposals for allocation and disbursement of fisheries assets, and Maori debate and opposition, the Trusts have expanded their activities in human resource development and social service outreach. For example, the Ngai Tahu established the Ngai Tahu Development Corporation in 1996 to develop social benefits focused on the social and economic needs of the tribe in the areas of culture and identity, economic security, education, environment, health and social well-being and housing assistance and advocacy. Since 1997, the Tainui Trust has distributed benefits from treaty settlement assets as solicited grants to Marae (52%), education (20%), Maori language (3%), sports (13%) and culture (6%) in the amount of NZ$ 2.3 million in 1997 and NZ$ 3.9 million in 1998.

Chapter Fifteen: Economic Security for All: A Necessary Condition for Eliminating Racial Economic Inequality

1. Effects of immigrant workers on the jobs and earnings of native workers in the U.S. are still in dispute, but a number of economists believe they have found negative effects. Economist Vernon Briggs (1990, 10) believes that the majority of immigrants must seek employment in declining sectors of goods producing industries (agriculture and light manufacturing) or low-wage sectors of the expanding service sectors where they compete with poor native workers. David North (1994) who studies immigrants in Los Angeles' labor market contends that the decline in pay in the secondary labor market is related to the high proportion of legal and illegal immigration. David R. Howell and Elizabeth J. Mueller (1998) have found significant support for negative earnings effects of recent immigrants on black male workers in the New York metropolitan area during the 1980s. On the other hand, Gregory DeFreitas (1998, 340) points out that studies of the entire labor market of specific cities like Los Angeles, Miami and New York have found that increased immigration had no overall effect on the unemployment of native-born workers, and several national studies covering multiple cities have produced similar results. The conclusions of an expert panel convened by the National Research Council are similar to those of DeFreitas in their view that immigration is a modest factor, if any, in the labor market conditions of recent decades, although DeFreitas thinks this could change with millions of welfare recipients forced to find jobs in coming years. See Smith and Edmonston (1997, 7). For other studies, see Hamermesh and Bean (1998); Bean and Bell-Rose (1999).
2. In Austria, popular support for Haider's Freedom Party rose to between 25 and 27 percent in 1999 and the party is now part of the governing coalition. In Switzerland, the Swiss People's Party, fueled by opposition to immigration and the EU, gained 22.5 percent of the vote; in Denmark, the ultranationalist Danish People's Party was the third most popular party in recent opinion polls; in Norway, the Progress Party, again fueled by fear of

immigration, has become the joint second largest party in Norwegian politics, winning 25 of the 165 parliamentary seats in the 1997 election; and in Sweden a wave of neo-Nazi violence including murders and bombings targeting immigrants has shaken this traditionally pacific country. See "Europe's Far Right," BBC News online: http://news.bbc.co.uk

3. Sir William H. Beveridge (1944, 18), the British economist who is credited with developing the concept of full employment during World War II, defined "full" employment as "having always more vacant jobs than unemployed men, not slightly fewer jobs." Today, we should amend that definition to include both men and women as "workers." For more on the concept of full employment, see Gingsburg (1983, 3–19); Collins, Ginsburg, Goldberg, Rosen, and Zaccone (1997); Collins, Ginsburg and Goldberg (1994, 46–47). Since 1947, a series of international treaties, declarations and conventions have established economic security (full employment, adequate wages, workers' rights) as positive "human rights" which governments are obligated to provide. See "The Universal Declaration of Human Rights," Articles 22, 23, 25; "The International Covenant on Economic, Social and Cultural Rights," Articles 6, 7, 8 9; "The International Covenant on Civil and Political Rights," Article 8; "The International Convention on the Elimination of All Forms of Racial Discrimination," Article 5, sec. e; "The Convention on the Elimination of all Forms of Discrimination Against Women," Article 2. At the Rio Earth Summit in 1992, as well as through previous summits, covenants and treaties, world leaders have come to recognize the critical symbiosis between economic development and environmental sustainability; including the recognition that poverty itself is a major cause of environmental degradation and environmental degradation a cause of poverty (Flavin 1997).

4. Ibid, 1. See also Franklyn Lisk (1999, 1), Director and ILO Representative to the United Nations.

5. In Latin America by 1996, the share of workers without contracts or with new, more flexible-work contracts, increased to 30 percent in Chile, 36 percent in Argentina, 39 percent in Colombia and 41 percent in Peru. In Latin America, 85 percent of all newly created jobs are informal. In Egypt, it is increasingly common to require new recruits to sign a resignation letter before taking the job. Belgium, France, Germany and the United Kingdom have all weakened their worker dismissal laws. See Ibid, 37. In the United States, between 5 and 33 percent of all jobs are contingent or "non-standard," depending on how "contingent" is defined. Mishel, Bernstein and Schmitt (1999, 21) put the percentage of workers employed in "nonstandard" work arrangements at nearly one-third of the total labor force in 1997. These "nonstandard" jobs ranged from independent contracting and other forms of self-employment to work in temporary agencies. Nonstandard workers earn less than workers with comparable skills and background who work in regular full-time jobs and are less likely to have health or pension benefits. Paul Osterman (1999, 103), however, defines "contingent" work more narrowly as "an employment situation in which an essential characteristic of the job is that the employee lacks the level of job security that a given employer makes available to 'regular' workers" (55). In 1997, he calculated that temporary employment accounted for 2.7 percent of total employment and contingent employment 2.4 percent.

6. OECD Latest Short-Term Indicators, 5. Available from the OECD http://www.oecd.org

7. A 1995 New York Times poll found 53 percent of the population reporting that they were "less financially well off than they had expected to be at this point in their life." The same proportion of those who identified themselves as "middle class" worried that they or some-

one in their household might be laid off soon. Seventy-nine percent reported that they were either just staying even or falling behind. See New York Times Poll, December 3–6, 1995. In December 1996, only 13 percent of respondents in another poll reported that they felt "very secure." See Steve Lohr, "Though Upbeat on the Economy, People Still Fear for their Jobs," *New York Times*, December 29, 1996. In the tighter U.S. labor market of the late 1990s, a little over half (56 percent) of respondents rated the economy as "fairly good," while only 28 percent rated it as "very good." See CBS/New York Times News Poll, 17–19 December, 1999. In a Gallup/CNN/USA Today poll taken around the same time even fewer (19 percent) rated the economy as "excellent," while 52 percent rated it as "good." See Gallup/CNN/USA Today Poll, 1–10 January 2000. These figures reflect some continuing anxiety about the economy despite the highest rates of employment in a quarter century.

8. Ibid.
9. The analysis of food insecurity was conducted by Tuft's University's Center on Hunger, Poverty and Nutrition Policy. It provided three definitions or levels of food insecurity. The first was defined as "food insecure without hunger." Such households could not afford to insure the nutritional quality of their food. The second and third categories were "food insecure with modest hunger" and "food insecure with severe hunger." See Press release, "State-level Study Finds Over 15 Percent of Households Food Insecure/Hungry in Seven States, Ten Percent or More in Two-Thirds of States" Medford, MA: Tufts University Center on Hunger, Poverty and Nutrition Policy, 22 October, 1997.
10. Figures compiled by the National Jobs for All Coalition from the U.S. Department of Labor, Bureau of Labor Statistics.
11. World Bank, *East Asia Regional Overview*, available from the World Bank at: http://www.worldbank.org
12. For an analysis of the history of the relationship between poverty relief and the American labor market and an analysis of the effects of welfare repeal, see Goldberg and Collins (2000).
13. In France in 1997, the National Front party of Jean Marie LePen won 15 percent of the vote in the 1996 presidential elections but came in first among the industrial workers and unemployed. In 1997, he swept to victory in several municipal elections, and over a third of the French people now say they sympathize with at least some of the National Front's ideas. The Front took off in 1983, writes Singer (1996), when unemployment was high and the Socialists began dashing the hopes they had aroused on coming to office, and it spread as the economic crisis deepened (Cohen 1997). Austrians, faced with rising unemployment and the shift of jobs to lower-wage areas in Hungary and the Czech Republic, are increasingly turning to the outspokenly anti-immigrant Freedom Party, which won more than 29 percent of the votes in a contest for the European Parliament and established itself as the majority party in the provinces of Salzburg and Carinthia (Hitchens 1996). Turks and refugees from the Balkans have been the object of skinhead attacks in Germany, and East Germans are increasingly seen as second class citizens by their fellow Germans (Whitney 1996).
14. In the much tighter labor market that has existed in the United States between 1998 and 1999, it is not surprising to find that unemployment rates fell and wages rose for black and Hispanic workers and even for the mentally ill (Nasar with Mitchell 1999; Johnson 1999).
15. Kofi Anan's, Citizens' Compact on the United Nations and Corporations can be found on the website of Corporate Watch at: http://www.corpwatch.org.

16. The growth of third parties and third party formations in the United States and the growth of public opinion in favor of third parties is one of the most remarkable features of the political landscape in the late twentieth century. Among the parties or party-formations that are of significance in this regard are Ross Perot's United We Stand, the Labor Party, the New Party, the Green Party U.S.A., the Politics of Meaning movement, and the Independent Progressive Politics Network. Among the movements that are developing coherent approaches to corporate accountability and responsibility are: Ralph Nader's Public Citizen; the Program on Corporations, Law and Democracy; the International Forum on Globalization; the International Labor Rights Fund; the National Labor Committee in Support of Human Rights in Central America and the Caribbean; and the National Jobs for All Coalition. Among the groups working to organize workers and communities around a vision of democratically controlled economic development are the Federation for Industrial Retention and Renewal and Sustainable America.
17. For an articulation of these goals, I am grateful to my colleagues in the network of activist scholars involved in the National Jobs for All Coalition. For a list of their publications, contact: The National Jobs for All Coalition, 475 Riverside Dr., Suite 832, New York, NY 10115.
18. For more information on Jubilee 2000, contact: Jubilee 2000/USA, 222 E. Capitol St., N.E., Washington, DC 20003.

Chapter Sixteen: If Not Affirmative Action, Then What?

1. Cornel West (1996) claims that another aim of affirmative action is "to put a significant dent in the highly controlled networks of privileged white male citizens who monopolized the good jobs and influential positions in America."
2. Jack Kemp is quoted as saying "I believe with all my heart that affirmative action is very much needed, but the right kind of affirmative action, small 'a,' is affirmative efforts to open up the type of educational opportunity, the type of access to credit and capital, the type of access to ownership and housing, the type of an access to the American Dream that every child of God has a right to expect...we want to open up in this country once again that type of an America in which any man, any woman, of any color, can get that education, get that access to credit and capital, get that housing, get that ownership... So that to me is an affirmative action program that goes beyond set-asides or preferences..." (*Reuters* 1996) Dole is quoted as saying, "...some believe the solution to these problems is quotas and preferences and set-asides. And I've supported race-based preferences in the past. But over time I realized that preferences created with the best of intentions were dividing America, instead of bringing us or bringing them together. What I do support and what I do define as real affirmative action is aggressive, determined and persistent recruitment of minorities and women by business, government and universities." (*Reuters* 1996)
3. See Myers (1999). The Minority Business Enterprise Legal Defense and Education Fund is an outreach, research and education fund that defends public policy promoting contracting opportunities for minority businesses.
4. In decisions regarding affirmative action remedies, courts have been demanding that the programs be tailored in the least intrusive and most effective, efficient means of achieving their goals. See *Regents of the University of California v. Bakke*, 438 US 265, 98 S. Ct. 2733

(1978); *Podberesky v. Kirwan*, 38 F.3d 147 (4th Cir. 1994) *cert. denied*,—US—115 S. Ct. 2001 (1995). See also Nelson (1996).

5. In describing affirmative action as a remedy, Mitch Pearlstein (1997), President, Center of the American Experiment says "...If I were in the market right now for a [position in higher education] I would much prefer to compete with another white male...[People] think affirmative action is a sham in the sense that it's not going to lead to protected class members' getting preference or even getting a fair shake. I believe...I would be at a disadvantage. Affirmative action is the kind of policy that somehow makes everybody mad." See also Eastland (1996); Bolick (1996); Lynch (1989).
6. Glenn Loury (1995, 116) states, "...my point here is not to question the legitimacy of affirmative action, but rather the efficacy. Using simple ideas from information economics, I have tried to illustrate how preferential treatment can have counterproductive effects by producing negative reputational externalities..." See also Sowell (1994).
7 For a variation of this illustration, see Myers (2004), "Equity and Social Insurance" in *Strengthening Community: Social Insurance in Diverse America*, Kathleen Buto, Martha Priddy Patterson, William E. Spriggs, and Maya Rockeymoore, (Eds.), National Academy of Social Insurance, Washington, D.C, pp. 44–46.
8. Susan Gluck Mezey (1992, 56) describes the difficulty in measuring discrimination in "mixed motive" case to prove that discrimination was the key factor in employment decisions. Justice Sandra Day O'Connor explained, "...in the context of the professional world, where decisions are often made by collegial bodies on the basis of largely subjective criteria, requiring the plaintiff to prove that any one factor was the definitive cause of the decisionmakers' action may be tantamount to declaring Title VII inapplicable to such decisions."
9. The assumption here is that the test is fair and a reliable indicator of ability. Psychologists have demonstrated the cultural biases in the tests. See Williams and Mitchell (1991); Franklin (1991). Shade (1991, 243), for example, points out that blacks transmit knowledge through "kinetic and tactile senses, through the keen observation of the human scene, and through verbal descriptions." Examinations such as the AFQT heavily rely on written skills using language that arguably deviates in substantive ways from normal English. Also see Smitherman (1991).
10. Among other findings, Leonard (1984a; 1984c, 1985; 1990) has found that goals set by firms are good predictors of those firms' future workforces, federal contract status has a positive effect on the employment of black men, black women, white women, and "other" men, that federal contract compliance and Title VII have a positive impact on minorities, and that affirmative action increases the productivity of women and nonwhite men. See also Darity (1995). In this compilation, studies revealing the success of affirmative action include: Leonard (1984b); Fosu (1992); Heckman and Payner (1989).
11. Myers (1996) discusses that race-based remedies often are justified by evidence of prior discrimination. They work when they benefit groups previously disadvantaged. This article examines one such remedy—minority business set asides—and its application in the award of public procurement and construction contracts by the state of New Jersey. Analyzed are contract awards to minority and non-minority/non-women-owned business enterprises in 1990, as well as in periods before, during, and after the imposition of a state minority set-aside program. Using a conventional decomposition approach, the article reveals significant discriminatory gaps in the success of minority versus non-minority-owned firms in obtaining contracts from the state of New Jersey. The analysis suggests that minority contracting success rates fell from the pre-set aside era to the set-aside era and that

discriminatory outcomes persisted. The particular remedy chosen—while justified based on evidence of prior discrimination—appears not to have reduced the original discrimination nor did it unambiguously benefit minority businesses.

12. Friedman (1984) describes the general concept of efficiency as "an efficient allocation of resources is one from which no person can be made better off without making another person worse off" (26). An efficiency principle with an individualistic interpretation is defined that "each person is the sole judge of his or her own welfare" (27). Then there is relative efficiency. One might want to compare "whether one allocation is relatively more efficient than another or whether an allocative change increases efficiency" (36). One can see how interpretations of efficiency may become muddled.

Contributors

GARY C. ANDERS
Professor of Economics, School of Global Management and Leadership
Arizona State University, West Campus

PINAR BATUR
Associate Professor of Sociology, Director of Urban Studies
Vassar College

COLIN BOURKE
Adjunct Professor, Centre for Australian Indigenous Studies
Monash University, Australia

ELEANOR BOURKE
Adjunct Professor, Centre for Australian Indigenous Studies
Monash University, Australia

SHEILA D. COLLINS
Professor of Political Science
Director, M.A. in Public Policy and International Affairs
William Paterson University

BRUCE P. CORRIE
Associate Dean, Undergraduate Studies,
College of Business and Organizational Leadership
Professor of Economics
Concordia University—St. Paul
Editor, www.policybriefs.org

FRANK DEALE
Associate Professor of Law, City University of New York School of Law

AUTAR S. DHESI
Professor, Honorable Research Fellow
Coventry Business School, Coventry University, Coventry, U.K.
Formerly Professor and Chairman
Punjab School of Economics, Grur Nanak University, Amritsar, India

JOMO K.S.
Assistant Secretary General for Economic Development
United Nations, New York
Formerly Professor, Faculty of Economics and Administration
University of Malaya, Kuala Lumpur

MARILYN E. LASHLEY
Associate Professor, Department of Political Science
Howard University

SAMUEL L. MYERS, JR.
Roy Wilkins Professor of Human Relations and Social Justice
Hubert H. Humphrey Institute of Public Affairs
University of Minnesota

RUPERT W. NACOSTE
Alumni Distinguished Undergraduate Professor, Department of Psychology
North Carolina State University

YANICK ST. JEAN
Visiting Assistant Professor, Department of Sociology
University of Wisconsin-Eau Claire

WALTER W. STAFFORD
Professor, Wagner Graduate School of Public Service
New York University

SUKHADEO THORAT
Professor of Economics, Centre for the Study of Regional Development
School of Social Sciences, Jawaharlal Nehru University, New Delhi, India

HERNÁN VERA
Professor of Sociology
University of Florida

Index

M

N

O

P

Q

R

S

T

U

V

W

Y

FSC
www.fsc.org
MIX
Papier | Fördert
gute Waldnutzung
FSC® C083411

Kolibri 360 GmbH
Ferdinand-Jühlke-Straße 7
99095 Erfurt, Deutschland
produktsicherheit@kolibri360.de

Druck:
CPI Druckdienstleistungen GmbH
im Auftrag der
Kolibri 360 GmbH
Ferdinand-Jühlke-Str. 7
99095 Erfurt